When Women Rebel

When

The Rise of

Lawrence Hill Books

Women Rebel

Popular Feminism in Peru
Carol Andreas

A toma de tierra *in Puno. (Alvaro Villaran)*

Library of Congress Cataloging-in-Publication Data

Andreas, Carol.
  When women rebel.

  Bibliography: p.
  Includes index.
  1. Women—Peru—Economic conditions. 2. Women—
Peru—Social conditions. 3. Feminism—Peru—History.
I. Title.
HQ1573.A53 1985   305.4'2'0985   85-27244
ISBN 0-88208-197-7 cloth
ISBN 1-55652-127-8 paper, previously 0-88208-196-9

  2 3 4 5 6 7 8 9

Printed in the United States of America

Contents

AFEDEPROM   women's association in Comas

ama de casa   housewife, mother, homemaker

ambulante   street vendor

amauta   teacher, leader

AP—Acción Popular   political party of President Fernando Belaúnde Terry, which held power in the 1960's and again in the early 1980's

APRA-Alianza Popular Revolucionaria Americana   originally an anti-imperialist party, the *APRA* later became North American business' principal defender in Peru; billed as "centrist" in 1980's

aprista   member of the APRA

asesores   advisers or assistants—the term does not imply authority

ayllu   assembly of all adult members of an indigenous community who came together to make decisions at the local level before the Spanish conquest

ayni, chachawarmi   Quechua and Aymará words for harmony or balance, especially in human relationships—mutual aid—*chachawarmi* literally means husband/wife

barriadas   shantytowns or communities of working class and poor people who live in the cities

barrio   neighborhood

campesinoa   either peasants (small farmers) or farmworkers; all members of indigenous communities began to be called *campesinos* during the government of Juan Velasco Alvarado

capacitación   general education provided outside the regular school system

CARITAS   Catholic Relief Services

CCP—Confederación Campesina del Perú   farmworkers' union

chacras fields, especially small family plots

chicha home-made fermented drink, usually prepared from corn, peanuts, or fruit

CITE state workers' union, *Confederación Intersectorial de Trabajadores Estatales*

comedor popular Peoples Kitchen (*comedor* literally means eating place or dining room)

comités de lucha popular struggle committees

comuneroa members of indigenous communities

compañera (f), *compañero*—comrade-in-arms, companion, member of a popular organization

comunidades indigenous communities

conquistadores Spanish conquerors

cuy guinea pigs, domesticated animals in Peru for thousands of years

directiva governing body

empleadas employees, term used in Peru to describe "white collar workers" as well as household workers

encuentro conference

eventuales contract laborers who lack job stability and are not eligible for work benefits

faena community work brigade

ferias country fairs or farmers' markets

fotonovelas publications resembling "comic books" but illustrated with photographs instead of line drawings

hacendados those who were given individual title to land by the Spanish crown, and those who inherited or acquired such land subsequently

hacienda large farm

historieta pamphlet or storybook, usually with pictures

huayno folk music of the Andean mountains of Peru

Incanato Inca administration

indígenas indigenous or native peoples

Izquierda Unida Left Unity, broad-based coalition organized in 1980 to run candidates in municipal elections

jefes, jefas (f) community leaders (what historians sometimes call "chiefs")

machismo style of male domination brought to Peru by the Spanish

masato drink prepared of manioc root, the *chicha* of the jungle

mestizas (f), *mestizos* those who are Indian or part-Indian genetically but who do not adhere to Indian customs

movimiento movement, social movement

mujer woman

obraje slave labor system used by the Spanish for production of fine cloth

OFASA Seventh Day Adventist organization set up to distribute U.S. food surpluses purchased by the Peruvian government

olla común meal prepared for a big gathering; cooperative eating arrangement

Pachamama protector and ultimate refuge of living beings on earth

patrón, patrona (f) boss or owner

peones laborers bound to masters through indebtedness or feudal "loyalty"

pobladores inhabitants of shantytowns or *barriadas*

promotoras local people especially trained to educate others like themselves

pueblos jovenes "young towns," name given by the Velasco government to the encampments of the poor

puna high mountain regions, as distinguished from fertile valleys of the sierra

selva regions characterized by jungle or tropical rain forest

senderistas members of the Communist Party of Peru, "for the shining path of Mariátegui" *(Sendero Luminoso)*

Shipibos natives of the Pucallpa river area

sierra mountainous regions

SINAMOS *Sistema Nacional de Apoyo a la Movilización Social,* institution established by the military government of the 1970's to mobilize support to carry out its programs

sinchis government counterinsurgency forces (the word means warrior in Quechua)

sirvinacuy trial marriage as practiced by Andean Indians

socios full associates or members of a cooperative business enterprise

SUTEP *Sindicato Unico de Trabajadores en la Educación Peruana,* teachers' union

tawantinsuyanos the four districts governed by the Incas

toma de tierra land occupation or takeover

UDP *Unidad Democrático Popular* an electoral coalition of the late 1970's and early 1980's, composed of several leftwing organizations

vecino neighbor

Yanesha known to anthropologists as Amuesha Indians, natives of the Pichis-Palcazú river area which feeds into the Ucayali river (the Ucayali feeds into the Amazon)

Prologue

ON THE EVENING of July 26, 1982, a newly elected Miss Universe was escorted rapidly out of the modern coliseum in Lima where pageant beauties had been competing for the crown. Bombs thrown at the entryway forced several thousand elegantly dressed pageant observers to leave by side exits. In the days leading up to the selection of Miss Universe Peruvian feminist protesters had been dispersed with tear gas and red water shot from U.S.-made antiriot tanks. Some had been jailed. Opposition newspapers had criticized government expenditures on the pageant, even as they ran daily photographic displays of the pageant contestants. Journalists had pointed out that most of Peru's women had to fight for basics such as food and water and the right to attend school. The pageant, they observed, was a gimmick to advertise the products of multinational corporations.

A young Indian woman from Cuzco, attending a farm workers' union meeting in Lima on the day of the Miss Universe pageant, told television reporters who asked her opinion of the contest: "What I'd like to say is that, really, the government is using these women, spending the people's money on women who sell themselves, who show themselves off. We've seen how they're taken from one place to another, sleeping and eating in the best hotels, all made up and dressed in fancy clothes, each one with a policeman at her side to protect her, while there are so many of us sick and poor—we give birth right on the ground, without any help. There are so many children without food, and the government spends our money on things like this! . . . Almost all of us here [in the women's meeting] are mothers. We have daughters who don't have shoes, sons who don't have a single decent pair of pants. We can't even buy a notebook to send to school with our children and have to put pieces of paper together from here and there to make one. As women, as farm workers, we're angry because we don't go along with the idea that people should be bought and sold for their beauty. This government is so sold out, so reactionary! How many times I've cried to God! Why doesn't this government give up and die so the people can take over? That's why we have to struggle. We women, now that we're organized, we're going to protest, and Señor Presidente Fernando Belaúnde Terry is going to have to listen to us whether he wants to or not. Even if he sends us to the Fronton*—even if he kills us— we're going to keep on protesting because we're not afraid of dying. We've had enough!"

This statement was never broadcast on Peruvian television, but it stands as testimony to an emerging consciousness among women in Peru's popular movements. Women at the farm workers' national meeting, held only once every three years, demanded 40 percent of the organization's budget for the purpose of organizing rural women, who are the major producers of food consumed in Peru. Women had been practically unrepresented in the union before this event.

Less than a mile away from the farm workers' meeting, women factory workers were beginning a hunger strike inside a church located near the government palace. The workers had been on strike for thirty-six days, demanding implementation of their legal right to have a child-care center at the factory, as well as cost-of-living salary adjustments. Unable to get the company to negotiate with them, they had taken over the church and were refusing to eat until their union was recognized.

Within a few blocks of the church, thirteen children and twenty-two women—most of them domestic servants or household workers—were facing eviction from the centuries-old build-

*El Frontón is an infamous prison island that had been recently reopened to house political prisoners.

ing that had served as the group's communal living quarters since the mid-1970s. They were fighting the eviction while calling on other young migrant women to join them in living collectively in order to avoid the abuse of live-in situations in the houses where they worked, as well as the traps of prostitution or early marriage.

While these events were taking place in downtown Lima, an estimated forty-six women prisoners, accused of subversion of the Peruvian government, remained secluded in Callao, a port city adjacent to the capital. None of these women had been proven guilty of specific acts of sabotage, nor did they need to be: Peru's newly declared "antiterrorist" law gave to the central government power to imprison anyone accused of being "dangerous to democracy." Several of these women had already lost their minds under torture. A reporter who had attempted to verify the names of political prisoners brought to Callao from outlying provinces was herself arrested. (She was later freed through public pressure.) The government had tried to isolate these prisoners by transporting them to the capital, but this move only widened their base of support and called attention to the government's inability to control revolutionary movements.

The events claimed the attention of the Women's Coordinating Committee, a loose affiliation of feminist organizations in Lima. Originally formed in 1979 to support a factory takeover by women who had been shut out of work, the committee had subsequently split over priorities for action. With increasing repression and the challenge presented by factory workers, farm women, and household workers, a series of regrouping meetings were held. The regrouping appeared to presage a national rather than citywide coalition. It also appeared to link women inside and outside political parties of the Left more closely, at a time when the parties were deeply divided over other issues. This was the situation when I left Peru in August 1982. In spite of repression, women were feeling powerful in ways not even imagined ten years earlier, when I had first come to South America.

I arrived in Peru in December 1973, having fled from Chile after a right-wing military coup. There I had been working with women in a farm workers' union during the last year of the Popular Unity government, hoping to make a permanent home in

Chile with my three children. I brought to Peru the same expectation of finding a niche for myself living and working in an environment where social transformation was underway.

Within a few months I had found a job teaching sociology at the National University in Huancayo, was again working in support of a rural union, and was living in an indigenous community on the outskirts of the city, sharing my life with a man who had returned to the mountains after having grown up in the slums of Lima.

My second semester of teaching ended with an extended strike of students and workers at the university, accompanied by generalized police repression in the city of Huancayo. At this time, we made a trip to the United States. In December 1975, we moved to Lima, where we lived in a barriada, or shantytown, together with the family of my *compañero,* Raúl, and participated in the neighborhood organizations born during those turbulent times. We returned to the Mantaro Valley near Huancayo at harvest time the following year, and I left the country soon after that.

Throughout my stay in Peru, I had sent periodic reports about political events to some thirty organizations and individuals in the United States who were concerned about increasing economic and political repression in Latin America. And after leaving Peru, I kept in touch with family and friends there. As I became aware of the growing rebellion of Peruvian women, I yearned to return. The death of my father in 1981 provided me with a small inheritance, and I decided to use it in support of feminist movements. I returned to Peru and, with the help of many Peruvians, prepared a slide show about the lives and struggles of Peruvian women. I subsequently toured the United States with it.

In the following years, I visited Peru again, with the express purpose of writing this book. I came to appreciate more clearly than before that most Peruvian women, unlike women I had known elsewhere, and unlike most Peruvian men, still carry with them "prepatriarchal" values, a legacy of social structures that gave women respect and power equal to that of men. While the women are often outwardly submissive and modest in the presence of outsiders, or feign ignorance in order to "get along in the world," they have a reserve of anger and assertiveness that can be tapped when conditions permit or require it. Most of them dress in native clothing and speak among themselves in languages not understood by outsiders, even as they aspire to gain knowledge of the modern world necessary to their survival. They mourn deeply the loss of collective values in their children. As some of these women articulate their problems and seek ways to organize themselves politically, they are discovering—re-discovering—who can be trusted and who cannot. Sometimes I have been more surprised than they to share these discoveries. In any case, I have taken upon myself the task of documenting their experiences, with the hope that this knowledge will benefit them and those who share their goals and aspire to be their friends.

I have not tried to give a "balanced" view of Peruvian history or women's movements in Peru. Rather, I have tried to emphasize the often hidden aspects of history that are crucial to the interpretation of social change. Many people who have some acquaintance with Peruvian political developments, even those who are themselves Peruvians, who are themselves women, or who consider themselves scholars or revolutionaries, lack an understanding of the sources of the collective power of women in Peru. Most know little or nothing about the forms of struggle and the ways of thinking of those women who are politically active in the barriadas of the cities and in the indigenous communities of the countryside and the jungle, or of those women who work in the streets or in private homes or industries, thereby serving the needs of "development" without reaping any of its benefits.

What I have done is to document information that has been systematically kept from the public, especially from the women who are themselves most likely to be affected. This information does not consist of scattered facts or isolated events. On the contrary, I have purposely sought to include facts and events that I believe are highly determinative in the history of women and in the history of Peru. In making them more visible, I seek to make them even more determinative.

The women protagonists of this book are literally battling for survival, struggling to ensure the survival of their families during a period of failed reform. Affected by the development of feminist movements throughout the world, they are also in the process of redefining their own history and purpose as human beings. They are forcing themselves into the leadership of popular and revolutionary movements in order to defend their own interests both as women and as legitimate representatives of the Peruvian people.

Because I am a partisan of the women about whom I am writing, I make no claim to be disinterested. I have tried to acknowledge my biases and to understand, as well, the particular interests of those who have provided me with information. In doing the research for this book, I have cultivated the habit of checking academic studies, official statistics, and journalistic accounts against my own observations and against the expressed opinions and demands of the women who are engaging in organized struggle. I utilize a wide variety of sources, but I do not take anything I have read or heard or seen "at face value." Where all sources agree, however, I allow myself to speak with authority.

I have made an effort to explain how women are inserted into the social and economic structures of the country, but I have avoided both the lengthy quotation of academic sources and the presentation of tables and charts. In order to make my writing easily accessible, I have tried, on the contrary, to let the events unfold as in a story. This story, however, is related only in its essential features, because, for one thing, we are only recently beginning to write women's history in Peru. In the introductory chapter, I have outlined centuries of history without having very much feminist scholarship on which to draw. The material is therefore somewhat controversial and provisional, but I think it is important to present it at this stage so that we can begin debating about these themes.

I have tried to be selective rather than exhaustive in choosing material for this book. My intention has been to stimulate thought and action rather than to document long lists of names, places, organizations, and events. In the second chapter, which is a description of women's experiences in the coastal fishing town of Chimbote and in the river valley surrounding it, I introduce the reader to the recent effects of foreign economic penetration both in the city and in the countryside. The effects of this penetration are a major theme of the entire book; by glimpsing the forms of struggle that have emerged in response to economic change, the reader can begin to grasp how different and how similar the struggles of Peruvian women are from the struggles of other women. The organization of women is extremely difficult, but it is also more likely to happen under conditions of "dependent capitalism" than under precapitalist conditions.

The third chapter is a description of the work and political life of the indigenous women of the Andean mountains, especially in certain areas where the campesina, or peasant, union has been most active. In this chapter I acquaint the reader with the effects of agrarian reform among inhabitants of the sierra. The reform government of the 1970s sought initially to include women in ideological or educational campaigns, but it did not make the structural changes needed to bring them real economic opportunities. This failure caused some of them to openly challenge the premises of reform. At last, the women were forced to confront the male-dominated union so as to make it respond to their interests and assist them in reclaiming effective power in their communities.

Chapter four focuses mainly on the development of neighborhood or barriada organization in the cities, to which rural people have been forced to migrate under the impact of industrialization. Learning about women's struggles for survival in the cities brings to the reader's attention the emerging conflicts between women and men within the political parties of the Left, between the barriada women and the feminists who live outside the barriadas. Apathy or fatalism, so prevalent among the poor, and historically encouraged by religious officials, is contrasted with the revolutionary activism stimulated by sharp economic crisis. This activism is illustrated by climatic protests on Mother's Day and by impressive strategies evolved to combat the manipulation of relief organizations and government bureaucracies.

Chapter five demonstrates the precariousness of women's entry into the money economy in Peru and the combativeness and imagination that women who work in the "peripheral sector" of the economy bring to their political struggles. Whether women work on contract or as small entrepreneurs, whether in private households, in factories, or in the streets, they have no illusions about their future. Strikes, factory takeovers, and efforts to establish communal living situations have provided a focus for female organization and consciousness-raising among women who work for money. These women, more than any others, find themselves competing with men and at the same time allied with them in struggles against the state.

The sixth chapter focuses on ethnocide in the jungle and in isolated mountain areas. Here the contrasts between the non-patriarchal cultural values that predate the European conquest of the Amazon and Andean region and those of mestizo or modern societies can be most carefully drawn. Solidarity within the community and hostility toward enemies characterize peoples threatened constantly with extermination; it is here that guerrilla warfare began in 1980. Centered in the mountains and led largely by women, warfare spread rapidly into the jungle and the cities. Guerrilla campaigns presented a challenge not only to the state, but to all the popular movements and organizations of the country, as their members were attracted by its successes and traumatized by its immediate effect on their lives.

The final chapter brings the book up to my last visit to Peru, in 1984. It provides a summary and review of the outstanding issues and prospects facing Peruvian women today.

The effort I have made to document and interpret the experiences of Peruvian women of the popular classes has not been an easy one. I have lived with many of them and traveled with some of them while I was collecting the material for this book, but I have not really lived as they live, although I have shared personally some of their struggles. Sometimes our association was dangerous for both of us. In an effort to be faithful to these women's needs, I have returned to their homes in order to read aloud what I have written, asking for criticism and suggestions.

Each visit to Peru brought me into more intimate contact with the women who are the subject of my book. During the first month of my most recent visit I stayed in a Lima barriada at the home of a woman whose many political activities included the organization of a neighborhood *refugio,* or shelter for women, and of a basket-making cooperative, as well as the planning of meetings of barriada women at the regional and national levels. The women in her neighborhood had organized a "people's kitchen" but had been refused relief allotments for it. (The refusal was connected with controversies over their support of Lima's new mayor, a representative of the Left Unity coalition.) As a consequence, in order to offer meals at low cost to members of their own families, the women sold lunch to men who worked in a nearby asbestos factory producing water tanks and roofing very popular in the shantytowns of Lima. Every time a bus rolled by our house asbestos dust was raised in billows. No one I talked with was aware that such products are no longer produced in the developed countries, where asbestos companies have been taken to court for knowingly ignoring the risk of cancer and other fatal diseases to customers, workers, and residents of the towns where factories are located. The experience of living in this situation made much more apparent to me the stark alternatives women face when choosing priorities for political action.

I spent several weeks during my recent trip to Peru accompanying a peasant union organizer on a visit to indigenous communities in Apurimac. Because of a severe drought lasting several years, the people of this central mountain region were eligible for special shipments of relief food. However, these shipments were reportedly being diverted to nearby provinces where the government was combatting guerrillas, although these regions were not affected by the drought. A part of my friend's work was to see that emergency aid was made available to the people of her district, especially to those who were most isolated geographically and had suffered most acutely from heavy rain and the ensuing drought. Both the extreme poverty and the political tension have gravely affected my friend's health and the health of her family: she is only thirty-nine, and three of her children have already died.

For all the hardships my friend and I endured during our stay in the countryside, we never made the twelve-hour uphill climb that would have established direct contact with the women of her own community, who live apart from the men. We had, however, talked with some of them when they came down to join the men in a road-building project. Although the women had lost their corn crop, and their animals were dying from a disease never before encountered, they did not think that migrating to a lower altitude, or to another area, would benefit them in any way.

Nevertheless, they seemed desperate for contact with other women and for knowledge about the world.

Returning to Lima from the countryside, I was able to spend part of my time with an old friend who is active in the newly developing native movement. I agreed to care for her baby during a conference that was to last several days. Both of us assumed she would leave the conference periodically to nurse her daughter and spend the night with her. However, a state of emergency existed in the city because of strikes and antigovernment protests, and no one was allowed to enter or leave once the proceedings had begun. As the hours and days went on—although the baby adjusted well to the situation—both her mother and I became tense about our inability to make contact with each other. My friend was elected to the governing body *(directiva)* of the organization and felt exhilarated that a number of women had participated in the conference, in spite of problems each of them had encountered in coming to the city and gaining admittance to it. But from our experience we both knew there would have to be a more permanent solution to the question of child care if women were to participate fully in the native movement. In fact, my friend, as a household worker, had criticized middle-class feminists for leaving their children with servants in order to engage in political activities, a privilege they took for granted. Certainly she did not have this option, and, besides, the women in her movement opposed it on principle.

While living and working with Peruvian women, I was always aware I was an outsider. I rarely expressed my own political opinions unless asked to do so, and I did not use tape recorders freely. Some of my closest friends thought I was being too cautious in this respect, but I knew from experience that it was a necessary precaution. An elderly man once said to me outright: "You must be a missionary or a CIA agent. Otherwise, what would you be doing here?" Fortunately, I had with me an article I had written about peasants. He sat down and read it out loud while other villagers listened. Some of them knew me from years earlier, and they were curious to know what I had to say about them, about men and women. They made useful comments, as did the man whose confidence I needed to win, and I was glad to have an audience for my views.

Only on one occasion did I intervene directly on behalf of women without having a clear invitation to do so. I was helping prepare a meal during a congress of the Yanesha Indians in the jungle. A man who was not participating in the congress was watching us cook and giving us orders from time to time. The Yanesha women ignored him for the most part; once they asked for his help and were refused. Suddenly, one of the logs under a big pot of soup gave way and it fell over. The man began to yell at the women, calling them stupid. I said to him, half joking, that he should have told us the pot was about to fall, since he had been sitting there watching it. That began a discussion during which I accused him of behaving like a *patrón,* or boss. He defended himself, saying he couldn't be a *patrón* because he didn't have a whip. One of the observers from the capital criticized me for intervening, when I recounted the story to him, but the women who were cooking with me were happy with the situation and tried to persuade me to stay and live with them. I eventually came to believe that the native man's yelling at the women was partly meant to impress me as an outsider and that the women were pleased I was not impressed.

During my recent visits to Peru I felt constantly rewarded by the appreciation people showed me when I shared with them what was happening in other parts of their own country. Most of all, what I tried to accomplish in a personal way was to give encouragement to women activists who were having all kinds of problems—material, personal, and political. This was something I had been able to do only rarely in earlier years, because then women's consciousness of their own situations had been weak. In the mid-1970s, when I encouraged women who were trying to gain some power in a union or community organization, for instance, my support could easily be turned into a liability. Men would tell them I was an outsider who was "trying to split their ranks by pitting women against men." On my visits to Peru in the 1980s, women were not intimidated by that line. And they were not "pitting themselves against men" either.

Women in the provinces were especially eager to share their ideas with me, and to ask me for ideas, without feeling compelled to agree with me. They were not asking me to take over for them in organizing, as had sometimes been the case earlier. They were already organized and looking for solidarity. Usually the suggestions I was able to offer I had learned from other women in Peru. My advantage was that I was free to travel around and to study while they were immersed in overwhelming daily struggles. They were looking for ways to break through the despair of other women, or to overcome the fear of those who naively hoped for "better days" at the hands of the authorities in return for "good behavior." When I was able to put them in touch with women who were having some success at organizing, it strengthened their cause and gave them new hope.

Learning can come from adversity and hostility as well as from the friendly exchange of ideas. One of the experiences important to my understanding of the struggles of women in Peru was the reception my ex-husband's grandmother gave me on my return to Peru. Mama Juana had helped Raúl and me get etablished on communal land and become part of her community of Huanca Indians. Then, in 1976, we separated. In 1981, Raúl's mother accompanied me to Mama Juana's house, where we both hoped to stay for several days before returning to Lima. Mama Juana screamed at us, began weeping loudly, and addressed her daughter through the closed door to her house: "Get away from here with your Carola, who made my little boy suffer so much!"

Mama Juana is a medicine woman. She had helped rear her grandson, Raúl. In her old age she had became a recluse, but when Raúl and I returned to her community in the Mantaro Valley, she began to open up to outsiders. Then, immediately after my departure from Peru, she was taken into custody for an entire week while police tried to get her to talk about our political activities. Today she is more of a recluse than ever, and has turned to sorcery to deal with her frustrations. Raúl and I had rejected Mama Juana's counsel when we married, before our trip to the United States. She knew that we were in continual conflict with each other, and that our marriage was therefore a violation of tradition, which requires a long period of successful cohabitation before marriage. Nevertheless, once the deed was done, she gave us both her full support. Later, after I left Raúl, she shared the trauma he experienced from our separation. Mama Juana's outburst toward her daughter and me on my return visit served to keep me humble, causing me to realize that the desire to promote solidarity among women had to be tempered with an understanding of my limitations. It also helped me to comprehend the anger Indian women feel toward foreigners who can choose to enjoy the benefits of community without ever having to assume its burdens and responsibilities completely.

On many occasions, I came to realize that the friendliness shown to me was a product of a particular investment in my good will; it was not a sign of generalized trust. Unconditional trust is more than any North American has a right to expect in Peru. I also came to realize that my commitment to writing a book did not automatically provide me with respect or cooperation. In the experience of most Peruvians, the printed word has not often served to enhance their cause. Even when I felt people understood and approved of my work, I often had to return repeatedly in order to find them with enough time to give me the help I needed.

For all of these reasons, I wish I could express publicly my heartfelt thanks to those Peruvian friends who gave me constant help and encouragement. Unfortunately, I must refrain from doing so, because, for many of them, anonymity will better serve their cause. That is the unkind world we have inherited; it is the world we are trying to change.

Outside Peru, among those who helped in the organization and development of this book are Jana Everett, Peggy Gleason, Florence Babb, Gloria Escobar, Irene Silverblatt, Barbara Millman, Urvashi Butalia, Inez Banchero, and Robert Molteno. Lydia Fraile offered her services in translating the manuscript into Spanish so it could be read and criticized in Peru before the final draft was written. She did this at a time when I had no offers of publication and nothing with which to remunerate her. Needless to say, her interest and her help were crucial in carrying this project through.

Since I have purposely chosen to write in a personal style, I have not always given explicit credit to those whose research and writing has contributed so greatly to my own understanding. Therefore, I would like to encourage the reader to look over the references carefully. Considering that practically nothing had been printed about women in Peru until very recently, the existence of

so many sources is itself impressive evidence of women's ferment.
Many of these are primary sources not readily available in libraries
or archives either in Peru or elsewhere. They are listed to inspire
collection and to make public the efforts of activists in the dis-
semination of information at the grass-roots level.

I would have preferred to continue gathering information and
photographs for many more years before committing this book to
print, since there is so much more to learn and to discover.
However, the writing of history is, in the final analysis, a collective
effort, and I feel some urgency about making this material available to others. I only hope this account of Peruvian women's
struggles will be more helpful to those whose cause it is meant to
serve than to their enemies, who will no doubt have easier access
to it than they will.

When Women Rebel

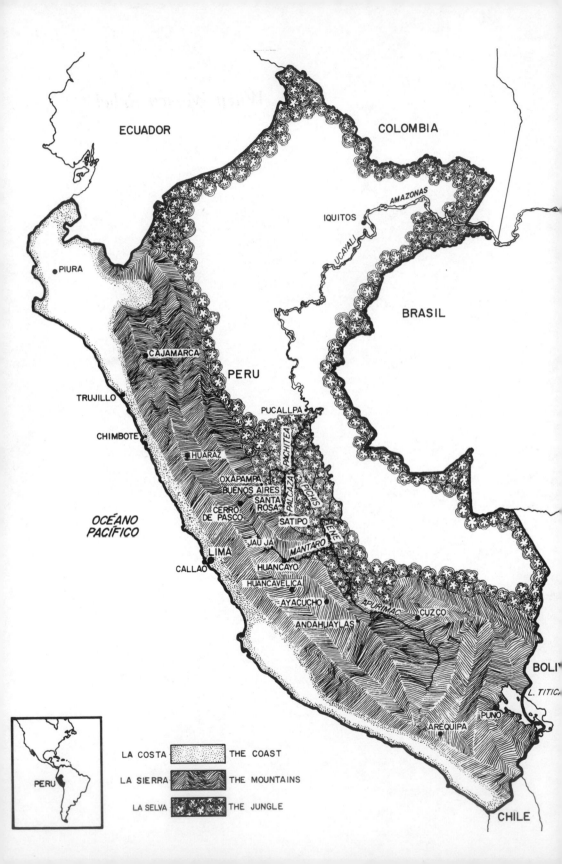

ECUADOR

COLOMBIA

IQUITOS

AMAZONAS

UCAYALI

BRASIL

PIURA

CAJAMARCA

PERU

TRUJILLO

PUCALLPA

CHIMBOTE

HUARAZ

PACHITEA

OXAPAMPA
BUENOS AIRES
SANTA
ROSA
CERRO
DE PASCO
SATIPO

PALCAZU

PICHIS

OCÉANO
PACÍFICO

JAUJA

MANTARO

ENE

LIMA

CALLAO

HUANCAYO

HUANCAVELICA

AYACUCHO

APURIMAC

CUZCO

ANDAHUAYLAS

BOLIV

L. TITICA

PUNO

AREQUIPA

CHILE

PERU

LA COSTA   THE COAST

LA SIERRA   THE MOUNTAINS

LA SELVA   THE JUNGLE

I : *A Look at Women's History*

Conquest, Subordination, and Resistance: The Incas and the Spanish

ACCORDING TO the narratives of the Spanish explorer Francisco de Orellana, he and his soldiers were opposed in battle by native women and men of the South American jungle, with women commanders in the lead. When their experiences were retold in Europe, the river on which they had floated eastward out of what is now Peru came to be known as the River of the Amazons— reminiscent of the stories of warrior women in southeastern Europe who had been known as Amazons. At this same time, in the early sixteenth century, female leaders, or *capullanas,* governed a majority of the Indian communities on the Pacific coast to the north of what is now the capital of Peru, Lima. After the Spanish conquest, the *capullanas* lost their power, and most refused to cooperate with the Spanish in any way. Many of their male counterparts, the *curacas,* succumbed to the crown in return for being made co-administrators of Spanish rule.

Diseases brought to the South American continent by Europeans, together with internal warfare, had destroyed half of the population even before Incan territory was taken over by the Spanish. Spanish soldiers never succeeded in conquering the people of the jungle—nor had the Incas before them. But in the rest of the Andean territory, conquistadores forced Indian men to work in gold and silver mines, exacted tribute from them, and appropriated community land. The resistance of the Indians, together with the continued spread of disease, eventually reduced the population to a tiny fraction of what it had once been. During this time, women lived in constant fear of sexual assault by the Spanish, which continued even after open warfare ended. As one historian remarked: "To view the individual case of rape as a desperate action of a sex-starved man is to miss the point, for viewed collectively, the rape of Indian women was an integral part of the drive for submission that characterizes all conquest."[1]

Legal marriage was a partial protection from rape by Spanish men. Marriage laws under Spanish rule made women literally the property of their husbands. Many women were forced to marry, or were given to Spanish men in lieu of tribute, or were sold into slavery by their own families. Hacendados, or feudal landowners, required Indian women to spend a night in the feudal manor before they were permitted to marry a fellow comunero, or member of an indigenous community. To escape abuse, some women fled to high mountain areas. Others fled to the cities. There they worked on contract for their conquerors and became the mothers of mestizo children.[2]

Whereas the Inca administrators exacted tribute from their subjects in the form of produce, redistributing the products of communal labor in times of hardship, the Spanish required tribute of individuals, using it primarily to enrich themselves. Only men were required by Spanish law to work in the mines, but when they ran away or died, or when they couldn't pay their debts, women had to substitute for them. Women were also isolated in small rooms where they were made to weave cloth for export   Spain. When families couldn't meet their obligations, community land was taken over by the Spanish. Parcels that communities had allotted to women were especially vulnerable. Women were forced to move to their husbands' communities—a reversal of traditional custom and a tremendous loss of independence for women.[3]

Inca society had been based on careful cultivation of land that had to be continually tended to maintain fertility. Complicated irrigation systems, terracing, and scientific calculation of lunar and solar cycles had made the land productive generation after generation. Storage of surpluses assured that no one went without food in times of severe drought. All this changed under Spanish administration.

The Indians' agricultural system was undermined by territorial grants given to the Spanish conquerors by the crown, and by the gradual introduction of private property and commercial relations. Women, who had been in control of agricultural production in most Andean communities, retained this control after the Spanish conquest. However, the mode of production established under Spanish rule did not permit the continuance of traditional practices. Women were forced to sell what they produced to gain access to money. Class divisions within indigenous communities, apparently already in existence under Inca administration, were reinforced and developed by the Spanish in order to control indigenous populations and gain access to their labor.

In most places Inca government had been characterized by autonomy at the local level. All adults participated in native assemblies, or *ayllus*. Women shared power with men and participated as equals in the work of the community. Sexual life was not degrading to them. Sexual freedom during youth was followed by temporary pairing, trial marriage, or *sirvinacuy*, and eventually by consensual union, which gave women and men adult status in their communities.

Although in most of the territory under Inca control there was no double standard for sexual behavior at the community level, Spanish narratives speak of "royal nuns," the "virgins of the sun." These women spent their lives weaving exquisite tapestries depicting the history of the Inca people and their relations with the gods. These tapestries were often burned in sacrifice to the sun. According to some reports, women were also sacrificed on occasion, and the Incas recruited women as mistresses for themselves or to give as gifts to men of outstanding achievement. Evidently the Coya, who was the wife of the Inca, did not have the same sexual freedom that her husband had, nor that common women had, but she was powerful as administrator of production and technical research in the areas controlled by the Inca. The Inca handled accounting, the resolution of political disputes, and the conquest of territory.[4]

According to Spanish sources, male-dominated empires had already been established in some places in South America before the Inca conquest. Here, according to the same sources, the Incas resorted to harsh methods of rule to subdue local populations, including massive deportations or forced migrations. Such was reportedly the case in the Andean territory of Cajamarca. It was in Cajamarca that the Spanish initiated the conquest of South America in 1532, gaining the allegiance of local leaders against the Inca, who lived in Cuzco. The Spanish, however, soon subjected the people of Cajamarca to a terror never before imagined. Slaves were imported from Africa to help subdue Indian slaves and to replace them when necessary. Women, apparently already reduced to slavery and concubinage, were further degraded and physically abused by the Spanish.

The foreign takeover of the coast of Peru was accomplished not so much through definitive battles but through slow genocide against the Indians. Very little remains of the native cultures whose technological and artistic achievements in weaving and pottery, skills mostly attained by women, are unsurpassed anywhere in the world.[5] The peoples of the Peruvian coast were the oldest known horticulturists in the Americas. Recently discovered remains in Paloma date back over eight thousand years, at which time inhabitants were storing food surpluses in grass-lined pits, much as the inhabitants of the jungle do today. The domestication of animals and the cultivation of cereals and roots was common throughout the territory conquered by the Spanish in the sixteenth century.[6]

It was in the southern Andes, in what is today central Peru, that cultural conflict with the Spanish became most intense. Indian women's resistance to foreign rule brought them into continual conflict with Indian men, to whom they had been systematically subordinated by the Spanish. By the eighteenth century, when native administrators appointed by the Spanish crown finally began to rebel against Spanish tyranny, Indian women were leading troops, composed of both women and men, and suffering terrible reprisals. Most remembered among these women is Micaela Bastidas, wife of the revolutionary leader Tupac Amaru II. She and her husband were brutally slaughtered by the Spanish on the central plaza of Cuzco.

Herbal remedies are offered for sale in a local market. Communal ferias bear little resemblance to the commercial activities carried out by street vendors in the cities. (Jorge Azañedo)

A mother and her children in the coastal town of Pisco reflect the racial mixture of descendants of native South Americans and African slaves. Both in the cities and in the country, stable family life has become exceptional. (Lynn Murray)

British and North American Dominance

Peru finally achieved independence from Spain in 1821, and slavery was formally abolished soon afterward. However, the plunder of Peru's people and resources was continued by the British, whose political defeat by the North American colonies had only increased their need for economic resources. The British extracted fertilizer and rubber from the country, exhausting these resources just as the Spanish had exhausted gold and silver. Meat, cloth, wheat, and newly discovered mineral resources were also exported. Temporary or seasonal migration from communities in the mountains to the coast and jungle became a pattern of existence for many men, who sought wage labor away from their families.

Women carried on community life and subsistence agriculture at home, always vulnerable to abuse by feudal landowners. Women had to confront landowners who killed animals that wandered outside communal territory. Landowners accused native women of stealing, and punished husbands if wives were slow to perform required tasks—tasks for which the women received no pay. Wives were also abused or punished for the insubordination of husbands or sons. They were continually on call to bring food to members of their families who were working the fields or pasturing the animals belonging to hacendados.

During the period when the Peruvian Republic was dominated by British interests, missionaries and outside colonizers successfully invaded the jungle. Spanish explorers and priests had been expelled from the Amazon region by natives, but mestizos, British, and other traders and colonizers were finally able to establish a foothold in the area. They offered needed products to the natives in return for work, raided their villages for slave labor, and recruited them to build roads and other public works. There are many accounts of the wanton abuse of women and children by the rubber barons of the jungle. Later, young women were lured or forced into prostitution by entrepreneurs and by Peruvian soldiers who came to the Amazon area to guard against Brazilian incursion. With the depletion of women in native communities close to military outposts, native men began raiding other villages for mates. The relaxed relations between women and men that had characterized communities of the tropical rain forest were replaced by male rule enforced by marriage and, occasionally, by gang rape.[7]

The British economic domination of Peru terminated at the end of the nineteenth century after Peru's defeat in the war with Chile. Chile gained control of the southern coastal regions that had provided the richest area of exploitation of nitrate reserves for the British. Since then, North American business and financial interests have dominated Peru's economy. The North Americans formed alliances with feudal landowners at the same time that Peruvian industrialists were beginning to establish capitalist enterprises, especially on the coast. Eventually, in the 1950s, North Americans allied with the industrialists or encouraged landowners to invest in industry and to modernize farming so as to increase export potential. Direct investment by North American companies was maintained where possible, while financial control became paramount. Reliance on foreign credit put Peruvians at the mercy of multinational corporations and the banks and other financial institutions with which they were linked.[8]

The North American presence accelerated class divisions in Peru, produced massive migration from the countryside, accentuated the centralization of economic and political power in Lima, and further separated women and men in work and community life. Women were left to oversee farm production where capitalist wage labor was not profitable, whereas men were encouraged to acquire skills enabling them to perform wage labor. Mining once more became the principal source of exports, along with sugar, cotton, coffee, wool, lumber, fish, animal hides, and cocaine. Meanwhile, the importation of machines and surplus agricultural products such as rice and wheat from the United States placed a burden on the local economy. Cereals grown on subsistence plots and on communal land were needed for survival, especially by those who had little access to money, but these products were grown less and less because they could not be sold competitively in the capitalist market. For the first time in Peru's history, potatoes were exported, not because they were more plentiful than ever, but because selling them overseas brought a higher profit than selling them at home.

As the subsequent chapters of this book will demonstrate, North American dominance of the Peruvian economy has affected women in specific ways in each of the major regions of the country—sierra, selva (or jungle), and coast. The sierra, cool and relatively dry, is thought to be suitable mainly for animal grazing, subsistence cultivation, and mineral extraction. The selva, warm and humid, is suited primarily to hunting and fishing and the selective cultivation and extraction of wood and vegetable products. It is also thought to contain large petroleum reserves. The coast is dry, except when irrigated, but it has been the site of industrialized farming and manufacturing, as well as extensive extraction of wealth from the sea. Tourism and production of handicrafts exist throughout the country.

Women of the sierra, who are the major producers of food for domestic consumption, as well as the major reproducers of the labor force needed by capitalist industry throughout the country, are more exploited now than ever before in history. They have nevertheless gained partial independence from their former overseers, the landowners who were expropriated by industrial interests. Indians had been demanding the expropriation of feudal landowners ever since the Spanish were overthrown, but it became possible only after Andean women joined men in the guerrilla movements of the 1960s, forcing the government to undertake agricultural reform.

Women's intransigence in popular struggle during this period is recalled graphically in an account of a meeting at which men were negotiating with government officials after a massacre of six hundred peasants: "Those who had the last word, those who refused all agreements, were the women seated on the floor of the prefect's office during the entire debate. These women, more than the lawyers and peasant leaders, represented the masses. They were the masses, an intransigent indigenous force, disposed to die for the cause—and the leaders were helpless to move them."[9]

Both women and men in the selva have been expected to accommodate themselves to the development of the petroleum industry and to the destruction of the jungle to make way for those who hope to make quick profits from lumber, animal products, coffee, cocoa, and cocaine.[10] The devastation of the natural en-

vironment is inevitably accompanied by the progressive impoverishment of the native populations and their transformation
into peons, continually indebted to colonists and forced to serve
them as laborers, servants, or prostitutes. In recent years, major
U.S. government investments in Peru have been concentrated in
the jungle. In those areas of the Amazon region now under territorial dispute, natives have been pushed further and further away
from the rivers, away from those areas where the soil is richest and
transportation is easiest. The "protection" of native territory from
incursion by colonists and foreign businesses has been promoted
periodically by reformers in the church and government, but in
the end these efforts have always served to provide a cover for the
acceleration of conquest. Recently, native groups have organized
federations to oppose incursions by multinational corporations,
and are meeting with increased government repression. At the
same time, women who are recognizing that there is no place for
them to live with dignity outside the jungle are helping organize
others to join in the struggle to reclaim native culture and
strengthen native economic life.

In the cities and on the coast, women's wage labor has been
exploited by capitalists, but always subordinated to that of men.
Women and children were the first wageworkers in the textile
industry in Lima. Later, women were recruited to work in fish-
processing plants. However, most men opposed the hiring of
women, and men replaced women after the initial labor struggles
had won better conditions or brought more machinery into the
factories. Because of their early recruitment into the labor force,
women fought and died alongside men in the early labor movements to win a shorter workday and to prevent the complete
destruction of the natural environment by industry. Nevertheless,
they were finally left to serve the interests of capital in marginal
employment as seasonal or contracted labor. Today they are demanding, with increasing militancy, recognition of their own labor organizations and representation in union federations.

Although regional and economic differences cause women to
be divided politically and culturally, there is a beginning of communication between mestizas and indigenous women within
women's movements. While women in the cities are reclaiming

their rights in the workplace, others, especially in the countryside, are publicly voicing doubts about the kind of education and technology promoted by men, and from which they have been excluded. They are beginning to reclaim their knowledge of traditional medicine and traditional methods of cultivation and nutrition. Some women from the cities are assisting them in doing this, and assisting them in tasks of organization. Though geographic and economic barriers constitute permanent obstacles to organizational unity, there is, even in the remotest parts of Peru, some awareness of the ferment that is taking place among women in other places.

The growing militancy of women can be seen in part as a drive to establish a permanent power base for women in revolutionary movements. There is no doubt that contradictions posed by the system have demanded this for a long time. The capitalist economy has benefited from the free labor of women and children in the home—a survival of feudal relations—yet it has been unable to provide conditions for stable family life. Women cannot afford to remain at home maintaining their families. They are forced continually to seek sources of financial support on their own because the men are unable to provide for their families. On the other hand, the exploitation of women and children as marginal or reserve labor contributes to the breakdown of family relations. Because the interests of women and men are redefined under capitalism, creating new contradictions between them both in the workplace and at home, the state is forced to intervene with programs of social assistance.

In countries such as Peru, called "dependent capitalist" countries by some scholars because their economies are subordinated to the interests of foreign capital, the state does not have the resources to provide even minimal public assistance for families affected by such phenomena as unemployment and inflation. Therefore, churches and other private agencies attempt to ameliorate the situation, often with money coming from outside the country. As will be shown in the later chapters of this book, church leaders in Peru have usually worked hand-in-hand with the government to persuade women to accommodate themselves to the needs of the economy through personal self-sacrifice, chastity, forgiveness, self-abnegation, hard work, honesty, and sobriety. Protestant churches also promote consumerism and saving by those who are fortunate enough to have steady incomes. Women have been chastised by both Catholic and Protestant church organizations for "meddling in politics" and propagandized to fear community efforts at cooperation as the harbinger of "communist tyranny." While they are actively discouraged from resisting exploitation through grass-roots political organization that demands social change, they are encouraged to participate in political movements which call for the defense of order and stability, home and family.

Within the Catholic Church, progressive elements have recognized the suffering of the poor as unjust. Rejecting the conservative idea that poverty is imposed by "God's will," they have sought to mitigate suffering through alliance with those who are organizing to make demands on the state. However, the Church rarely questions the family system itself as one of the props to an exploitive economy and a source of special suffering for women, who are expected to put the needs of their husbands and children before their own and to put up with abuse to assure domestic peace.

Individual resistance has prevented Peruvian women from being entirely subjugated by Church and State. Women have retained property rights within marriage. Indigenous couples continue to respect and practice trial marriage.[11] But even those traditions have come under concerted attack under modern "reform." Ignorant of women's traditional strength in community life, reformers have consistently undermined women's status and power.

Among the notes of North Americans who staffed a much-heralded "development project" in Vicos, Peru, in the early 1950s, was the following account of one woman's resistance to the dispossession of community land in the name of "progress."

The subject was apparently settled, and the *mayorales* about to start discussing something else, when Ojeda's wife (she looks much older than Ojeda), who had been lurking in the doorway, sprang into the room and screeched a diatribe against Rodríguez and Villar. She declared them lazy *pingas paradas* (erect penises) who stood up and screwed other people. If Rodriguez wished to dispose of her *chacra* [land under cultivation] she said, he would have to kiss her *chucha,* and the only way a *pinga* like him could get near her *chucha* was if she were dead. At this point, Rodríguez interrupted her, demanded that she leave, and said he refused to be talked to in such a way. He said it was not proper for her to be addressing the *mayorales* anyway since the affair concerned her husband and not her. She refused to leave, but stood there yapping away harshly. Mario Ricaldi asked her husband to eject her, but Ojeda did not move. Ricaldi then told Tadeo to eject her, but he did not move from his seat either. Ricaldi then got up from his seat and approached her and put out his hands as if to push her, upon which she sat down on the floor and refused to move, talking all the while. Ricaldi pushed against her with his shins until, still declaiming, she got up from the floor and Ricaldi and Enrique Ona walked her to the door and out the gate. She remained outside the gate for a minute or so, shouting through it.[12]

The person who recorded this incident undoubtedly thought it was "cute." Official project reports make no mention of the effect of what they call "development" on the lives of women, other than to note that "women have not moved apace with men."

Since the rebirth of feminist movements in Europe and North America in the 1960s, there has been a change in the attitude of personnel in those agencies concerned with facilitating capitalist development in Peru. Specific attention is given to women's needs through the funding of special projects giving women skills in accounting, communication, and leadership, and helping them to secure credit for small business ventures. Given the over-all situation of the economy, and women's double role in it, such isolated efforts seem destined to create rivalry among grant recipients while doing little to satisfy the needs of the majority of women.

The Growth of Political Consciousness

Women who live in the cities are the most hopeful of finding a way out of desperate poverty. But the vast majority are confronted with a lack of housing, health services, and sanitation and such basic necessities as water and transportation. They are forced to try to make a home for their families under intolerable physical conditions, while continually seeking ways to augment the family income. While these women have had no real voice in determining national and international policies, the burden of the solution of urgent problems created by these policies inevitably falls on them.

The growth of women's political consciousness in the cities can be understood primarily as a reaction to the ineffectiveness of male political leadership in addressing the problems of workplace and community felt most acutely by women. In the barriadas, or shantytowns, the double burden of home and work keeps women out of neighborhood organizing once the family is settled, but when confidence in male leadership is shattered, the latent organizing force of women emerges.

This process could be seen in Lima a few years ago in the threatened removal of shantytown residents from a site they had occupied since 1961. The government had declared their settlement illegal. During the years of litigation, the pobladores, or shantytown dwellers, lost confidence in their leaders, who seemed about to give in to government authorities. Then a man appeared on the scene and accused community leaders of having pocketed money given them to carry on the struggle. By appearing to be a leftist representing the interests of the poor, he gained the confidence of the community. Then he betrayed them, signing an agreement behind their backs that ratified their removal to the desert area Canto Grande. He called a general meeting, intimidating the residents by inviting the police and identifying those mothers and housewives who complained as agitators and terrorists. All of this motivated the pobladores to organize in defense of their community: "Women of all ages, single women and married women, tired of being dominated, manipulated, and deceived, took to the streets and formed an Emergency Committee in which the majority of the leaders were mothers. Our spirit of struggle, kept dormant for so long, manifested itself on the fourth of February [1981], when, at a meeting of the community center Segundo de Mayo, representatives of the Housing Ministry and the Department of Civil Defense tried to convince us to move temporarily to Canto Grande, and later to San Agustín. Over a thousand of us, in an energetic and disciplined way, said NO, and they were forced to back down. . . . Even though we were in constant struggle over this matter, on March 8th, International Women's Day, the women of our settlement, Primero de Mayo, and others from a neighboring settlement, decided to join the march in downtown Lima together with other women who carried their own banners. We marched with our signs denouncing the imminent danger of eviction from our terrain, and it was an inspiration to know that so many of us are abandoning the passive role that society has assigned us for so many years, that we are now assuming the defense of our own rights."[13]

Those who have felt excluded from political participation, or frustrated working in political organizations that seek only to manipulate or use them as women, find their own strength and their own kind of wisdom and inspiration by joining forces with other women in political struggle. Wherever political struggle occurs, women are taking on new responsibilities that bring them into direct conflict with the government and alert them to the dangers of entrusting the direction of their lives to men.

In both the city and the country, women's immediate concerns for securing the understanding and cooperation of men have caused them to reexamine the nature of their ties to men in the family and community.

A group of women from both the country and the city came together in Cuzco in 1980, at the invitation of grass-roots community leaders, to discuss their urgent problems. These included abuse by men who had succumbed to alcoholism or who had become irresponsible toward their families and inconsistent in their defense of community interests. The conversation turned to the institution of the patriarchal family, an institution which has brought little security, not to mention happiness, to its members. One woman concluded: "If we stop getting married, others will go on doing it anyway, and they'll have the same problems we're having. We'll never change things that way. I think we have to find a real solution, decide whether women should marry or not, how we can organize our lives, what alternatives there are."[14] Hers was the expression of centuries of frustration felt by the hundreds of thousands of Peruvian women who have seen their husbands turned into tyrants, their land taken away, their children die in

Gleaning has helped sustain growing families, but the fields of modern farms are seldom accessible to women. Efforts at birth control are frustrated by institutions that seek to manipulate or use women rather than help them and their children prosper. (Jorge Azañedo)

Women and children carry water for household use. The availability and quality of water are issues of primary concern to women; as "development" progresses, access to water is often restricted. (Jorge Azañedo)

infancy or disappear from the community to become outsiders, mestizos—forced to be either scoundrels or victims in capitalist society. Her statement, made in the context of an organized effort to confront important contradictions experienced by women, was a big advance over the desperate personal appeals women have made over the years when faced with exclusion from community power.

Peruvian philosophers who are founders of indigenous movements have questioned the structural foundations of capitalist patriarchy or what they prefer to call "western individualism." These scholars are labeled utopianists by both the Left and the Right in Peru because they base their critique of modern society on a view of the *incanato* that is in dispute.[15] They reject the idea that the *incanato*—the government established by the Incas—was patriarchal or despotic in any way. They describe the Inca economic system as "agrarian communism" based on direct democracy at the community level and "confederate centralism" at the national level. Western individualism, they say, declares the minimum expression of humanity to be the male, who seeks "his woman" to serve his needs, while indigenous philosophy sees the human pair in service to the community as the fundamental entity of society. One author says: "In the times of the *tawantinsuyanos* there were large communities governed by women, perhaps even more than were governed by men. . . . The supreme power over everything was our protective mother, *Pachamama.* . . . All the children of the community were legitimate for the simple reason that they were all natural children, or children of *Pachamama;* even if children knew who their individual biological fathers were, all the men of the parent generation treated them alike, as fathers or uncles."[16] Another indigenous scholar says: "The community was responsible for each child until the fourth year, and all the men of the *ayllu* were its father and all the women its mother. After this, the child began formal education, and by seven years of age the child had the basic knowledge of an 'oldtimer.' . . . In spite of 460 years of western subjugation, no one has been able to destroy the community. The *ayllu* is invincible simply because it is the maximum expression of socialist relations."[17]

Indigenous leaders have called for the rebirth of the Nación

Andina-Amazónica as a modern expression of socialism. Most of the organizations they have founded have not, however, seriously taken up the cause of women or sought to bring about radical changes in family structures imposed by the European conquest. Women's organizations, born out of men's inability to support their families, men's abandonment of women, and men's failure to lead in the popular struggle against the government have, however, begun to take up this cause.

The Effects of Military Rule

Women were given unwitting assistance in asserting their power during the late 1960s and early 1970s—the early years of progressive military rule in Peru—by the government itself. The military wanted to appear modern and revolutionary. Its reform program was labeled Christian Humanism by its proponents, and included a program for the *revalorización,* or reassessment, of women's contribution to society. Certain health and work benefits for women were written into law.

The military had come to power in 1968 through the failure of the Alliance for Progress to modernize the economy. Feudal landowners had opposed agrarian reform, and peasants fought to push the reform beyond what was envisioned by representatives of industrial capitalists who were its authors. A number of young military officers had acquired some familiarity with socialist ideas as students at Peru's Center for Higher Military Studies in the 1960s. They became convinced that the military government could unify the country under the slogan "Neither capitalism nor communism." Apparently, the military also thought they could not modernize Peru's economy without the cooperation of North American financial institutions, and so they sought credits and technical aid from them. Expropriated North American companies were compensated by allowing them to reinvest in new and more profitable ventures in Peru.

The military reform government was destined to fail. Export industries continued to take priority over production for domestic consumption. In fact, those industries which were expropriated from private owners and intended to be administered by the workers were particularly oriented toward export markets. The devastating effects of world-wide recession, falling prices for products, skyrocketing interest rates, and escalating prices on imported technology brought increasing government control in the management of production. Promises of worker control were revoked. Reforms giving women some access to education, child-care facilities enabling them to enter the work force (albeit without the same salaries or prerogatives as men), promotion of the general idea that women should be considered the equals of men—all were forgotten or reversed by government under the impact of recession. Many women had been admitted to universities for the first time, yet found there was little they could look forward to after graduation. In practice, *revalorización* had brought women little concrete improvement in their lives. But those whose hopes had been aroused or whose vision had been expanded did not forget.

As the military regime headed by Juan Velasco Alvarado began to implement *Participación Popular* without popular consent, thugs were hired to fight social activists and assassinate union leaders. Extreme right-wing elements in the government, closely allied with the United States, were able to take over. Velasco was removed and replaced by the former prime minister and minister of war, Francisco Morales Bermúdez. Under Morales Bermúdez' rule, from 1975 to 1980, inflation averaged 70 percent per year and unemployment or underemployment soared to over 50 percent. The country nearly went bankrupt through indebtedness, and was bailed out temporarily by a Texas oil company that paid the first installment on its debts to U.S. banks. Peru was placed under a caretaker committee of U.S. bankers until its debt problems could be ameliorated. Government austerity in social programs was accompanied by new concessions to foreign investment. Strikes and popular protest increased, in spite of periodic declarations of martial law. Escalating class struggle culminated in three successful general strikes in the period of two years.[18]

During this time of hardship for the Peruvian masses, women participated heroically in land take-overs, student protests, and strikes and internsified neighborhood organization in the shantytowns. In 1978 and 1979, women were the backbone of a nationwide strike by school teachers that gave voice to the frustations of the masses of the Peruvian people. "There wasn't a single day in which the streets weren't filled with teachers, demanding to be heard. Bombs and tanks no longer affected them. The Jirón Unión [a street in downtown Lima] belonged to the union and almost every evening it was impossible to pass by there without encountering a demonstration. . . . On June 16 a compact mass of 3,000 occupied the last block of the street and encountered the most brutal repression that had ever taken place during the strike. One tank and hundreds of police attacked this heroic mass from behind and from in front. The men tried to distract the police, but the women didn't need protection. They withstood the tear gas with the help of those who threw water at them to diminish its effect, resisting and counter-attacking. They only dispersed after some of them obtained an answer from the President, who agreed on a date to meet with the union leadership. . . . On June 26, the women demonstrated their heroism once again, taking over the Iglesia de la Merced [a church on the same street] where they stayed three days and nights, propagandizing for the strike."[19]

In spite of their active involvement in the popular struggles of the 1970s, women were excluded from formal leadership in popular organizations. Women were seen as a kind of logistical support for the struggle. "*Comités de damas* worked constantly and untiringly in support of mining strikes, went out on the streets to march, prepared meals and watched the children. Women were beaten up when encampments were overtaken, they were worried when, in the confusion and the violence, they lost their children. Even state workers, secretaries and public employees went out to march and agitate, scribbling picket signs while police were swinging their clubs and throwing their tear gas bombs."[20] One feminist recalled bitterly: "The repression doesn't distinguish between men and women—the only ones that apparently maintain this inequality are our comrades of the political parties of the Left."

Criticism directed toward women who raised the issue of male domination of politics only raised women's consciousness. A spokesperson for a newly formed feminist group said in an interview published in a magazine of the Peruvian Left: "The problems of women aren't problems of the 'superstructure' that will go away when the structures of the society are changed, nor are they problems that come from 'petty bourgeois thought.' They are an aspect of general oppression that demands our analysis." She went on to declare passionately: "The street vendor cooks before she leaves her home, runs with her baby on her back when the municipal police chase her to take away the things she's selling, fights sleep as she changes her baby's diapers, depositing them in a cardboard box under her cart. She gets sick, dies for lack of attention during childbirth, passes out from bleeding when she resorts to a primitive abortion, accomplished with a piece of wire introduced into her vagina, in order to kill a child before it's born rather than seeing it die of malnutrition or bronchitis afterward. . . . And in spite of the *fotonovelas* and *Buen Hogar* [cheap novels and magazines written especially for women], in spite of sick children and abusive husbands, women have demonstrated that they are capable of going into the streets to defend the rights of the workers. . . ."[21]

Once women gained a hearing in the popular organizations of the poor, they began to raise political questions of particular concern to them, adopting positions that sometimes directly challenged those previously espoused by men: "Because 'family planning' programs have been part of imperialist aggression, the Left has refused to deal with the real necessity of birth control; almost like a mechanical reflex, they have hoped to avoid the problem. We've arrived at the conclusion that it's important, not to compulsively control the population, but to make information available to couples and to make contraceptives readily available. We need to recognize that couples have a right to be able to regulate conception and to make this knowledge their own. In the case of abortion, there's a religious attitude, very masculine, that denies women a whole series of rights. This attitude is backward and reactionary on the part of our brothers, who may be very 'progressive' leftists, but who refuse to take into account this elemental right that is specifically ours as women. . . . Hiding these matters or pushing them aside, we can't make any progress, because there are going to be abortioins anyway, there's going to be birth control, but it will be left in the hands of the Reaction. . . . In our neighborhood, abortion is a daily practice and it's practically the only 'contraceptive' that women use—even if they don't admit it."[22]

Some women separated themselves from parties of the Left to organize specifically around questions related to women's rights. Others who had been agitating for women's rights for nearly a decade without declaring themselves in favor of revolution began to define their positions in more radical terms. A leading feminist declared that "reform" demands made by women, such as access to salaried work, public child care and control of the reproductive process, are actually revolutionary in Peru "because dependent capitalism creates a situation where such reforms cannot be realized without revolution."[23]

Return to Civilian Rule

By the end of the 1970s the Peruvian military government, faced with popular insurrection even more threatening than the guerrilla movements of the 1960s—which had been dealt with by calling for help from the U.S. Green Berets—was promising elections and a return to civilian rule.[24] However, during the year in which elections were being planned, the government increased its attacks on the poor. Left-wing leaders who planned to stand for election were deported from the country. Publications of the Left were suppressed.

In the United States the Carter administration, while propagandizing the upcoming elections as a personal victory for Carter's human rights program, continued to press for an economic austerity program so that U.S. business interests would not suffer a setback under civilian rule. A U.S. congressman revealed the embarrassment that Peruvian unrest was causing in Washington when he inserted in the *Congressional Record* of May 25, 1978, an excerpt from a *New York Times* article of the day before:

Rioting, strikes and bloodshed in Peru have created a profound dilemma for the Carter Administration, which has been groping for a way to balance at least two competing and, some officials argue, inconsistent foreign and economic policy objectives.

While the Administration is supportive of Peru's planned return from military dictatorship to democratic, civilian rule, the United States is deeply committed to a program negotiated between the International Monetary Fund and Peru. The program is designed to cut inflation, reduce imports, stabilize currency exchange, limit government spending and bring Peru's balance of payments into equilibrium. The announcement last week of the austerity measures required by the I.M.F. stabilization program, as the agreements are known, touched off the turmoil. That, in turn, forced the military government to declare martial law, suspend constitutional guarantees of assembly and free speech, and postpone the Peruvian elections.

Once economic conditions favorable to North American business were achieved, the elections were held. Leftists were at first unified behind the popular hero Hugo Blanco, who had been a leader of peasant movements of the 1960s, but they were defeated when they subsequently split into five factions. The party favored by the United States, the APRA (Alianza Popular Revolucionaria Americana), was also favored by the military regime under Morales Bermúdez. However, the founder and long-time head of APRA, Víctor Raúl Haya de la Torre, died before the elections, and the party suffered at the polls for having supported the repressive military government. The man who triumphed was former President Fernando Belaúnde Terry, of Acción Popular. Poor people who voted for Belaúnde apparently forgave him his vacillation in carrying out reforms during the 1960s, in the hope that he would now allow democratic processes to operate to the benefit of the people. Belaúnde had spent the years of military rule in the United States.

In the 1980 elections many women voted for the first time in the country's history.[25] Illiterates had been previously excluded from elections in Peru. Nevertheless, few women were elected to public office, and none who even claimed to represent feminist interests. The newly elected parliament was controlled by the Right, and it promptly gave the president powers unprecedented in the entire history of the Republic. He used these powers to continue and even accelerate the subordination of the Peruvian economy to North American interests.

The most that Belaúnde was willing to give women was

increases in relief programs and a renewal of self-help schemes called Cooperación Popular. A critic of the Belaúnde government said: "Instead of solving problems of housing, we are given a square plot in the desert; instead of providing health services, we are given bricks to build a 'module.' Now, instead of eliminating unemployment, some agency is brought in to distribute food from U.S. AID."[26]

Relief and public assistance were not just woefully inadequate; they were not seen by anyone as a permanent solution to the problems of women and their families. In recent organizing efforts of women priority has been given to establishing neighborhood and community kitchens, child-care centers, and popular education to counteract the power of foreign and government programs and to establish stronger bases for mass protest. For many, these efforts have been viewed as a prelude to a general insurrection. For some of those already engaged in insurrectionary activity, they have been seen as a waste of time. The opinions of women activists were weighed in regional and national meetings during 1983, held under increasingly difficult conditions, while male comrades awaited the results hopefully or disapprovingly—but in any case nervously. Other people were busy, as usual, trying to calculate how best to exploit women's organization so as to use it for their own ends—or, failing that, to crush it once and for all.

2 : *Entering the Global Economy*

Chimbote: Its People and Their Problems

CHIMBOTE, an industrial town with approximately 300,000 inhabitants, lies an easy day's journey by bus or car north of Lima in the Department of Ancash. Chimbote is not in any way typical of Peru, but the problems created by Peru's rapid integration into the international economy can be seen in this coastal town especially clearly. In the early 1980s, steel, shipbuilding, and fishing industries attracted people from surrounding rural areas in search of work. However, less than one third of the women and men in the work force were able to obtain regular jobs. Hundreds were turned away from factory gates daily, even though thirty new fish canneries had opened up in only a few years.

The vast majority of Chimbote's inhabitants are immigrants from the countryside, and they live in some forty shantytowns, or barriadas, many of which lack running water, electricity, sanitation, and medical facilities. The growth of the barriadas reflects the conditions of Peru's general economy. Great disparities exist between those areas affected by "modernization" and those which feed into this sector without getting anything back. Peru's increasing dependence on external financing for capitalist development and its increasing dedication to production for export leaves the country with enormous debts and an inadequate supply of food for domestic consumption. In spite of twelve years of military rule, during which major industries and banks were nationalized, the burden of foreign debt dominates public policy.

Discontent among workers has caused multinational corporations to mechanize factories wherever possible, displacing the work force and weakening the buying power of the people. Inflation and periodic devaluation of the official currency further aggravate the differences between rich and poor, and between Peruvians and their North American "benefactors." When I visited Chimbote in 1982, the interest rate on bank loans was an astounding 56 percent. Six months later it had jumped to 108 percent.[1] Government officials constantly expressed concern for the resolution of social problems created by the economic crisis and the massive migration from the country to the city. But as the crisis deepened through the entire country, social problems worsened, especially in places like Chimbote.

The situation of women in Chimbote has been particularly affected by the vagaries of the fishing industry. By 1982, approximately eight thousand women were working in fish canneries, comprising 80 percent of the work force in the fish-processing industry, the city's major economic activity. Another five thousand women were hired by private households as domestic servants. Many more sold food in the streets and markets or peddled contraband clothing from Ecuador and Chile. Some worked as prostitutes in officially regulated brothels, dancing clubs *(casas de tolerancia),* or hotels *(casas de cita).* Underage women solicited at bars, discotheques, and moviehouses as clandestine prostitution became increasingly common. (So, too, was clandestine trafficking in drugs.) Having come to the city hopeful of improving their life chances and those of their children, women found themselves increasingly degraded and entrapped by a society over which they had little control.

The Fishing Industry

The fishing industry in Chimbote was developed during the Second World War in response to the need for food for allied troops.

The industry attained its peak in the mid-sixties, when the town was the world's largest exporter of fish products. Fishmeal, used to feed animals, became one of Peru's major export products, along with copper and sugar. With the decline of anchovy in the waters off Peru's coast in the early 1970s, the fishmeal industry nearly collapsed. Overfishing and the wasteful use of fish harvests contributed to the industry's decline. When the companies began to transfer capital elsewhere, massive layoffs took place. The military government that had come into power in 1968 was forced by popular pressure to buy out the private companies. This was accomplished in 1973. However, the overexploitation of the natural resources of the sea continued. In 1976, when new layoffs were threatened, the fishermen's union, which had been practically run by the government, became more militant. Leaders favoring management were thrown out. The government responded by passing a law permitting the sale of three hundred fishing vessels to private companies and claimed, fraudulently, that former workers were the new owners. This touched off major strikes and protests in Chimbote and Lima, but they did not secure a reversal of government policy.

The fishing industry has brought higher profits to private investors than any other sector of the Peruvian economy (with the possible exception of the recently developed underground market in cocaine) and is characterized by extreme competition among companies. In the late 1970s, because of overfishing in northern European and Japanese waters and the discovery of huge new reserves of sardines along Peru's coast, investment in fish-canning in Chimbote was accelerated once again. Exportation of fish products jumped from 15 percent of production in 1975 to 74 percent in 1980. By 1979, two North American companies, COPES-Starkist and CAROLINA, had taken over 56 percent of the fish-processing industry. The government, responding to pressure from the industry, declared it exempt from labor regulations as a "nontraditional

A young woman of Chimbote. The city attracts rural people in search of work, but the boom-and-bust economy makes life precarious, most of all for women and children. (Jorge Azañedo)

export." This meant that processing plants were under no obligatin to hire a stable work force.

Most women who work in the fishing industry in Chimbote are hired as "temporaries" or contracted labor. They may lose their jobs at the slightest infraction of discipline, indication of poor health, or family problems. They enjoy no job benefits. Women workers have to wait long hours, without pay, for the arrival of fishing boats or refrigerated cars. If there are no fish, there is no work. When there are fish, workers must sometimes put in double shifts of twelve hours each. They wait four to six hours in between shifts at the factory, also without pay. If canning operations terminate in the middle of the night, the women are left to find their way home in the dark. Family members often come to wait for them outside the factory gates. Anyone who is not willing to put up with these conditions can easily be replaced.

The most common health problems among workers at the fish-canning plants are caused by the constant handling of cold or icy fish and by the long hours of standing in water. Arthritis, rheumatism, varicose veins, tuberculosis, pneumonia, swollen feet, and back problems are common among the cannery workers, and all cause the women to lose their jobs. Workers complain that anyone who is sick and asks for time off is fired. I know of a teenager who began her job when the factory first opened and later contracted tuberculosis. The doctor she went to prepared a request that she be given time off to recuperate from her illness. Instead, she says, she was fired, told to go home and rest. She had worked nine months for the company.

The canning companies in Chimbote generally provide no medical care for contracted workers, even though a percentage is taken from their paychecks for it. Gloves and boots are seldom provided. Women's hands become sore from handling bony fish, strong spices, and chemical cleaning agents. Accidents are frequent: women cut themselves when sleepy or exhausted from overwork. Night work is especially hard. In the words of one worker: "When you work at night, it's terrible. You're always cold because you're working in water and fish waste; those who work stripping fish are soaked from head to foot, and their hands are full of sores from the fish bones, and white and wrinkled from being in the water all the time. It's a long time since they said they were going to give us gloves and boots, but they never have."[2]

In Chimbote's canneries, women are subject to a constant speedup when machines are introduced or pay increases are won. In describing the pressure of supervisors' demands, one woman said: "The supervisors want us to work at the same speed as the machine. If the machine cuts twenty fish in a certain amount of time, we have to do the same. So we're not treated like people, but like machines."[3] New recruits who can't keep up are let go after working without pay during a trial period. Those who work at piecework rates seldom earn the minimum wages paid in other industries, even after months of experience.

As better conditions are won through struggle at the workplace, men are recruited to replace women. If women do become part of the regular work force, the contract they are asked to sign may contain a blank piece of paper which can be used later to exempt the company from certain legal obligations. Anyone who questions this practice is refused a contract.

In November 1981, a group of women workers in COPES-Starkist, one of the oldest and largest fish-canning plants in Coishco, a district of Chimbote, attempted to organize fellow workers to oust male union leaders who had been handpicked by management. One woman who was fired for raising the issue of company unionism told me: "The company knows that we women are stronger and more insistent than the men because our problems are bigger. They're afraid of us. Even the men in the union are afraid of us, but since we don't have bad habits like they do, they put us down by calling us 'skinny' or 'shorty' or making light of our anger by saying we go around *con el hígado en la mano* [carrying our livers in our hands]."[4]

In the course of the struggle at COPES-Starkist, the company was forced to accept new union leadership. Workers won widespread support in the city. The struggle included work stoppages at CAROLINA and other factories, a hunger strike, a short takeover of the plant, marches, demonstrations, and then an extended strike. Although the company was forced to compromise, it refused to accept as union representatives any of the women who had led the strike. Several of these women sued to get their jobs back.

During the same period, workers at PRODUPESCA (*pesca* means "fish") who had organized a union the year before, in 1981, attempted to get a contract approved. The company balked and withheld Christmas bonuses to punish them. During this struggle, fifteen workers were fired, of whom twelve were women. Workers decided to take over the plant and were able to hold it for fourteen days, in February and March of 1982. They occupied the factory in two shifts, with those who were outside working to get public support for the demands. When the takeover ended, military-type control of workers at PRODUPESCA was instituted. But the struggle did help to create more respect for unions in other factories.

One of the workers who was fired from PRODUPESCA told me she had been part of a group of specially privileged workers before the struggle began, that the creation of privileges for certain groups was one way the company had tried to control workers. She lost those privileges when she participated in the protest activities at Christmastime, and she is not interested in returning. Having suffered severe health problems because of the high humidity in the plant, she expressed a common opinion of those who work in the canning factories: "It's a job that will kill you in the end."

The takeover at PRODUPESCA and the union reorganization at COPES-Starkist are two of a number of such struggles that have taken place in fish-canning factories since 1980. In one of the first such actions, two company officials were taken hostage by four hundred workers at ACTIVIDADES PESQUERAS. The workers demanded the rehiring of three women who had been fired a few days earlier just before completing three years' service. The firing was related to a list of demands workers had presented to the company. Because of their action, they say, the company was forced to negotiate.

By March 1982 a group of women workers from various fish-processing factories in Chimbote had prepared a motion to present at the seventh congress of the workers' federation of Ancash.

A hunger strike at a fish-processing plant, COPES-Starkist, is supported by family members and fellow workers. (Jorge Azañedo)

Women lead a protest as cooperative farm workers of the Santa Valley demand lower interest rates and lower prices for fertilizer. In recent years, the government has lowered investment in the agricultural sector of the economy. (Jorge Azañedo)

Previously, these women had not been members of the federation, and most had not been active in unions at all. In the motion the women pointed out that they represented a big majority of the work force in the fish-processing industry and that their conditions of work were uniformly terrible, even worse than those for men. They also pointed out that as women and mothers they had special problems that male workers didn't have, problems that hadn't been addressed by the unions. In order to gain equality in union representation, they demanded the formation of a women's commission within the federation and the creation of a parliamentary commission in Lima to make their situation known to the whole country. They also introduced a list of specific workplace demands and called for a public meeting of all women working in the fish-processing industry, whether unionized or not.

According to women who were present at the meeting, male workers responded enthusiastically to the women's intervention. Even though the women had experienced constant frustration in their attempts to break into unions individually, their organizing successes during the two previous years prepared the way for their entry as a group in 1982.

Some of those who introduced the women's motion at the workers' federation of Ancash were members of an organization called Movement for a New Woman, which had bases in nearby Trujillo as well as in Chimbote. It was one of several feminist groups in the area which had been active among housewives and had only recently begun to gain members among factory workers.[5] Among their main concerns was winning women the right to work, both concretely through greater availability of jobs, maternity leaves, and the implementation of other rights (some of which were already theirs by law, but had not been respected) and psychologically through acceptance by the husbands of women's going to work. In many cases women feel they have been forced to go to work because their husbands cannot support their families, yet once a woman begins to work, it often happens that her husband abandons her, saying that now that she is working, he is no longer responsible for supporting the family at all.

Women feel a sense of desperation both at home and at work, yet their feelings cannot be shared with the members of their own families, especially with husbands. One woman says: "I started working at the factory because I have five children in school and what my husband earns isn't enough. He's a fisherman, and sometimes they catch fish and sometimes they don't. There are weeks and sometimes months when there aren't any fish. One day I decided to go out and look for work, and I went to the factory without saying anything to my husband. I waited 'til they called me to work before I said anything to my husband. I've worked eight months now, on contract. All of us suffer a lot at work, but we put up with it because we have to . . . ."[6]

In spite of the problems created by going to work, those women who have worked and then got let off feel restless. Most important, they miss the economic independence their work provided, and they miss the contact with other workers and the feeling of doing something productive. The common problems of women who work create a sense of community among them. In the words of one worker: "When there's plenty of fish, we stay at work until eleven or twelve at night, and sometimes until three in the morning, when it's hard to get buses or rides home. I live in San Juan and I walk to work. For several months I didn't know any of the other women well. I came home alone because I was usually the last to leave. I decided to ask my twelve-year-old son to come to the factory and wait for me so he could walk home with me. He came with other friends and they waited for hours at the factory gate, and nearly died of the cold. Now we women know each other. The ones who live near where I live wait for me. Some live in San Pedro or Pensacola, and when they leave the factory late they sleep at my house. When we're on night shift, which starts at 11, we go early and wait at the factory until they let us in."[7] Testimony such as this is often repeated. It provides a strong sense that collective activity, no matter how difficult, is important to women's self-esteem.

The Decline of the APRA, the Movement toward the Left, and the Beginnings of Feminist Consciousness

When I descended from the mountains by bus on my first visit to Chimbote, loudspeakers were blaring homage to Victor Raúl

Haya de la Torre on the third anniversary of his death. Haya de la Torre is an important figure in Peruvian history because of his relation to the North American presence. He was born in Trujillo, a coastal city directly north of Chimbote, and founded the Alianza Popular Revolucionaria Americana (APRA) in 1924. An estimated three thousand of his followers were massacred by government troops in 1932 after an attempted takeover of military posts in Trujillo by sugar workers on U.S.-owned plantations. But by the end of World War II the APRA had made its peace with North American business interests. This happened because of pressure from middle-class constituents in other parts of the country and because of government repression. The APRA entered electoral struggles and began courting sections of the military. Because Apristas were never able to gain decisive power in the central government during his lifetime, Haya de la Torre escaped being held personally accountable for the subsequent increasing impoverishment of the country. He is still a popular, if fading, hero on the northern coast even after his death. In Chimbote, however, there was no great celebration in his honor during my visit. The loudspeakers resounded through otherwise quiet streets. Restaurants and stores were empty, and the distant sound of factory whistles and ships were a reminder that the real business of life was not going on in the Avenida Pardo, Chimbote's wide main street.

The declining popularity of the APRA was directly related to the political struggles of workers in the fishing industry. It affected women primarily through their participation in these struggles.

In October 1976, ten thousand fishermen went on strike to protest the government's action in returning the industry to private companies. The government refused to negotiate, declaring the union to be communist. A near civil war broke out in Chimbote. The families of fishermen prepared around-the-clock meals in the union hall. When government troops came, women, men and children fought them off for hours before succumbing, then moved to the city's central park, where they were joined by the families of steelworkers, teachers, and others who were opposing government repression of their own unions.

Because of inflation, Peruvians had experienced a fifty percent loss in real income in one year's time. Only the military got commensurate salary increases. Strikes by workers in strategic areas of the economy were declared illegal, and public demonstrations were banned. Chimbote was placed under martial law, an eight P.M. curfew was declared, and more than one hundred labor leaders were rounded up and imprisoned. Police entered the homes of anyone suspected of harboring those sought by government authorities, causing terror. All this happened after the military government of Juan Velasco Alvarado was taken over by right-wing generals. Those officers loyal to Velasco were labeled communists and exiled from the country.

A media campaign launched by the new president, Francisco Morales Bermúdez, an APRA sympathizer, blamed fishermen for the economic problems of the country. The government organized the Movemiento Laboral Revolucionario (MLR), a paramilitary group which carried out assassinations and broke up workers' meetings. The United States Central Intelligence Agency was reputedly involved in the MLR, as it had been linked to the fishermen's union for a period of time in its early years. The APRA was discredited among Chimbote residents during this time because of its involvement with the CIA and with the increasingly repressive government. For women, this meant the questioning of values that the APRA had promoted, including the idealization of their own roles as transmitters of conservative ideology in the home.

One woman who left APRA recalls the longstanding frustrations of women in combatting this ideology: "We were greatly disappointed when we invited [Haya de la Torre] to speak to us. He began speaking about the home, about the care given by women to their husbands, about how marital harmony can only be achieved when women 'understand their husbands' situation.' I was at his side and told him, 'This isn't what they're interested in. Talk to them about other things.' The women had come to talk about politics, about Marxism . . . women of the popular classes were hearing about Marxism and they came to find out what it was really about, and Haya came to talk to them about how to be good wives and mothers."[8]

In the late 1970s, the opportunism of the APRA became more evident than ever in its open defense of capitalism and clear alliance

with the upper classes. In 1977 and 1978, further strikes of steelworkers and shipbuilders occurred in Chimbote.[9] Women mobilized in *organizaciones femeninas* and *comités de damas,* and
participated in neighborhood *comités de lucha* (struggle committees). They propagandized the strikes, defended union headquarters, and prepared meals for strikers. They also organized the
sequestering of fugitives in shantytown homes and brought pressure to bear on reluctant strikers. As women worked along with
men in these activities, they also participated in political discussions and began to form their own opinions.

   Finally, in 1978 and 1979, Peru's schoolteachers initiated a
struggle that was to lay the groundwork for the abdication of the
military government and bring the promise of elections that
would prevent civil war. In the teachers' strikes, women were not
only the support forces, but also, since most teachers were
women, there was solidarity among both strikers and community.
Although male teachers were the leaders of the union, female
teachers were most active in carrying out militant actions. The
mothers of schoolchildren affected by the strike organized their
neighborhoods to protect demonstrating teachers and to provide
food and blankets for them. These organizations continued in
existence when nuclei of women determined to educate themselves, to secure employment, to confront the daily problems
presented by motherhood, domestic and neighborhood violence,
and lack of health care, public services, and educational opportunities for their children.

   In all of these struggles, women experienced new power
outside their homes. They had to confront husbands to be able to
carry on political activities away from the home once specific
crises were over. These experiences raised women's consciousness
about their own situation in the world. The discovery of machismo as a social evil, something that not only caused personal
suffering but weakened the common cause of the people as well,
gave women a permanent issue around which to rally. The accumulated experience of power in social struggle against the government gave them reason to believe that the battle against male
domination could be fought successfully, and that it *had* to be
fought if social struggle was to continue.

   It was evident to me during my visits to Chimbote that men

were "preferred" as community leaders even by many women in the *barrios*. But in every community there were women who were publicly challenging such ideas, and gaining the support of some men by doing so. Within the political parties of the Left, women were forming discussion groups, and men who discouraged or prohibited their wives from attending were criticized. The process was slow. Sometimes an initial meeting would attract twenty women and generate a great amount of enthusiasm. At a subsequent meeting only a few would show up. Women were often slow to discuss the causes of their reluctance to continue, but under questioning would finally reveal the pressure they felt at home. It was one thing to participate in an emergency situation in which men's interests were very evidently at stake and women were needed to give help to men. It was another thing entirely for women to meet on a regular basis as women to explore their resources and give strength to each other in confronting daily problems, which includes problems with men and male domination both at home and in the society at large.

A woman who has been active in organizing women both in her own neighborhood and across the nation said: "Whenever there are meetings for women to begin looking at the specific problems of women, some husbands will remove their wives forcibly, or if they don't do that, they wait till their wife returns home to hit her or punish her. 'What were you doing there? Listening to propaganda, I suppose, wasting your time, or maybe carrying on with some other man?'—even though he could see the meeting was all women."[10] Although many men have accused women activists of trying to "divide men and women" and thereby weakening the cause of fighting economic and social oppression, clearly it is the men who separate the struggles of the workplace from those of the home and neighborhood.

Instead of retreating defensely, some women have increased their feminist activity when they come under attack, publishing tracts and leaflets and bulletins calling on women to examine their own lives together and to continue to challenge men:

It's true that the New Man will be formed when material conditions are changed through revolution; but the complex process of the disintegra-

Grafitti denounces a union leader who betrayed the workers' cause. When jobs are scarce, women who seek work are expected to provide sexual favors to employers. (Jorge Azañedo)

Women take a lunch break at an asparagus canning factory, Santa Valley. "Nontraditional" enterprises oriented toward export are exempt from labor regulations. (Jorge Azañedo)

tion of old values and the creation of new values doesn't have to wait. As we look to the future, we have to begin walking toward it.[11]

The emergence of feminist consciousness has been linked historically with the active participation of women with men in social struggles important to them both and to the subsequent changes this struggle brings to the relations between women and men. The entrance of women into the paid workforce has also been associated with the origins of feminist movements all over the world. A third factor, less often discussed theoretically, is the emergence of feminist activity in "frontier towns" or "boom towns" where the culture of machismo is manifested in increased prostitution, alcoholism, delinquency, and rape. In Chimbote, women's efforts to protect themselves from physical aggression by men, especially on paydays, when men hang out with each other and feel they have a license to abuse women, give them cause to examine their common situation as women and to demand more control over community life.

Women in Chimbote were not unaware that the general poverty and social disorganization were caused by the government's policy of orienting economic and political life to the needs of international markets. They knew, for example, that the fishing industry, which was begun to provide food for allied forces during World War II, is today oriented to feeding North American pets. Feeding cats has a higher priority than feeding the children of Peru's workers. Fish are more expensive in Chimbote's central market than they are in Lima, and the per capita consumption of fish is lower in Chimbote than in the nation as a whole. But the immediate sources of frustration among women relates very often to the lack of support or understanding by men. Husbands and sons frequently spend their paychecks on beer and prostitution instead of buying food or clothing for their own families. The pay that women receive from their own jobs—which include prostitution—is more likely to be spent on shoes, medicine, school supplies, and bread for their families. Furthermore, women do not have time to engage in "street life" unless being in the street can bring them some income.

Women bear another special burden. They frequently have to look after family members who are jailed, whether for delinquency or for political activism. Because of the responsibilities they bear, women can less "afford" to risk going to jail, and they know it is less likely that there will be someone to look after their needs or visit them there. Visits to jail are the province of mothers, wives, and sisters, who wait in long lines to enter, one by one, to take food, blankets, and comfort to family members.

The Effects of U.S. Programs Directed Toward Mothers

As if being a frontier town were not enough, Chimbote experienced a major earthquake in May of 1970. The United States Food for Peace program was activated to allow the Peruvian government to purchase surplus food from the United States with local currency, which U.S. officials in Peru could then use to pay local staff and support local programs. The food was distributed through Mothers' Clubs which were organized by the Catholic Church through CARITAS.[12] More than eighty Mothers' Clubs were formed at this time. Recalling their experiences in these clubs, women activists told me they resented being treated paternalistically and being required to attend classes and carry out projects obviously designed to reinforce roles and beliefs fostered by the Church. Women generally welcomed most the offer of classes in sewing. But a lack of facilities and teachers limited their effectiveness, and the classes did nothing to broaden women's view of themselves or give them new power in their communities or families.

One outcome of the Mothers' Clubs was rivalry among neighborhood women for control of food distribution and other favors made available through the churches. But when some women demanded more from the clubs than the program was designed to offer, independent leadership emerged. New women's organizations were formed, and occasionally the clubs were transformed into centers for neighborhood organizing and general education of women.

In 1975, a Central Committee of Mothers' Clubs of Chimbote was formed through the initiative of the local government. Discussions ensued over the functions of the committee and over the legitimacy of the women who claimed to be representatives of local clubs. Women became polarized over issues that were sometimes personal but which also had political implications. When Francisco Morales Bermúdez ousted Juan Velasco Alvarado as president of Peru in August 1975, the government turned its back on the women's organizations. Since the local government was short on funds, the Central Committee of Mothers' Clubs continued in name only. However, the earlier contacts and struggles among women had laid the basis for renewed organization later on. Then with the end of military rule in 1980, municipal elections brought into office leftists who gave their support to Mother's Day protests.[13] These protests called attention to the daily problems of poor women and to the exploitation of women through consumerism and the idealization of self-sacrifice for women. A number of Mothers' Clubs were represented in these protests through a reactivated Central Committee.

After 1980, President Fernando Belaúnde Terry so centralized authority in his own hands that the legislative and economic power of local government in Peru became extremely weak. Unless municipal governments were partisans of the president's party, their function was mainly symbolic. But women took advantage of Belaúnde's eagerness, during his first years in office, to present an image of democratic rule to the world.

To the extent that women's organizing energies were directed exclusively toward gaining legal rights, government authorities perceived their protests to be relatively harmless. In fact, where women raised demands for contraceptives and for legalized free abortion, U.S. AID encouraged their organization, and the Peruvian government had to adopt certain programs to promote population control. The United States was concerned primarily about its inability to manage capitalist development in Peru. Its goals were to develop a profitable export economy and a local market for U.S. products, but the attempt to achieve these aims fostered class divisions and a growing population of the poor and the unemployed, a potentially revolutionary force. The U.S. concern for birth control grew out of its frustration in the face of this contradiction and out of a need to explain increasing poverty by blaming the people for having too many babies. For those women who lived in the city slums, where children's labor is not a major contributor to family welfare, a woman's right to control her body was a growing demand. The desire for birth control programs thus coincided in part with U.S. objectives. However, the U.S. programs were criticized for not focusing on educating women about their health needs and alternative methods of birth control. Rather, women said, the focus was on propaganda and experimentation and on the marketing of dangerous or worthless products.

Between 1972 and 1981, the Foster Parents' Plan in Chimbote adopted an extensive and controversial birth control program. In fact, contributions from private individuals in the United States were used almost exclusively for the promotion of "family planning" rather than for the education and maintenance of adopted children, the stated goal of the program. Finally, after staff members who worked for the plan disclosed internal documents, the Foster Parents' Plan was closed down and population control programs were transferred to other agencies.

In describing similar activities carried out in Peru by the Peace Corps, the Alliance for Progress, Rockefeller Foundation, and Ford Foundation, one resident of Chimbote noted that the major ideological objective of all these programs has been to convince the people that their problems are caused by their own ignorance or lack of personal initiative. Noting that the history of resistance to such indoctrination has forced population programs to be transferred to United Nations agencies, he complained that the United States nevertheless maintains control over the policies of these organizations by contributing most of the funds provided for population control.[14]

In response to popular protests about the lack of disinterested assistance in birth control, the United States has established a program through the central government of Peru for the training of midwives in the insertion of IUDs (intrauterine devices). It is thought that midwives will be more readily accepted than doctors as agents of birth control. The job of one North American woman working in the Department of Ancash was to "prove that government mid-wife training programs are not established solely for the purpose of birth control." Though she emphasized to me that she was hired directly by the Peruvian government, locally contracted employees are well aware that money for the "study" came from U.S. AID. Understandably, birth control continues to be seen as an issue related to outside interests.[15] The use of Depo Provera, a birth control drug produced by Upjohn, was banned in the United States in 1975. It is now being tested in Peru as well as in Chile and Mexico.

Women affected by population control programs are criticizing not only businesses and governments, but church leaders, doctors, judges, and husbands, all of whom are seen as manipulative and insensitive to women. Both the Peruvian government and the Church keep reversing their positions regarding contraceptives, but neither recognizes a woman's fundamental right to voluntary motherhood without jeopardy to her health. For this reason, the Church's recent entrance into the campaign for "responsible parenthood" is not exempt from attack. One feminist remarked, "They've considered women as the essence of sinfulness. In order to save her from her sinful condition, she is redeemed through motherhood, making it self-sacrificial, and her whole reason for being." The Church has now organized a Program for the Promotion of the Family (at first called the Movement for the Christian Family), which, she says, distributes birth control pills "to save women from the sin of producing too many children."[16]

Whether or not women in Chimbote are inspired by feminist issues, most have gained enough political experience during the past decade of struggle to be suspicious of any and all attempts to manipulate them with promises and threats. For many, their first contact with authorities came in defending terrain that they occupied when they first came to the city.

Practically no housing is provided for workers in Chimbote, or anywhere in Peru. Those who migrate to the city looking for work usually find temporary accommodations with relatives. Periodically, shantytown dwellers organize to stake out new territory in surrounding areas, "invading" desert land which is unproductive and unoccupied, but to which they have no legal claim. While the men who have jobs go to work, others—mostly the women and children—cling to temporary shelters put up overnight, resisting police repression and building solidarity for the invasion among other sectors of the population until such time as their claim is recognized. Each new invasion is a cause around which pobladores (the inhabitants of the shantytowns) can unite.

The official repression usually ends with a negotiated settlement or with an agreement stipulating that the invaders will move to a site selected by the government and begin procedures to secure title to individual plots in return for tax payments to the government. New struggles are then begun to secure public services for the newly established community.

Among the many issues that concern pobladores is the problem of sanitation. In barriadas where working-class people live there is usually no municipal garbage collection service. Rather, as one neighborhood organizer declared, "What we do see frequently are the well-known signs saying 'No Dumping Permitted,' in a vain attempt to keep pobladores from getting rid of their garbage in the streets. But what are we supposed to do? Where are we supposed to dump trash?" The lack of collection causes garbage to mount up in certain places, contaminating the environment and endangering the health of the people, especially the children. Since there are no parks, the children play in the garbage. Meanwhile, the city launches well-publicized campaigns to beautify downtown areas of the city so that Chimbote can change its reputation as "one of the dirtiest cities in the country."[17]

Problems of this type result partly because government resources are not made available to the residents of shantytowns, especially in regions outside Lima. This affects the election process in municipalities. Those candidates who can demonstrate that they have "pull" in Lima have an edge over those who cannot, even though such "pull" often means that candidates do not have genuine ties to their own constituents. The shantytown dwellers have responded to this centralization of government power with centralization of their own—of the community-based organizations that will better serve their interests. The impetus for nationwide coordination came from the community leaders in Chimbote, where a larger segment of the population lives in shantytowns than in any other city in Peru.

In September 1980, a federation coordinating the struggles of shantytown dwellers in the provinces of Santa and Casma (where Chimbote is located) held its third congress. All of the officers elected were men, even though a majority of those in attendance were women. By 1983, when another congress was to be held, women were in a much better position to assume leadership.

However, by then a national state of emergency had been declared, and popular organizations were, for a time, forced underground.

Because women in Chimbote have become active politically during the past decade, especially at the neighborhood level, they have also begun to be active in political parties of the Left. These parties had no meaningful base in the region until the late 1970s. In 1981, a U.S. AID team, alerted to this situation, was sent to the area to conduct a study of the effect of work opportunities in "nontraditional" production on women's political attitudes and involvement. The study was carried out among women workers in an asparagus canning factory. It was hoped that the opening up of new factories would diminish women's need for organization in their neighborhoods, keep them busy, and pacify them enough to prevent "vulnerability" to leftist ideology. The results of the study—which was never published—showed that because women shared common problems at work and were angry about being hired and then fired at will, the experience of working only increased their militancy in protest against the government.[18]

Apparently, the overall economic situation of women in Chimbote has increased their awareness of their own potential as human beings at the same time that it has increased their suffering at the hands of business, government, and men. Women are also increasingly aware that the problems of Chimbote are closely connected with the problems of those who live in the surrounding areas, and in the nation as a whole.

Rural and Regional Organizing

The steady stream of migrants to Chimbote from the countryside is a constant reminder that the crisis in the city is related to the crisis in Peru's agricultural system. Although this system stems from colonial times, the crisis has developed in recent decades. The agricultural reform begun in the 1960s was not sufficient to prevent the growth of revolutionary activity in the countryside. Even where reform was carried out rigorously by the Velasco government, especially on the coast, it increased production without improving the lives of those who lived there. Reform meant women lost power in both the family and the community because they were excluded from regular paid agricultural work on modernized cooperative farms.

While life was extremely hard under feudalism, and women were overworked and physically and sexually abused by landlords, they were sometimes given privileged tasks in the household of the hacendado, such as cooking, cleaning, and child care, animal tending, or gardening. They had gleaning rights in the fields, and were hired as peons during planting or harvest. Women worked alongside men on family plots and on land belonging to the community. They were responsible for the care of animals belonging to their families and for the education of the children. Most important, men and women fought together against an oppressive landlord system.

With the introduction of agrarian reform, men became associates, *socios,* in state-administered cooperatives. Young men were encouraged to attend school to learn the skills needed for mechanized agricultural production. With greater decision-making power in agricultural production, men assumed more power over women at home. In the coastal areas, women were increasingly confined to domestic work. They became dependent on men for survival. Women were expected to carry meals to the men who worked in the fields. When hired as contracted labor by the cooperatives, they had no voice or vote. Only divorced or widowed women could become *socios* of the cooperatives. Contracted workers, *eventuales,* did the unskilled work and received inferior wages for it.

The technical education that women did receive under reform did not prepare them for paid work outside the home. Rather, they were taught to sew with machines in their own homes and for their own families; but this work isolated them from the collective and public activities from which social power is derived. Thus, even those few aspects of reform that were supposed to benefit women increased their separation from men and from access to the social and economic resources that would have promoted equality with men. While traditionally most men sewed and some earned

Campesinas in Cajamarca have organized a Democratic Women's Front to give women more power in their communities and to protest government policies in the region. (Jorge Azanedo)

money as weavers or tailors, agricultural reform turned sewing into a homemaking skill, one that was to be pursued by women without remuneration, confining them more than ever to the house. In coastal areas where these processes have been more pronounced, illiteracy among women, always high, has increased markedly.

Government officials sent to the countryside to administer agrarian reform have generally been insensitive to the women's loss of power under "development." Male *socios* and farm union leaders have been equally insensitive. As women were less and less represented in community affairs, union leaders avoided dealing with women's complaints. In one coastal farm community I visited during the early years of agrarian reform, women had been attending literacy classes for one year at the urging of a female employee of the government who had been conducting a statistical study there. The women were angry because the all-male *directiva* of the cooperative had subsequently denied them literacy classes on the pretext that they were neglecting their duties at home. The women's call for group child care on the farm was also opposed by the *directiva*. The one woman who brought these issues to the farm workers' union was eventually harassed out of the union. This was not an isolated case, according to more recent statements by rural women.

In the Santa Valley surrounding Chimbote, the agrarian reform program is in such serious trouble that farm workers have been forced into permanent confrontation with the government, a situation which has given women new possibilities for reentry into community life. The farmers' immediate problems have to do with the rising prices of fertilizer, pesticides, machinery, and seeds; high interest rates; falling prices for farm products; and the difficulty in obtaining credit for the industrialization of farm production in the countryside. The central government blames the cooperative structure itself for these problems and pushes for the "restructuring" of cooperatives. Farm workers see this as a move toward parcelization, a gradual liquidation of the cooperatives and a return to private ownership, which they believe would mean eventual domination by the multinational corporations.

Rural people complain that they are expected to provide

schools, clinics, water, and other services out of their own earnings, even though the law obligates the government to do so. The government insists that farm workers and peasants continue payments to former landlords to compensate them for expropriated land, while campesinos find this to be an intolerable burden, especially since they say the land was theirs to begin with.

In several cases in the Santa Valley, cooperative members have not been paid for six months to a year for cotton sold to the government. They are finally paid only after persistent protest. When the government is charged with corruption in managing the sale of farm products, it threatens reprivatization. Reprivatization would mean the eventual return of the landlord system, most likely with multinationals as the new landlords. It would also mean a loss of any hope for women who have been demanding equality within the collective structure and an escape from domestic servitude. It is not in women's interest to return to relations of servitude on the hacienda. Neither is it in their interest to reinforce present relations of private servitude to men. Reprivatization would be especially damaging to women because most of them are not now *socios* of cooperatives and would therefore not be eligible for parcels of land when cooperatives are broken up. Those who are contracted or seasonal laborers are thrown off the land entirely when parcelization takes place. Small plots cannot support growing families and cannot solve the problem of massive migration from farm to city.

Women of the Santa Valley began meeting as early as 1981 to discuss how the economic crisis affected them and how they could best organize to confront it. Pilot projects of collective child care and vegetable gardens run collectively by women were planned. These organizing activities by rural women did not retard protest activities carried out together by men and women. In the Chimbote area, a twenty-four hour *paro,* or work stoppage, on the cooperative farm Rinconada was followed by a regional *paro,* which was later reinforced by a work stoppage at the national level organized by the farm workers' union. The initial protest at Rinconada was made to demand overdue wage payments to workers and to oppose the threatened parcelization of the farm, which would have left 1,500 contracted employees without work. The success of these protest activities could be attributed in part to the advancement of women's organizations in the countryside, according to testimony by the women themselves.

The situation at Rinconada is one among many which have united workers from the country and the city. In Chimbote, unity has been enhanced by the participation of the Social Justice Commission of the Catholic Church, which reflects the social struggles of its parishioners.[19] These struggles have put pressure on church officials to mediate between the poor and the government. In 1981, Catholic Church leaders in Chimbote became the first in the country to openly criticize the government for the systematic torture of political prisoners. As activists met repression from the government, and within the Church, some retreated from public roles as the "conscience of the nation." Nine priests were transferred from the area. Nevertheless, church leaders continued to articulate the demands of the poor before the government.

On March 8, 1982, the Social Justice Commission of the Church, together with the Cultural Commission of the province, unions, and feminist groups, organized a celebration of International Women's Day in Chimbote. For the first time, feminists called on all progressive forces in the local government and churches, unions, and political parties in the opposition to join forces in articulating the general concerns of poor women in Chimbote and surrounding areas. The recognition and legitimization of women's leadership in popular struggle and of women's demands in political programs for revolutionary change had been won through several decades of activism at the grassroots level. Women's battles were just beginning, but their place alongside men as makers of history had finally been secured.

3 : *Agricultural Reform in the Mountains*

THE QUECHUA and Aymará-speaking women of the Peruvian Andes have an impressive history of resistance to Spanish culture. This, together with their heavy responsibilities in maintaining communities, has provided them with a kind of respect unknown to mestizas. They they are also objects of discrimination and extreme exploitation. They receive little remuneration for their work and have almost no access to medical attention or other social benefits available to many other Peruvians. Birth rates among Indians in the Andean mountains are high, and children are greatly valued, yet nearly one-third die during the first year of life. Illiteracy has been the common condition of Indian women. While their need for formal education has increased because of involvement with the money economy in recent decades, their access to schooling has decreased. Indian women work in the "traditional sector" rather than in the "modern sector," and identify their own future with the future of the land and their culture.

Women of the sierra have repeatedly demonstrated militancy in defending their communities. Nevertheless, it is probably true that only in the past few years have they begun to view themselves collectively as participants in historical events. In a complex and conflictive political environment, Andean women are trying to define a new place for themselves as community members, workers, mothers, daughters, and leaders in popular struggle.

Indigenous Struggles with the State

Most of the people of Peru who consider themselves Indians—
nearly half the population of the country—are members of officially recognized indigenous communities. Spanish conquerors
conceded certain community rights to Indians, who were confined
to *reducciones* that resembled the *ayllus* of preconquest Peru, where
women and men held parallel power. Even though male-dominated state and municipal governments were later imposed by the
Spanish on comuneros, or community members, and reinforced
by the British and their successors, community structures were
never obliterated. In some mountain provinces land-use rights are
still inherited by daughters from their mothers and by sons from
their fathers, in spite of legal stipulations that official land transactions be mediated by husbands. Often daughters are given more
land than sons, in recognition of their greater bond with the
community, even though male community members are the only
ones elected to municipal government. Men and women work
communal land together. Often women work *chacras,* or family
plots, alone, and in some places they pasture animals alone, far
from their families. Paid work outside the community is strictly
segregated by sex, always to the advantage of men.

Indian resistence to the usurpation of community land by
outsiders and to the cruelties continually perpetuated on them has
forced governments to enact periodic reform throughout the four
centuries of European and North American domination. Under
reform, communities retained title to certain portions of their land
which remained in common cultivation or as pasture for the
comuneros' animals, even as land seizure by non-Indians remained
a constant threat. Legal battles pursued by the indigenous communities usually resulted in victory in the courts, while actual control
of the land often remained in the hands of usurpers. Indians
initiated land takeovers sporadically, and women were always
readily mobilized for the struggle, even at the risk of massacre.
Finally, in the 1960s, higher levels of organization by indigeous
people resulted in a series of successful campaigns against landlords especially in the central sierra. Young women who joined

guerrilla forces insisted on fighting alongside the men, sharing with them such auxiliary tasks as cooking and sewing.

Because of pressure from insurgents, land reform was promulgated by the Peruvian government, and supported by the United States government as part of the Alliance for Progress. Reform was, however, opposed by powerful feudal landholders. The military coup of 1968, which brought reformist generals into power, had as one of its main priorities the formal recognition of indigenous communities, with their rights and obligations carefully defined by law. The promised benefits of reform pertained almost exclusively to men; nevertheless, women supported land reform because it meant expulsion of hacendados from community land.

During the early 1970s, land reform continued to be carried out slowly in mountain areas, where most indigenous communities existed. The successful expropriation of foreign-owned plantations along the coast, and their conversion into modern collective capitalist farms under government regulation was easier than expropriation of mountain land.[1] Coastal farms, more readily cultivated with machinery, and more oriented toward export of farm production, were a natural priority for government programs. In the mountains land-holders were able to exert pressure on local governments to postpone reform. Even where land was expropriated, indigenous communities were given little government assistance in improving production. Where credits and technical training were provided, these were never made available to women. Cooperatives set up to administer production under agrarian reform had no control over the sale of products. Workers were unable to make mortgage payments with which the government intended to assist former hacendados to invest in urban industry. Taxes imposed on the use of water were a terrible burden brought about by reform. And former landholders, mostly mestizos, were permitted by the government to take away animals and equipment, and even to dismantle buildings, before returning the land to the Indians. Some divided up property among relatives or sold off portions of it privately in order to avoid expropriation.

General Velasco, who was president of Peru during this

period, was himself born into an Indian family. He hoped to unite the country by the development of national sentiment. He sometimes spoke Quechua to the people and promoted the revival of cultural traditions that would enhance Peru's attractiveness to tourists. However, in order to prevent a resurgence of indigenous movements, which could serve to unite Indians against mestizos and whites, the government introduced the word campesinos (peasants) to describe those who work on cooperatives and others who are members of comunidades, or indigenous communities, discouraging use of the word *indio*. Actually, the *comunidades campesinas,* as defined by the agrarian reform, came to overlap with cooperative state-regulated farm structures. In some places, *comunidades* even merged with municipal government, a process that always weakened the woman's position in family and social life.

The designation of Indians as peasants or campesinos was propagandized as a way of ending racial discrimination against *indios,* and was supported by major political parties of the Left. Even those parties or organizations that were profoundly critical of reform, because it was linked with capitalist development and subordinated to imperialist interests, organized to enforce implementation of those aspects of reform programs that would provide a foundation for more radical change. None of these organizations criticized agrarian reform laws for giving secondary status to women.

Obstacles to the implementation of reform in the sierra, and the encouragement, under reform, of production for export at the expense of production for consumption, meant that farmers in the least productive areas were pressured to provide more and more of the food needs of city-dwellers. The prices of their products were determined without consideration for the investment made by campesinos. In the sierra, water became increasingly unavailable to subsistance farmers and those producing for local markets. Families were unable to survive in the countryside. The promise of jobs in urban industry, together with the impoverishment and extreme exploitation of campesinos, stimulated massive migration from the countryside to the city. This migration had begun in the 1950s, but it accelerated rapidly under reform.

The Confederación Campesina del Perú, founded in 1947,

became active in the mid-1970s to guarantee that campesinos' rights under agrarian law were respected and to lay down conditions for implementation acceptable to them. The CCP was strong enough to lead in massive land takeovers where agrarian reform had been delayed through collusion between government officials and hacendados. More land was restored to control of comuneros in the central sierra in 1974 than at any other time in the country's history. Over forty thousand campesinos mobilized in one province alone to reclaim 150 haciendas.

When revolt was channeled through the union it could be coordinated on a nationwide level. Through union action, campesinos opposed heavy taxes and debts imposed by the government. They opposed the government's orientation of production toward private profit by former landholders who had been given government posts. They exposed the hacendados' attempts to speculate on land not immediately subject to expropriation, and they exposed corruption in marketing and distribution of products.

The rural rebellion was linked with urban strikes and uprisings directed against the government, which was also reneging on promises made to workers and shantytown dwellers. *Ligas Agrarias* (agrarian leagues) were set up by the government to counteract the CCP; the premise of the new leagues was that, since "the land belonged to the worker," a union was not necessary. But these new government organizations were taken over by union sympathizers, and the government was thus unable to stem the opposition. Eventually, the government sent military troops to occupy those areas where opposition was strongest. Many campesinos were imprisoned or killed.

During this period, rural women formed special brigades to assist in the expropriation of hacendados' land. They punished men who were slow to participate in land takeovers, using such tactics as painting men yellow and handing them over to landlords. Women also held landlords captive by tying them down while campesinos gathered to enforce land takeovers. Women were always in the forefront of marches and land takeovers. Yet they did not, as a group, question the union's acceptance of provisions of reform that directly threatened female social power; nor did they collectively oppose the process of "modernization" that was forcing the migration of rural people from their communities.

Most Indian women of the sierra who emerged as leaders in the land struggles of the mid-1970s returned to their homes and fields when military repression ended their political activity in 1975. Like other campesinas, they pastured their animals, sometimes sold meager products of their agricultural labor in local markets or in the street, helped repair adobe houses after the rains, carried water home for cooking, washed in the streams and rivers that remained available for their use, and, where possible, sought to sell handicrafts and food to tourists. They were rarely incorporated in the cooperatives administered by agrarian reform; few were active in the Ligas Agrarias set up by the government.

The active participation of women in the campesino union was not sought by men. Those few who participated in the union seldom brought up questions relating to women's special situations—problems relating to child care, schools, health needs, and domestic violence—or to the discrimination against them within the union. To do so would have meant the loss of whatever personal power they had been able to achieve within the organization—and almost certain punishment at the hands of husbands who, while sometimes defending them in public, would severely criticize them in private. Women were expected to prepare meals during union meetings. If they came to listen after the meal was over, they were thanked profusely for the contribution they had made in serving the *olla común,* and then invited to retire to their houses.

Only within the *comunidad campesina* did women's participation continue to receive some legitimacy. Women were expected to attend and vote at community meetings, especially in the absence of their husbands. This was a marked contrast with union meetings. Meetings in the indigenous community were a survival of

A campesina from Huancavelica asks to speak before the Sixth National Congress of the peasant union, Confederación Campesina del Perú. Women's intervention brought cheers from male delegates who had previously conspired to keep women subordinate to men in the union. (Ernesto Jimenez)

the *ayllu,* and were typically conducted in native languages. Women sat in a group, as they had since pre-Inca times, when they held power comparable to that of men, but their active participation was reduced to murmuring among themselves. Even this activity was frowned upon by men: *"¿Porqué hacen bulla?"* (Why are you making so much noise?) Sometimes a woman would speak up, but she was usually ridiculed or ignored. Women were expected to approve whatever the men had decided. Occasionally, when women as a group perceived their interests had been violated, one woman would intervene in the meeting on the group's behalf. At such times, a major reorientation of the proceedings took place, and a female spokesperson occasionally assumed the role of president of the community.

Finally, under the impact of continuing economic recession in the 1980s, the systematic subordination of women came increasingly into question. Women all over the country began consciously to increase their participation at the community level, to reproduce the process of "noisemaking"—as we shall see later on—this time on a national level, thus preparing the way for their entry as a group into the campesino union and other organs of popular power.

Survival in the Andes

Confrontation with hacendados and with the government in the 1960s and 1970s brought rural women into active participation with men in political life from which they had been barred for many years. It also brought formal recognition of the indigenous communities for the first time in generations. But agrarian reform threatened community structures in new ways, because it accelerated the processes of capitalist development. Not only were more women and men than ever forced to leave the indigenous communities in search of paid work, but many more men began to leave their communities for seasonal work on coffee plantations at the edge of tropical rain forests or with petroleum companies in the heart of the jungle. Those campesinos who migrated to the city found that few men, and fewer women, were able to find steady work there. Women who accompanied their husbands to the city could not even count on feeding their families potatoes and corn. They began to realize that their abandonment of rural communities left them without a base from which to struggle for some control over the future, and for the preservation of cultural values they hoped to pass on to their children.

The community structure gave meaning to women's lives. They were impelled to find ways to continue in its defense, with or without the encouragement of husbands and fathers, and in the midst of the most extreme deprivation they as Indians had faced since Europeans invaded the continent.

Today, many more women than men remain in the Andean mountains. And the higher one goes into the mountains, the fewer men. Men who migrate to the cities without their wives often establish ties with urban women. They cannot be counted on to support their families in the sierra. Traditionally, women and men work together on difficult jobs. For example, the men hold sheep down while the women sheer them. Today, the products of the alpaca and the llama have become a major new export commodity monopolized by four North American companies and one state-owned company. Even those men who work for wages as shepherds on expropriated land in the sierra are away from their communities for long periods of time and are seldom available to work communal or family plots together with women.

Women do not receive the technical or financial assistance needed to make production on communal land competitive with mechanical farming. They must spend increasing amounts of time traveling to towns to sell what they produce in order to get cash to buy salt and kerosene or other commodities they have come to rely on for daily survival. Restrictions on water use have reduced its availability to comuneros for irrigation and domestic use.

My own experiences while living in the Mantaro Valley, where women as a whole are better off than in other regions of the sierra, helped me to understand the stark reality of rural life in Peru. When I first came with my family to live in an indigenous community outside Jauja, a neighbor offered us two eggs and two cups of milk daily. She was happy to save herself a trip to town by selling to a neighbor. I was upset to learn, however, that her own

Herding sheep in the Mantaro Valley. In places where partnership between women and men in daily work has been the structural basis of community life, many women are now left to work alone or to suffer the violence of men who are afflicted with alcoholism. (Jean-Pierre Perpoil)

In indigenous communities, women have preserved a semblance of equality with men but often meet with resistance from men when they speak at community meetings. (Jean-Pierre Perpoil)

family seldom ate either eggs or milk, since these were their main source of cash. I had been hanging salted meat to dry outside our front door for some time before I realized that these products, too, were never available to most of my neighbors, even though they pastured animals regularly. We walked about a kilometer to get water from a pipe that was connected to a mountain stream. Not until the pipe ran dry and we had to resort to taking stagnant water from the irrigation ditch did I realize that my neighbor had no access at all to piped water. The pipe had been installed for private use by a wealthier member of the community, who offered to share it with us because we were newcomers who had been invited to the community.

The increasing impoverishment of women and children in the countryside is for the most part not recognized by the government as a social problem. Women's contribution to the economy in bearing, rearing, and maintaining the future work force for rural and urban industries has not been reflected in official reports, nor have women been recognized as agents of social change. Rural women are considered ignorant and incompetent because they are not as likely as men to speak Spanish or to read and write.

In the sierra, if a young girl is permitted by her family to attend school, which is unlikely because her work is highly valued at home, she will usually attend only up to the third grade. On weekends when young boys are not in school, they are likely to be playing or studying, while young girls who do go to school seldom have time to study or play. Schools offering courses beyond the primary grades are far away, and it is risky and costly to let daughters go on buses to school and return late at night. For those who live in the high altitudes where there are no teachers, attendance at school is impossible.

Once rural men have received some education and are fluent in Spanish, they generally refuse to carry loads on their backs or do other chores they consider beneath their dignity. Even my *compañero,* Raúl, who was conscious of the inequality of women and men and was committed to struggle against it, found carrying water degrading. He thought that being seen carrying water would jeopardize the position of leadership he had been given as the community was about to form a cooperative on expropriated land. He was also afraid that comuneros would be critical of me. Actually, I found that women, at least, were quite willing to sacrifice such customs for greater cooperation between spouses. Nor were men critical of me for questioning ther traditional division of labor because they saw that I was more than willing to work on communal projects, doing whatever I could, including digging ditches and cutting wood. They noted that I shared their "love for the land," and while they admired my companion's enthusiasm for defending community interests, they also recognized that he had taken on mestizo ways.

As the process of "modernization" increasingly separates indigenous women from men, women in some regions have been left to do agricultural work practically alone. The transport of products to market, the care and pasturing of sheep, cattle, and small animals on communal land, as well as the crafts of weaving, knitting, spinning, and so on are being left, more and more, to women. Men seldom help children with their homework or teach them the religious or cultural values that might be important to their survival.

Women are so busy making do, and so overwhelmed by the gap between their own knowledge and that which is identified with modern technology, that they are forgetting what they once knew of nutritional balance, herbal medicine, steam therapy, body massage, midwifery, and other natural health practices. Very few are teaching these skills to their children. Yet modern medicine is not available in most areas where campesinos live, or if it is, it is practically useless, since they cannot afford prescribed medicines, vitamins, or treatments involving the use of expensive equipment.[2]

The diet of Indians has changed with the introduction of a money economy and government subsidies making available manufactured products such as soda pop, noodles, and refined sugar. Pesticides and chemical fertilizers have polluted water supplies. Sometimes government agents sponsor educational programs criticizing campesinos for eating poorly, but without recognizing the processes by which nutritional balance has come to be violated.

Even as the consumption of refined and processed products has weakened campesinas physically, their daily work has become harder. With fewer men there to help with the heavy jobs, and with less to eat, women are often totally exhausted. Many suffer terrible pain from an illness known as *recalco,* a product of exhaustion combined with the penetration of cold in high altitudes, that can leave the sufferer partially paralyzed.

Because the rural women of the mountains live in poor health and poverty, the burden of repeated pregnancies terrifies them, yet the labor of children is needed for bare subsistence. Women are eager for sex education so they can space their pregnancies, and they complain bitterly about the lack of help and care during pregnancy and childbirth. Those who try to practice birth control are often punished by husbands who feel it threatens their own power. A woman will sometimes lie to outsiders about her knowledge of contraceptives rather than admit that her husband forbids their use and accuses her of "laziness."

The precariousness of life in the countryside is increased many times over by the high level of alcohol consumption, especially among men. Women rarely drink except on special occasions, such as weddings or funerals. But among men, drinking is a social activity and they have taken to drinking more bottled beer than homemade *chicha. Chicha* or *aguardiente* is consumed by everyone on festival days, but the beer the men drink regularly comes from the city; it must be bought with money, and it makes them lethargic and sometimes violent. Campesinas always associate male violence with alcohol, and they complain that the men drink to get out of working: "sometimes the men get drunk and go to bed and we have to do everything." Both men and women chew coca leaves to ward off hunger and fatigue, women perhaps even more than men. Used regularly as a substitute for food, the leaf is likely, according to campesinos, to cause *"embrutacimiento"* (disorientation, stupidity). Its use as a medicine or stimulant on special occasions is, nevertheless, defended by Indians as an important part of their culture.

Violence toward women is present almost everywhere in Peru. In the cities, one sometimes hears that rural men are not violent toward women, but the evidence today is to the contrary. What does seem to be true is that domestic violence is more common where mestizo influence is greatest. Rape, especially, is

identified with Spanish-style machismo. Among indigenous couples, tussling, teasing, and mock fighting are more traditional, and women are just as often the "aggressors" as men.[3]

Aside from cultural practice, there is a good case to be made that male violence toward women is a product of colonial and present government policy, for it gives men effective power over women by making women economically dependent. Male power is reflected in property and tax laws, marriage laws, church practices, agrarian reform structures, and municipal governments, and all are linked with commercial interests. Loss of self-esteem among women is produced largely by their weak position in the money economy. Women still do nearly all the bartering, but money transactions are usually handled by men. The lack of formal education contributes to women's silence in defense of rights they seek both at home and in public life. Those Indian women who are well-dressed, have some formal education, and are successful entrepreneurs or landholders are invariablly treated with respect by Indian men.

Campesinas universally feel they work more and harder than men, and many complain that any respect they receive from men is given grudgingly. As one campesina remarked, "We get up at 5:00 in the morning and go to bed at 9:00, working all day long. Sometimes men give us some recognition but generally they don't. They even insult us." Indian women feel insulted not only by men, but by anyone who has received some formal education, even their own children. Although they are sensitive to the disdain of others, they do not underestimate the importance of the work they do. "The women who know how to read and write leave home to go to Lima or Cuzco. We illiterates stay in our communities . . . taking care of our animals, of our *cuy* [guinea pigs], cooking, and working in the fields. The people who know how to read don't like this kind of work and they go away anywhere they can." Some campesinas work as peons for others, either because there is no land available to them or because their land is insufficient for survival.

Washing clothes is "women's work." Most women who wash in cold water all day eventually succumb to respiratory illnesses. (Jean-Pierre Perpoil)

The powerlessness of women at home and in the community must be seen as both a cause and a consequence of their powerlessness before the government. In describing her frustration at the government's imposition of official prices on farm products, one campesina testifed: "We've gone to the Ministry . . . it was a trick they played on us, because now we're indebted up to our necks. Our potatoes bring terribly low prices and they haven't considered how much we have to pay for fertilizers, how much it costs to treat diseased potatoes. The people who set the prices haven't worked in the fields, suffering the heat and the cold, washing in cold water. They just sit there and say, 'This one's worth so much, that one's worth so much.' "

Many such statements came out of *encuentros,* or conferences, held in Cuzco, Huancavelica, and Andahuaylas in 1980, where campesinas chosen by their communities met for several days with academics to explore the needs and opinions of rural women. The results of the meetings were publicized and served to stimulate organizing activity among women and to generate a climate of debate with regard to relations between women and men as well as a questioning of the priorities of government.[4]

Through questioning of campesinas in similar group situations, I learned of many cases of suicide by women who felt completely overwhelmed by poverty, overwork, disrespect, abuse, and abandonment. Poisoning and throwing oneself into a river are common forms of suicide. Sometimes women kill their children before they kill themselves.

Women also threaten to kill their children as a form of protest. Popular theater that flourished in Peru (before it was repressed in the mid-1970s) made the killing of children because of poverty the theme of one of its street pantomimes.[5] In the pantomime story, the main character discovers there is no food in the house, catches a rat as it is escaping, convinces the hungry children that the soup will be very tasty, and then puts rat poison into it before giving each child a spoonful. Since, when I saw the pantomime, the artists were men and were not wearing costumes, I assumed the central character was the children's father. Only recently, when I began to collect stories of women's lives in the Sierra, was I able to feel the story with full force. The main character was meant to be a woman.

Official Reform, Repression, and Popular Education

The special suffering of rural women was part of the focus of a short-lived campaign for the emancipation of women carried out by the Velasco government in the early 1970s, evidently at the urging of the Communist Party, its main publicizers. As capitalist development was promoted, government officials no doubt saw some possibility of women's entering the workforce in greater numbers. This possibility was never realized. The percentage of women doing wage work is lower today than it was before industrial development began. The worldwide capitalist recession and the special conditions of development under dependent capitalism make the integration of women into industrial development problematic.

When Velasco decreed that women should have certain rights in the workplace not previously accorded them, he also gave illiterates the right to vote, although no elections were permitted at that time. A government office, staffed by volunteers, was established to draw up plans for women's general education *(capacitación)*. Social scientists were sent to the countryside (under United Nations auspices) to evaluate the progress of women under agrarian reform. The findings of the studies were largely suppressed, and the entire program was ended abruptly with the demise of the Velasco regime in 1975. Even pamphlets and documents calling for equality between women and men were recalled. However, as a legacy of this period, political parties of the Left began discussing the issue of women's emancipation, something most of them had never done.[6]

The government's promotion of reforms for women coincided with my 1974 teaching term at the Universidad Nacional del Centro in Huancayo. In the year before my arrival, students had taken over the sociology curriculum and demanded an end to the use of materials from the United States Information Service. They insisted on the teaching of Marxism as the central focus of study. The student organizations that had demanded that other North Americans be ousted from sociology faculties accepted me on the basis of my experiences in Chile. In fact, I was hired on the initiative of these students. They were critical of government programs and policies that propagandized about women's emancipation but did nothing to improve the basic conditions of women's lives. Nevertheless, the attention the government was giving to women was a challenge to which students and others were responding. I was able to introduce studies about women and about social change in the countryside, even though I never succeeded in introducing a special course on women.[7] Some of my female students formed a women's study and action group outside the university, and a student organization sponsored a forum on Women and Social Revolution that drew a crowd of several hundred people.

After 1975, student movements were repressed, and curriculums came increasingly under the control of conservatives, although the universities did not return to the kind of U.S. domination that had existed before.[8]

Government-sponsored studies and services to campesinos were cut off or were severely restricted with the end of the "first phase" of military government, as the reform period came to be called. However, nongovernment institutions, funded by progressive Europeans and staffed largely by Peruvians—social democrats, leftists, or former employees of the government—took up work as investigators and technical advisors to campesinos. These projects were solicited by indigenous communities. The advisors were less bound by bureaucracy and better accepted by campesinos than government agents had been. Most important, they were able to oppose or criticize official policies. They did this at their own risk, however, as the government became increasingly hostile to criticism.

Some two hundred centers to assist popular movements were established throughout the country at this time, many of them in rural areas. Staff members worked with permanent residents of rural communities who were expected to carry on later without outside assistance. Such trainees were called *promotoras,* just as government trainees had been. Some urban women who joined popular education projects began to work with local *promotoras* in such a way as to learn from them rather than to impose "modern" ideas. In one case with which I am familiar a staff member having

Young girls bear heavy work responsibilities at home, especially in the countryside. (Jean-Pierre Perpoil)

a degree in nutrition from a foreign university learned from campesinas that altitude, climate, temperature, cooking methods, and the state of health of individuals all figure importantly in a native woman's understanding of nutritional balance. So she began helping elderly campesinas to record systematically their knowledge of nutrition, native medicine, and birth control. Combining this knowledge with what she had learned from her formal studies in Europe, she helped women prepare their own educational materials, teaching them at the same time to read and write. They also learned to identify harmful foods and drugs that were being imported from foreign countries.[9]

Through popular education projects such as these, rural women were encouraged to evaluate their own situations historically and to identify and develop agricultural and other technologies appropriate to their needs. Women's traditional interest in seed selection and horticultural technique was recognized and legitimized. Since popular educators had no need to cater to the desires of business interests to produce immediate profits at the expense of long-term goals related to conservation of natural resources, popular education projects were able to experiment with the use of natural fertilizers and natural methods of pest control. Needless to say, women were more enthusiastic about such projects than they had been about earlier efforts to involve them in rural education programs in which the goals of learning were obscure. Government *promotoras* had often given up on women, declaring them to be uninterested in education, if not actually resistant to it. Through popular education, women not only shared useful knowledge among themselves and gained new knowledge, but also gained self-esteem and political awareness.

Popular education was effective in preparing some campesinas for community leadership, but it did not reach many, and it could not by itself create conditions for progressive social transformation in the countryside. More than anything else, education made obstacles to such change more visible. Municipal governments often came in direct conflict with community advisers who defended the interests of poor campesinos. Staff from experimental and educational projects sometimes suffered persecution at the hands of those whose commercial interests were threatened by their activities. Businessmen tried to run them out of town or have them arrested.

By the end of the 1970s, the government's undeclared policy of support for reprivatization of the economy in the countryside forced government officials to view attempts to promote self-sufficiency among comuneros as subversive activity. Encroachment on communal land was tolerated by the Morales Bermúdez government, and by the Belaúnde government which replaced it. Efforts by indigenous communities to fight against encroachment were punished. Women's emerging leadership in the countryside came to be symbolized by the death of Toribia Flores, a Cuzco woman who led protests against the encroachment of a private developer on community land. She had been well-known as secretary of defense of her community and had been able to inspire campesinos throughout the region with her oratory. In June 1981, during a mobilization of campesinos who were sitting on the highway to cut off traffic, she was shot and killed.

Foreign Investment

The government's support of reprivatization of the land in order to further capitalist development in the countryside was related to Peru's dependency on foreign capital. The Belaúnde government declared that direct foreign investment was preferable to heavy government indebtedness, and U.S. AID programs were invited to Peru in the 1980s to prepare the way for massive foreign investment.

AID personnel, in contrast to personnel from the popular education projects, have little respect for local history and customs. This is not simply the result of ignorance, but precisely because the intention of AID is to help usher campesinos into "the modern age," the age of the multinational corporation. Where AID officials are forced to recognize local demand for popular technology, it is translated into "intermediate technology," something the multinationals can accommodate within their own operations.

In the Mantaro Valley, investment by U.S. companies in

pesticide and chemical fertilizer plants became a high priority. These plants were given access to the electricity generated by the huge hydroelectric project which has been operating for some time on the Mantaro River. Electricity generated there has mainly served Lima, hundreds of miles away. For years campesinos in the valley have been demanding access to electricity for their own needs, with little success.

From such experiences the campesinos understand that both the government and the multinational corporations are primarily concerned with the exploitation of natural resources and human labor, not with service to campesinos. The corporations not only remove workers from control over production, but also from the possibility of benefiting from what they produce. The most obvious examples, of course, are the mining companies, which spread poison over the countryside and produce nothing at all that is of use to local populations.[10] But this is true even where production is geared to the Peruvian market. Monopolization of the dairy industry by Carnation Milk (LECHE GLORIA) and Nestlés (PERULAC) is an example of this process. Nestlés operates in Cajamarca and Carnation in Arequipa. Government subsidies protect these companies from loss; as a result, fresh milk is not available to consumers—even in milk-producing zones—and the campesinos cannot afford to buy canned milk. Subsidies also mean that tax money flows out of the country, and that dependence on foreign technology increases. The process of canning milk is so expensive that imported powdered milk is cheaper. This has caused a decline in dairy production in Peru. Similarly, a North American company has achieved a monopoly on chicken production. Its mass-produced "modern" chickens (grown rapidly in controlled environments with undisclosed amounts of hormones added to their feed) are available only at high prices, primarily to those who dine in restaurants; chicken consumption in the country as a whole has declined.

In the mountains, where women's unpaid agricultural labor is vital to the economy, women have seldom been incorporated, even marginally, into production by the multinationals. They have, however, increasingly flooded into the cities, working in the streets as prostitutes and vendors, to serve the needs of those who have been able to get jobs in industry.

Indian women's special skills in the production of artisanry have not gone unnoticed by foreign investors. Protestant missionaries have often become involved in making these skills marketable, as part of their effort to convert campesinos to Protestant evangelical faiths. Both evangelization and small business activities tend to accelerate the process of class division within communities, blunting solidarity in popular movements. Those families who are receptive to missionary programs and influence aspire to become the privileged class within the community. Male members are often able to take over municipal offices and manipulate commercial interests, weakening indigenous communities. Traditional fiestas are used to demonstrate and consolidate personal status rather than to express unity among comuneros. Women's education is promoted, but only in subjects and themes that do not violate the missionaries' ideas of what is properly women's sphere. The presence of missionaries tends to cultivate in their followers a taste for the consumer items that missionaries use, items which are then flaunted by those campesinos who have been able to acquire them. The missionary presence seems inevitably to encourage individuals or families to enter into the money economy at the expense of the larger community.[11]

Because of the assault on indigenous communities by capitalist development, in its various guises, customs of reciprocity and mutual helpfulness among comuneros have often come to be seen as evidence of backwardness. University students in my sociology classes in Huancayo all agreed that avoidance of communal work was a mark of prestige.[12] They were at first reluctant to discuss class divisions in their communities, because doing so created personal conflicts for them between their professed desires for social revolution and their own privileged status in their communities.

Within each indigenous community, there were a few campesinos who were able to exploit the labor of at least several others—what scholars sometimes identify as an "emergent bourgeoisie." Others were essentially self-sufficient. Still others, the

majority, were forced to work for wages at least part time. The expropriation of large private landholdings under agrarian reform and their conversion into cooperatives made possible the reunification of comuneros who became associated with these, but many others remained outside agrarian reform structures.

By the late 1970s, rural women who under the impact of capitalist development were most affected by the out-migration of husbands and children began organizing, sometimes informally and at other times very consciously, to reestablish reciprocal ties through communal labor, mutual aid, and exchange of products. They did not do this with the intention of remaining entirely outside the national economy, which most campesinos considered impossible. These Indian women knew they had to coordinate their efforts on a wider scale and secure the cooperation of men through active participation in political organizations if they were to ensure that their organization was integrated with movements for social change.

A Victory in the Union

Only a handful of women attended the fifth national congress of the Confederación Campesina del Perú, which met in Cuzco in 1979. These women, tired of seeing their own concerns as women relegated to last place—or nowhere at all—requested that a Secretariat of Women be set up in the union. They could no longer keep silent in the face of men's inability to recognize the desperation felt by campesinos in general, as the union appeared to be falling into bureaucratization and division among leaders. Their motion was accepted, but a man was voted in to head the secretariat. For three years, the secretariat remained inactive while indigenous women in various parts of the country organized their own bases to face crises in the countryside and to confront the union membership at its next congress.[13]

One of the groups that came into being at this time was the

Watching military maneuvers in Huancayo. The demise of the military government brought civilians to power, but military occupation of the country increased. (Lynn Murray)

United Front for the Rights of Rural Women in the Department of Puno. Among the activities of the front was the political education of campesinas. An organizer of the front recalls that many women were told by their husbands that they were "just looking for excuses to get out of the kitchen." Her own husband left this organizer because she insisted on going to meetings: "My husband abandoned me when I began getting involved in these things, because I understood the problems we women have, that we have to learn something about our reality . . . My husband never let me go to the meetings; I have two daughters by him, and he even refuses to recognize the second child because of my going to the meetings. But this doesn't humiliate me. It gives me pride, because with this experience I have the spirit to dedicate myself even more to my *compañeras* [women comrades]."

Dedication to the organization of women was seen by the women themselves as part of the liberation of the entire country from economic bondage, but that was clearly not enough to win the support of husbands. Another woman declared: "If my husband wanted to order me not to come to this meeting, well, I'd just tell him he was wrong . . . That's what we women have to learn, to not let the men impose their whims on us. Why? Because, even if we never see socialism, our children must see it, our grandchildren. We have to do this so we'll have a new kind of family in the future, in a free country, a socialist country, where everyone will participate equally, where everyone will eat meat, where everyone will drink milk. It's not like that now."[14]

Over a hundred women, many of whom had already been organizing others in the countryside, came to the sixth national congress of the CCP which was held in Lima in July 1982. Since I was able to attend this congress, I was witness to the outpouring of frustration, intense mobilization, and triumph of women that took place there.

The first night of the congress, a woman from the Department of Puno asked to address the more than two thousand delegates in attendance. She rose from her seat in the audience, grasped the microphone firmly, and electrified her audience by calling on women to end the centuries of abuse they had suffered in their homes and communities. She sought redress from men who had denied women their rightful place as union leaders while

A grandmother in Jauja. Older women, though lacking formal education, retain knowledge of nutrition, medicine, and agricultural techniques that are threatened by the penetration of foreign industries and by an export-import economy. (Monika Lupescher)

using them opportunistically in times of crisis. She spoke urgently and fluently, in Quechua, even though the congress had been conducted up to that time in Spanish. She did not hesitate or retreat in her message when the cameras of the press rushed to focus on her.

When I began to comprehend what was taking place as the representative, from the Puno Women's Front made her initial appeal to the members of the campesino union, her words sounded to me like thunder over fields parched by years of drought. When she was finished she sat down to protracted and excited applause. The long-overdue, but still largely unanticipated, rebellion of rural women had culminated in the first public recognition by the campesino union of men's wrongful consipracy to keep women subservient both socially and politically.

In response to the groundswell of protest by women, a Commission on Women and Youth was established by the executive committee of the CCP. When the commission met during the sixth congress, a young man complained that the women were showing "poor discipline" by not limiting their conversations to Spanish. The question was discussed at length, and a vote was taken, resulting in a unanimous decision to continue in several languages, as the women had been doing. A discussion then took place about the need to restructure the meeting, since the problems of youth and women could not be adequately dealt with in a single commission. Some participants said that the intention of the executive committee in putting the two together had undoubtedly been to dilute their anger as women. Nevertheless, the women agreed that they could take advantage of the situation to impress upon the congress that one of their main concerns was the loss to indigenous communities of children affected by poverty and alienation.

Women expressed the desperation they felt at not being able to provide a future for their children. The loss of children to the city, especially to delinquency, prostitution or drugs robbed the community not only of the productive contribution these children had made at home, but also robbed women of the motivation to persevere in their own extremely difficult situation, for it put in doubt the continued existence of the community. Women called for a resurgence of cultural pride that would enable young people to overcome alienation and dedicate themselves to revolutionary struggle as a way to combat poverty and despair.

Women agreed to call on the union to set up schools in the countryside where young women and men could learn about their history. In this way it was hoped young people would be motivated to fight for their right to remain in rural areas. "We mothers are going to die anyway. Things are very bad for us. But we have to give our children something. We have to inspire them and educate them to respect themselves and fight for a better world. We've been walking along behind our menfold long enough. We have to build an organization that won't accept false promises and that won't be complicit with all the corruption and failure that has been such a common experience in our lives."

The young man who had intervened earlier to rebuke the women for speaking Quechua was inspired by the women's strength and unity in defining their own terms for political struggle. He had come to listen to a discussion of the problems of youth. At first he had been disappointed that youth were outnumbered by women, who seemed intent on their own agenda. While listening to the women's analysis of young people's alienation, he was transformed from a follower to a leader. He thanked the women for the lesson they had taught him and said that he himself would approach the Executive Committee to notify them that the young people were about to set up a commission of their own.

As the Women's Commission meeting continued, the dominant theme which developed was the need of women to organize to fight machismo and male domination in their personal lives, in their communities, and in the political struggles of rural people. "The men don't treat us with respect, they don't pay attention to what we say. They think we are stupid, and sometimes they will even beat up a woman within a few weeks after she has given birth. We have to let them know we won't let this happen anymore." Women complained that they had been repeatedly used in the fight for the land and then told to "go back to their kitchens." Not only did that deprive women of their own political rights, but it produced leaders who were opportunists. Campesinas agreed that men had demonstrated their incapacity to lead the popular

movement in the countryside by misspending community funds, mishandling equipment, drinking instead of disciplining themselves for battle. "We are tired of being slaves—slaves of men and slaves of government . . . We women have to take over the leadership of the revolutionary movement in the countryside, not because we think we are better than men, not because we oppose the men. We want the men to talk with us, to discuss things with us, to help us in our work, to be responsible to the community. Maybe we don't know how to read or write. But that doesn't mean we aren't intelligent. We know how to talk and we know how to think. We're not lacking in intelligence—what we're lacking is organization."

The misspending of funds attributed to machismo included such things as building soccer stadiums instead of assuring a reliable water supply and health care in the countryside. During land takeovers, women also felt men were too willing to negotiate and compromise because their tie to the land and to the community was not as strong as was that of women. Women felt that men's infighting in the union was due in part to personal power struggles that were a reflection of machismo, that by organizing themselves as women they would be able to demonstrate unity and overcome the sectarianism that had debilitated the union. At the community level, it is women, they said, who have been forced through extreme hardship to help each other with their work. The women felt it was time to revive traditions of common child care and to oppose all practices that cause competition for status among comuneros.

Campesinas brought to the congress printed materials, sometimes with cartoons drawn by the women themselves, or by their children, run off on small silkscreen-type presses. The pamphlets described their local organizations, the reasons for which they came together as women, the frustration and anger they felt after so many years of sacrifice. Women's associations had been formed

Market day in Jauja. Accelerated "development" has forced many people to leave provincial towns in search of paid work in the export sector of the Peruvian economy. (Jean-Pierre Perpoil)

in many places to produce baskets, blankets, sweaters, and other handmade articles both for sale within the country and outside. By forming associations, the women had been able to exercise control over quality, to obtain materials on a more regular basis, and to teach each other skills. Even though women had been encouraged in some instances by missionaries and by government and private agencies to form such associations, it seemed to them that the result had been exploitation by these same agencies, and further impoverishment of campesinas. Meanwhile, the government subsidized both those who imported food products and those large-scale businesses that exported food products, leaving the women who produce on family or community land without a viable market. Women said they were expected not only to feed and clothe their own families without any help, but that they were increasingly expected to feed and clothe other peoples' families at the expense of their own. In order to buy fertilizer or hire someone to plow, for instance, they had to sell products they needed for their own family's consumption or use.

The campesino union, in dealing primarily with the immediate financial problems of cooperatives established under agrarian reform, had begun to lose sight of the issues that had inspired formation of the union in the first place—the right of indigenous peoples to live in community and to reestablish control over the land, the productive process, and the product of their labor. Out of concern for these issues, one of the women who presided over the discussions of the Women's Commission was chosen as a candidate for secretary of Technology and Production in the union.

When the commission meeting adjourned, those who had attended put their arms around each other spontaneously and shouted slogans that expressed the broad range of their concerns and the energy they had felt from coming together for the first time.[15] What came through most clearly was the powerful sentiment that women weren't going to put up with any more infighting and ego-tripping (*divisionismo* and *egoismo*) among the men nor with any more humiliation or abuse from men. And they were committed to maintaining their own unity as women dedicated to the radical transformation of Peruvian society.

Among the observers at the meeting were leaders of barriada movements and household workers' movements. They expressed their support for rural women and emphasized the need for women's unity throughout the country. The mandate of the Secretariat of Women was defined in the following terms: ". . .to foment an enormous movement of rural women, to break their silence, to speak for those who have been forgotten thousands of times over, to coordinate with women workers, street vendors, hosuehold workers and housewives in the barriadas of the cities, building a powerful national movement, a Popular Front of Women, to fight for their own rights, linking their struggle with that of our entire people who are oppressed and exploited."

The energy from the women's meeting had not failed to attract the attention of the other commissions, seated on the ground in groups scattered around the outdoor coliseum. However, the Women's Commission was not scheduled to address all the assembled delegates until the "regular business" of the congress had been completed. On the fifth day of the congress, the delegates met all night, seated on bleachers in the indoor arena. Not until six A.M. was the Commission of Women called upon to present its report. At least half the delegates were either sleeping on their benches or wandering around outside in search of coffee or bread to help them stay awake. I had managed to get a little sleep myself curled up in a blanket on the floor of the room where women had been running off copies of their motions and making last-minute changes in wording. Each commission was strictly limited to half an hour in which to present motions and hear debate, and the women were determined to take full advantage of the time allotted them. I was awakened in time to reenter the arena and take my place beside other observers from the Province of Jauja, with whom I had been credentialed.

The person who had been chosen to present the motions prepared by the Women's Commission was president of her community in the Department of Cuzco. She was one of the two or three women who had attended union congresses before. She walked out to the long table in the middle of the arena where a line of men were seated before microphones. She appeared confident and serene. As a woman's voice was heard through the loudspeaker system, delegates began to stir, to open their eyes and sit up. The motions had been written in Spanish, but after reading each motion, the representative of the Women's Commission punctuated these with earnest appeals in Quechua explaining the seriousness of women's situation and the long history of abuse that women have suffered. Before long, everyone was not only awake, but standing on their feet and following each appeal with noisy applause, drums, horns, and shouts of support. When the reading of the motions was over, women from various delegations representing bases in different parts of the country held up their hands to ask for the use of the microphones, which had been attached to long extension cords. They spoke forcefully, one by one, emphasizing the importance of women's leadership in the union and the importance of mobilizing rural women all over the country in defense of their long-forgotten rights. Each speech was supported by standing ovations and the shouting of slogans: "Down with machismo!" "Down with male domination!" "Long live the Confederación Campesina del Perú!" Whatever the private thoughts and feelings of campesino men, they were emboldened to give women support long overdue. The half-hour allotted for the women's report extended to over an hour, as the chair was drowned out with cries of *"Otro!"* *"Otro!"* (More! More!) each time he attempted to move on to the last item of business or to end the women's intervention with defensive comments such as: "We are not against women—we support you—this is not a battle between women and men."

In the end women gained two seats on the Central Committee, including that of secretary of technology and production. And the union gave high priority to conducting regional women's meetings throughout the country during 1983 in order to develop women's programs and to recruit rural women into the union.

After the campesino congress was over, some men continued to give active encouragement to women. Others expressed open concern lest things get "out of hand." Personal defensiveness was often expressed through joking. Men who were most comfortable with the event were those who had been serving as *asesores* (helpers, advisers) to women's organizations where their special skills had been sought. They saw their participation in a new light, however, after the events at the congress, giving women from their own communities more respect than before.

Before the Congress I had visited one leader of a women's organization at her home in Huancavelica, in the presence of a male *asesor*. Each time I asked her a question, the man took it upon himself to answer. He even explained to me pointedly that "we need to educate and organize our women so they can help us when we are in conflict situations." Actually the women had established their organization in spite of male opposition, and had subsequently recruited men as helpers. Nevertheless, the *asesor* insisted on seeing himself as the initiator of the women's organization, and was interpreting its function so that it was not inconsistent with continued male leadership of the community. (This was a community where women far outnumbered men.) After the women's intervention in the CCP, in which they made public their frustration with male domination and their capability for leadership, the patronizing attitudes of men could no longer be sustained.

The powerful presence of a relatively small number of determined women at the sixth congress of the CCP laid the basis for a transformation of the relations between women and men in the union—perhaps in the country—as campesinos entered a new era of hope and struggle. A cogent expression of this transformation was the remark made by one eighty-four-year-old man who had befriended me during the meetings and who had told me he had in his personal library the writings of Dolores Ibarruri (Spanish revolutionary who is his contemporary) and Flora Tristan (eighteenth-century French revolutionary-feminist, of Peruvian parentage). He said he had wondered all his life when the women would rebel.

The demonstration of women's strength at the campesino congress went practically unmentioned in the official and published reports on the congress. This did not seem to surprise or bother campesinas, who were more interested in consolidating the ties they had made among themselves and in transforming their experience into action at the grassroots level. For some of the women present at the congress, the crescendo of women's rebellion in the meetings had been their first experience of the development of collective consciousness among women.

The significance of the campesino event was not just that women had begun to take control of their destinies, in spite of the enormous obstacles that had been put in their way. The eruption of female determination to restore the CCP to what they thought to be its rightful place as the representative of the rural poor was a powerful expression of the confidence women felt in themselves. It was also a response to the threatened total subordination of their interests to the demands of capitalist development, inevitably centered in the cities. The indigenous women in Peru are the rightful leaders of the defense of the land and the community. As the most exploited sector of the economy they will not be bought off or intimidated as a group, and they cannot seek to establish themselves as a new class of rulers, to reserve for themselves the power that belongs to the entire people.

By themselves, campesinas would not be able to assert enough power to force social revolution in Peru, nor would *indigenas* as a group, but as we shall see, they were not alone in their struggle.

Easter in Huaraz. In spite of elaborate festivities connected with the Catholic Church, which enjoys official support in Peru, campesinos honor Pachamama *(Mother Earth) before planting. (Lynn Murray)*

4 : *Organizing in the Shantytowns*

THE HOMEMAKER who lives in a working-class district of a Latin American city is engaged in a constant battle: every day, from early morning until late at night, she must struggle to provide the necessities of life for her family. A middle aged woman most likely has five or six children. She lives with the hope that one or more of them will escape from the precarious economic situation of the family and so be able to provide some security for other members. That puts a terrible burden on the children as well.

In Lima, where only 20 percent of the families have a regular income, most mothers (married or unmarried) have to keep their families fed and clothed and sheltered on less than half of what their own government declares to be a "minimum wage." A mother who lives in a shantytown may spend half or all of her daylight hours selling in the streets, after leaving her children at home alone, or sometimes taking them along. She may do piece-work in her home to add something to the family income. If her children are sick and in need of medical attention, she may leave them at home to die instead of taking them to a hospital or a clinic. She doesn't have money for bus fare or medicines or enough cash to bribe a doctor to secure the kind of care she feels her children need. When medicines are available free of charge, she stands in line for hours waiting for them, frequently to find out that the supply of whatever she was waiting for "just ran out." If members of her family are picked up for delinquency or crime, she must usually borrow money from friends or relatives to bribe someone to get them out of jail.

If a woman is lucky enough to have a husband who is employed in a factory, she is expected to carry his lunch to him at his workplace. The factory has electricity and running water, but her home, as likely as not, will lack these amenities. Though her water supply is inadequate at best, the woman who lives in a shantytown or barriada washes all the family's clothing by hand and prepares meals from food purchased daily at the local market. Often she must stand in a long line to get a bucket of water, or fight over it with neighbors; and in spite of this she may take in the washing of others.

If a mother succumbs to tuberculosis, which is increasingly common in Peru, she feels terribly guilty, seeing herself as a complete failure. Women who try to perform abortions on themselves in order to make their lives a little easier and save their children from poverty and suffering, risk four years in jail. Authorities are usually notified if complications from an attempted abortion force a woman to seek medical help. Nevertheless, abortion is the leading cause of death among women of childbearing age in Peru. There are cases where members of a woman's own family send her to jail out of fear that another attempt will claim her life.

Housewives who try to join with others to organize for better living conditions are often accused of neglecting their families. A husband may even punish his wife physically. Conservative neighbors and government or church officials will surely pressure her to stop *"haciendo política"* (mixing in politics, agitating). Family networks that have helped her survive in the city after migration from the countryside may not help her when she finds herself drawn into wider community affairs. Relatives, fearing reprisal, will accuse her of "wasting her time" and of threatening the personal "advancement" of family members.

Despite these harsh realities, women of the barriadas have become a major social force in Peru's developing revolutionary movement and have reached out to rural women and to women factory workers, encouraging them to fuller participation in political processes of change.

Those Who "Invade" the Capital

Nearly half of Lima's population live in barriadas that are the result
of squatter invasions by migrants. Groups of shantytown
dwellers, young couples and others who do not yet have homes of
their own, organize to occupy empty terrain and claim it for a new
settlement. Every woman who has participated in the establishment of a barriada settlement has a story to tell that reflects her
courage, fear, and determination to survive. Some women, unable
to tolerate living with in-laws or relatives who preceded them in
coming to the city, have participated in *tomas de tierra,* or land
takeovers, without the support of their husbands. They have often
ended up alone with their children even after the *toma* was successful. One woman tells of her experience:

My husband didn't agree with me and said, "No! Who wants to go to a
sandy desert where there's no water—nothing?" I waited 'til he went to
work, and came here at 10:00 at night with my blanket. I went to the
open field without anything, with just my blanket, and stayed in the
open air with my three children. We slept there.

The next day . . . I looked for poles [to make a shelter] but I didn't
have enough money and I had to feed the children, so I bought two
carrizos [roots], went to the field again, and put up my tent with the
blanket that I had. We stayed five days.

I was out of food for the children when my husband came looking
for me, angry. "Why did you come here, leaving the house like that.
Look at the kids, all full of sand!" The children were filthy and hadn't
eaten and my husband said "Come on!" "I'm not going," I said. "Then
I'll take the kids!" he said, and left me angrily with them. I stayed two
more days. Then I couldn't take it any longer because I was seven months
pregnant and was thinking about the children. I got to the house and
luckily my husband wasn't there. I took the kids and came back, bringing along a small burner.

I was there a month. . . . My husband came just to give me a week's
allowance and said, "Get yourself prepared because the police are coming," but he told me he wasn't staying and that I should head for the hill.
I did, mainly for the children, but the other folks made me come back
because otherwise we wouldn't have been able to defend ourselves. I had
to leave the kids way up the hill and help defend against the police when
they began to arrest and beat up the leaders. We all armed ourselves with

Birth of a shantytown, Heroes del Pacifico, Chorillos, Lima. Half the population of the capital lives in barriadas established by the invasion and defense of unoccupied land. (Ernesto Jimenez)

A panoramic view of the barrio El Cenicero, El Agustino, Lima. (Ernesto Jimenez)

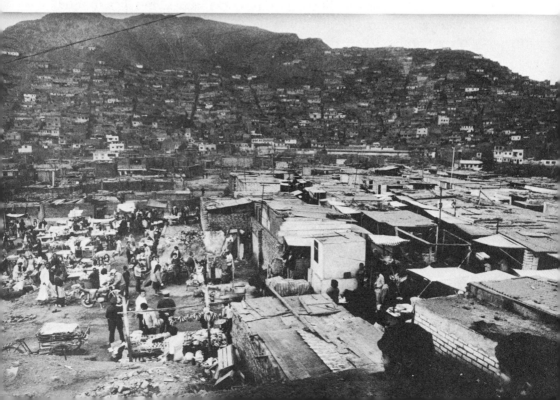

sticks and stones and defended ourselves. The police left, but they had given us a hard time. After that we stayed, all women, to defend our children, and one woman, I don't remember who, took a strong stand when they wanted to take away our leaders. The rest ran away, but she said, "You'll have to carry me away dead." I was real timid in those days.

Afterwards I had my baby and my husband came, brought our things, and we built a little shelter. I was there two years before I got a lot assigned to me. My husband never came back. I was there all alone, fending off the thieves who never stopped bothering us.[1]

Some pobladores, or shantytown dwellers, died while crossing the Rimac River in Lima to escape from police pursuing them on horseback during a *toma de tierra*. Each barriada has its collective history of struggle reflecting the solidarity that marked the formation of new communities in the city. Women are the unacknowledged heroines of those struggles.

Comas was one of the first of Lima's barriadas to be formed by a land takeover. Villa El Salvador is one of the latest. Each now comprises over 500,000 inhabitants. Villa El Salvador, sprawled out along the sandy seacoast, has no paved streets, and many of the houses are made of straw mats or other improvised materials. Comas is built mostly on hillsides of rock and infertile black sand. Some streets in Comas have sidewalks and streetlights, but there is no regular garbage collection. Rats, cockroaches, and flies abound. Water and electricity are not available to everyone, nor to anyone on a regular basis. Transportation is extremely inadequate and unreliable.

Mama Berta, the mother of my *compañero* Raúl, participated in the *toma de tierra* which eventually became Comas. Over the years, as a street vendor and entrepreneur, she was able to save enough money, with the help of her husband and children, to build a cement house equipped with running water and electricity. She developed heart problems, however, and was unable to walk the mile uphill to her house from the highway leading to the city. She was also in continual conflict with her husband, who spent most of his time at La Parada, a huge flea market in downtown Lima. So she joined a group that was staking out territory in Villa El Salvador. There she put up a house and store made of *esteras,* or straw mats. The community had built a school, but it had collapsed during an earthquake. So Mama Berta woke her children every day at four in the morning and sent them by bus to Comas, two and one-half hours each way, to attend school. During the day she watched her store and cooked and served meals to bus drivers who stopped there at the end of the line. She couldn't leave the premises because she might risk getting robbed or miss the truck which came by at odd hours every few days selling water. When the children were home, especially on weekends, they ran the store so she could get away to make major purchases for her business. Even though the family had no electricity, they kept the general store as well as the restaurant open until midnight, using kerosene lanterns, and playing records of *huayno* music from the sierra on an old battery-run Victrola.

Mama Berta was more successful than many barriada mothers. She had the occasional support of her husband, who had an old truck and brought provisions for her to sell in her store. She charged him for the meals he ate in her restaurant, but she took him in when his health was bad or his truck out of repair for a long time. When one of their five children was sick, he was sometimes able to help pay for medicine, and he contributed toward their education, usually after a prolonged battle. In Comas, he had been involved with her in the *toma de tierra* and had served as a delegate in negotiating with the government for pobladores' title to the land. He had also held things together when Mama Berta went to jail for spitting in the face of a public official who was campaigning against the proliferation of street vendors in downtown Lima. In comparison with neighbors the family was prosperous. Mama Berta was tireless in pursuit of long-term goals for her family, and was not inclined to use her energies toward the realization of community goals. Yet the contempt with which pobladores were regarded by government officials eventually impelled even people like her to commit themselves to popular struggle.

The Politics of "Development" in the Shantytowns

The Peruvian government first began to concern itself with the politically explosive situation in the barriadas twenty-five years ago. The United States had an interest in developing housing projects for the poor who were flocking to the city to work in U.S.-owned factories. With U.S. aid, and the cooperation of U.S. savings and loan companies, the Peruvian government made low-interest loans available to shantytown-dwellers. Both the Alliance for Progress and the Peace Corps were involved. These projects were closed down in 1970 when the inhabitants of various barriadas met in Comas to form their own organizations, protesting inequities and corruption in the U.S.-run programs. The Peruvian government then attempted to counter independent shantytown organization by mobilizing inhabitants of the barriadas under a new organization, SINAMOS,[2] part of the military's reform program for Peru.

Renaming the shantytowns *pueblos jovenes* (young towns) to emphasize the pioneer aspect of barriada life, the government promised free building materials in return for donated labor to put in wells and tubing for water and sewage, sidewalks, and electric street lights. Labor was not voluntary, however. Each family was expected to contribute a worker or pay a fine. Widows and single mothers were expected to provide drinks and snacks for work crews. The military sent well-paid officials into the *pueblos jovenes* to administer the work and handle distribution of materials. Competent technical supervision was not provided, however, and pobladores complained of corruption in the securing of materials and of having substandard products dumped on them. Promised materials did not arrive on schedule and projects were left half-finished because funding was cut back. As neighborhoods began organizing on their own to get the work done and to make demands on the government, SINAMOS officials began serving as intelligence agents in the barriadas, informing the government about "troublemakers." Whatever enthusiasm the government had generated among pobladores in the early years of its reform program gave way to open antagonism between officials and the inhabitants of the barriadas.

In order to get the smallest thing from the government, we have to prepare petitions, organize marches, and sit in government offices for days and days, almost as if we were employees of the government—and even so we end up without improving the situation in our neighborhood. Everything we've achieved has been through our own efforts. Sometimes people think that things are given to us. Not at all. We're reduced to behaving like beggars, but it still comes out of our own pockets. Sometimes we have to bribe . . . otherwise our requests don't get dealt with and we're told to come back the next day or the next week—in spite of the fact that it's their obligation, they're paid to do it. They live off us and don't have any understanding at all.[3]

Spontaneous uprisings in the *pueblos jovenes* occurred in the mid-1970s whenever bus fares were increased due to devaluation of Peruvian currency. Wages were not keeping up with inflation, in spite of strikes and protests. Community improvement projects were at a standstill. Pobladores were aware that luxury hotels and beautiful boulevards were being constructed in the downtown areas, that public services were provided free of charge in the more affluent sectors of the city, and that government officials were spending lavishly on projects that catered to the needs of factory-owners and foreign officials. Yet progress toward getting their own urgent needs met was impossible.

Representation of pobladores' interests could not be secured through SINAMOS. As government repression replaced promises, SINAMOS officials—at that time called agents or spies by pobladores—were run out of the *pueblos jovenes*. Shantytown dwellers began organizing their own *comités de lucha*—struggle committees—to bring pressure to bear on the government, and to protect themselves against soldiers and police.

Women began involving themselves directly in neighborhood organizing when it became obvious that organizations set up by the government were not accomplishing anything and that the government's concerns were directly opposed to their own. One woman explains how she began to participate in community meetings after an experience she and a neighbor had while attempting to aid a teenager who had been attacked by police during a strike:

We saw [in the distance] a youngster who had been thrown on the ground and was bleeding. He was about seventeen or eighteen years old, and it gave me an attack of nerves to see him bleeding and breathing heavily. . . . My neighbor said to me, "I don't think it's your son—I'll go and

see." I covered my eyes while she looked. My neighbor lifted the boy's
head, but it wasn't my son. We had to decide what to do. The youngster
was going to die if he didn't have help. A policeman approached and
ordered us to leave. "Why?" I said. "This boy has to have help, or he'll
die." There were no cars in the street, but a crowd soon gathered,
shouting at the police, "Assassins!" We all went to the commissary to
speak to the head policeman. "Señor, please help the boy! He's about to
die!" But they didn't want to do anything, and they talked to us brus-
quely, which alarmed me: "Go home or we'll shoot!" he said. I left in fear
because he seemed entirely capable of shooting. But I went through the
streets shouting and crying, "A boy is dying and nobody wants to help
him!" The policeman was still at the side of the boy, a gun pointed at
him. That's how I started to participate.[4]

The first *comités de lucha* were formed in 1976. The organizational
structure that had been set up by SINAMOS was respected for the
most part. Block meetings were held to elect delegates. A quorum
was required for decision-making. However, SINAMOS had stip-
ulated that only taxpaying "family heads" (i.e., men, by Peruvian
law) who had title to their land and who had lived on it for ten
years or more could be elegible for block representation. In contrast, the *comités de lucha* called on all the people of the community
to participate. Sometimes former block delegates legitimized the
demise of SINAMOS by handing over their positions formally to
newly elected delegates. The new delegates were often young
people and mothers.

When I was living in Comas, I participated in the neighborhood *comité de lucha* as a block delegate. Women came to block
meetings regularly and always outnumbered men. They were
terribly concerned about the overflowing or backed-up sewage
flowing down in the middle of streets, and the cutback on water
supply. Whereas pumps had been turned on all day after they were
first installed, we had running water for only one or two hours in
the middle of the night. Someone had to get up and fill barrels and
make sure the house didn't get flooded. Sometimes there was no
water at all. The problem was caused by the malfunctioning of one
pump and the pirating of water by building speculators outside the
community. Pleas and petitions had been to no avail. "Before, we
couldn't install plumbing because we needed money for the pipes,

and we didn't have any and we had to begin buying a little at a time. Now that we've laid the pipes, there isn't any water." No matter what the other problems, the problem of water was always paramount.

The other major concern of pobladores was transportation. Buses arriving in the district from the city were so crowded that only strong young men could fight their way onto them during rush hours. Service up the hill was sporadic or nonexistent. The streets were not safe for people returning home after dark. Other issues were poor medical and educational facilities, a lack of progress in the development of parks and playgrounds, and a lack of sanitation services or garbage collection. But the meeting usually focused on the primary concerns—water, sewage disposal, and transportation.

At first, women who came to the meetings expected men to assume the leadership. For the women, attending a meeting one evening a week was already a big problem, because they had to leave work undone at home or leave their families unattended. As time went on and the pace of struggle increased, meetings were held nightly, and more and more pobladores attended. Women rarely spoke up, however, unless asked for an opinion. When asked, they usually had well-developed ideas, but were hesitant to express them, fearing the men's ridicule for "lack of education." They were not experienced at preparing the papers *(oficios)* necessary for presentation to government authorities, at writing leaflets for distribution in the barriada, at public speaking, or at handling debate at community meetings.

During this period, young people who lived with their families in the barriadas and who had attended universities and become involved there in political parties of the Left played an important role in urging women to participate actively in neighborhood organizations. They taught individual women how to read and write, prepare documents and organize public presentations. They helped women stand up under family pressure and under ridicule from men, and supported them when they took radical positions and assumed leadership of neighborhood campaigns.

In spite of impressive successes in organizing at the neighborhood level, the streets did not get paved, the garbage did not get collected, and public transportation did not improve. Water and sewage services did not keep pace with continuing in-migration from the countryside. As one poblador said, "We pay taxes for everything, even for the bread we eat. The people pay, but those who benefit are the 'important people.' In their residential areas all the public services are automatically installed, and in ours—nothing." The only response of the government was to harass and threaten organizers and their families. Because the same process was going on in every *pueblo joven,* neighborhood organizing drives posed a tremendous threat to the central government.

The Teachers' Strike

When teachers went on strike in 1978, housewives *(amas de casa)* were quick to recognize the teachers' struggle was linked with their own. Even a writer for the *New York Times* conceded: "The people without any voice of their own because of government repression, rallied around the strike and made it their own."[5] Teachers aimed their attack at government priorities and at the heavy-handed way the government was implementing educational reform. They complained that the government was not providing material resources for schools while insisting that teachers spend long hours in indoctrination sessions. Policemen with five years of elementary schooling and six months of training received salaries 50 percent higher than experienced teachers. The teachers' union was not recognized by the government even though over 90 percent of the organized teachers in the country belonged to it. Government attempts to form a parallel union had failed miserably, giving the relatively young Union of Peruvian Educational Workers (SUTEP)[6] prestige and power among the extremely poor, who had experienced similar attempts to manipulate their own movements.

The SUTEP strikes of 1978 and 1979 became the major foci of political activity for all sectors of the society opposed to the Morales Bermúdez regime, which had replaced the Velasco government. Within the union, formal leadership was male, but the vanguard organizing force was female. Female teachers led in the occupation of churches and plazas and stood up to police in the face of fierce repression. Schools and colleges were taken over for days and weeks at a time, while SUTEP supporters provided vigilance against police and brought food to teachers and students. Finally, **prolonged** strikes by other sectors of the workforce and a series of general strikes or temporary work stoppages throughout the country brought the government to its knees.

In all protest activities centered in neighborhoods, housewives were the most important support force. In Comas, mothers fought off police who tried to arrest teachers occupying a school building. Mothers and fathers marched with teachers in public demonstrations. In Villa El Salvador the government closed down the schools in the face of massive parent support for the teachers strike.

Eventually, the Parents' Association (Junta de Padres de Familia), a nationwide organization set up by the government to facilitate transference of responsibility for education from the state to the neighborhood, took a position alongside the teachers. This was not automatic, however. The experience of El Planeta, a *pueblo joven* near the center of Lima, illustrates the process through which activist mothers brought the more conservative and male-dominated *juntas* around.

When the teachers' strike was first declared, a meeting of the Parents' Association in El Planeta supported the State against the teachers. Parents were called on to send their children to school even though the teachers were on strike. Mothers who had been active in the local *comité de lucha* took an opposing position and were forced to become active overnight to prevent the association's decision from taking effect. It was a formidable undertaking because on its face the decision made sense. The pobladores had worked hard to build the school. At the urging of teachers, some of them had volunteered many hours of labor to build furniture. Lotteries, bingo games, and benefits had exacted great sacrifice from parents, who had been required to participate in the association in order for their children to attend school. The parents saw education as the only hope for their children to escape from the cycle of poverty into which pobladores had fallen, and keeping the school open was a primary concern. Now the teachers were refusing to come to school. If the strike were allowed to go on, a whole year of education might be lost. Even though salaries of teachers were low, they were more than what most pobladores made.

A decisive factor in the parents' decision to keep the children out of school was the dedication of the teachers. The very teachers who had been most concerned about the problems pobladores were having in the economic crisis were those who were leading strike activities. One parent explained it clearly: "The teachers also support us in our struggles. Maybe they didn't before, but lately they have. . . . There's one teacher who teaches my son's class, who has been helping many children who have problems. . . . This teacher has gone to the houses of students where parents are having problems."[7]

Political parties of the Left and center eventually overcame their differences in order to take public positions supporting the strike. But much of the hard work of neighborhood canvassing was done by housewives. The mothers of El Planeta who mobilized to convince pobladores to support the strike eventually won out.[8]

Because of their own experience before the government in neighborhood struggle, mothers in Lima's barriadas—and across the country—joined forces *en masse* with grade school teachers, 90 percent of whom were also women, keeping their children out of school during the strike. Mothers also sent children to school during the days of temporary takeovers by strikers. They set up soup kitchens to feed the children of teachers living in the barriadas and the children of community members who had been arrested or were working full time to propagandize for the strike and engage in solidarity activities.

One teacher told me how she and other strikers had escaped repression with the aid of pobladores during a school takeover. A youngster who had been serving as watchman atop the wall surrounding the school spirited the teachers out one side while a group of mothers were distracting police on the other side. After they escaped, the teachers realized for the first time that over fifty police were still in the area and not headed in the other direction, as they had supposed.

Mother's Day Protest

The teachers' strike, more than any other event of the late 1970s, forced the military regime to promise elections and a return to parliamentary government. But the popular forces that had united behind the strike were unable to coalesce around candidates for public office.[9] Mothers who had supported the teachers were dismayed by the proliferation of candidates on the Left. Some voted for former President Fernando Belaúnde Terry in protest against both the military regime, whose supporters were also running for election, and the Left parties, which were too numerous to provide a clear alternative.[10]

Shortly after Belaúnde took office as president, his wife toured the barriadas and promoted ideas about women's sacred tasks in the family, the importance of their sacrifices, and the "great interest the government has in helping women serve their families better." The First Lady had failed to calculate well the aspirations of the people. Most of the women in the barriadas had not voted for Acción Popular, the president's party. Even those who had were in no mood to make even more sacrifices. They recognized that the president's wife was attempting to woo them with reactionary ideology as their actual life situations were steadily worsening. Women's organizations that had formed during the teachers' strike began preparing their own platforms of women's rights, which included the right to remunerative employment, community health services, child care at public expense, and price controls on basic food items. From past experience, the women knew that Mother's Day would be the occasion for renewed emphasis by the government—and by their own families—on the virtues of self-sacrifice for women. In May 1980, Mother's Day was chosen as the occasion for massive protest against all the policies and practices that keep women powerless, both in their homes and in public life.

The Mother's Day protest was a watershed for the politicizing of *amas de casa* in Peru. In Lima it was spearheaded by the Secretariat of Women's Affairs of the FEDEPJUP,[11] a federation of the barriada organizations of the entire metropolitan area. The federation, formed in 1979, had bases in thirteen *pueblos jovenes,* includ-

Mass protest in Lima on Mother's Day, 1981. Women demanded an end to the exploitation and abuse of motherhood, rejecting the use of Mother's Day to manipulate the public. (Ernesto Jimenez)

Inside the home of a barriada family in the pueblo joven El Progreso, Lima. Women in the barriadas struggle to gain popular control of Mother's Clubs that have been organized by churches and government agencies for the distribution of relief commodities. (Lynn Murray)

ing Villa El Salvador, El Planeta, and Comas. Five thousand delegates from these bases attended the first meeting, on March 30, 1980. At that time women from the barriadas joined forces with feminist organizations in the city to discuss the issues of health, birth control, food, child care, and neighborhood organizing. It was at this meeting that the issue of Mother's Day was introduced. An International Women's Day demonstration, the first week in March, had focused on some of the same issues and called on Peruvian women to show solidarity with the women of Nicaragua, who had helped defeat Somoza and U.S. imperialism. This event, which had been organized by independent feminists, helped to prepare the ground for the meeting of barriada women. The Mother's Day event then brought together all the progressive women's organizations of the city and provided specific support for those who had taken over factories that had been closed down illegally (see Chapter Four). For the first time in the history of the city, women from all sectors of the economy—workers and intellectuals, housewives and street vendors—came together as women to protest their situations. They called on the government to reinstitute price controls on basic foodstuffs and to finance health care and child care in neighborhoods. They also demanded freedom from government repression and from violent abuse by men. Some picket signs demanded the decriminalization of abortion, a subject that had not been widely discussed in the barriadas.

One mother of seven children who lives in El Progreso, a Lima barriada, writing by kerosene lantern after her family had gone to bed, expressed the concerns of women like herself on Mothers' Day, 1981, when protests were occurring throughout the country. In an open letter to a women's publication, she addressed her husband:

For how long are men of all ages and social classes going to make victims of their mothers, wives, and sisters because of their frustrations, bad moods, and unfounded jealousies? . . . How long will it take you to realize that as women we get twice the trouble this oppressive society has to offer? Every day things cost more, and in order to get a little better price from the butcher, the milkman, the baker or the vegetable man, we have to smile at his bad jokes and foul language, just so we'll have something to give you and your children to eat. . . . In our workplaces, we have to put up with insults from our bosses and fellow workers in order not to lose our jobs, in order to earn a little money to help you, and at the end of an exhausting day you start yelling at me and injuring me, without even caring if the children are listening or hurt. If you can't start changing the way you behave, please don't come around hypocritically offering me gifts on Mother's Day.[12]

Years before this Mother's Day protest, my youngest son had brought me an invitation to a Mother's Day program at his school in the Ocopilla barriada in Huancayo. I was the only mother who attended. I knew the other mothers had work commitments, but work was only partly responsible for their absence, as I learned from talking with some of them afterwards. They had no taste for sitting in school and listening to eulogies about the nobility of women who suffered and served their families. In them Mother's Day programs inspired only anger and resentment, and they didn't hesitate to let their children know how they felt. Now in 1981, the mothers of Ocopilla, like mothers in towns and cities across the country, performed theatre outside the school, letting their children know through dramatic portrayal how it felt to be a mother— and what they thought of Mother's Day.

Although slow to mobilize in the face of incredible abuse and hardship, mothers demonstrated solidarity and radical understanding through their unwillingness to "celebrate" their own exploitation. Finally, they turned a commercially inspired celebration of motherhood into a nationwide protest.

The anger that women directed toward men on Mother's Day arose from an understanding that women's personal happiness was linked with the vitality of their communities. Women saw men's personal transgressions against them as a violation of community spirit. This point of view enabled them to express their anger forcefully without in any way distracting attention from the overall struggles of their people. Since Mother's Day was established by the State and seized upon by business and religious interests to reinforce their own ideological precepts, women could call upon their families to join them in protesting these precepts. They asked family members to change their own behavior toward mothers so as to further the causes which united them.

The strategies adopted by Peruvian women in mobilizing to protest Mother's Day made it possible for the disparate movements of poor women to be seen as one movement. From then on, feminists in the cities began to see that "women's issues" were those around which women needed to mobilize as a group to achieve goals men were unable or unwilling to pursue. Violence toward women and women's right to reproductive freedom were concerns that would come to be addressed by all women as their collective strength grew. In neighborhoods and villages, however, the initial impetus for organization had to arise from local circumstances and experiences. For the housewives of the barriadas, these centered on the rising cost of living and on their inability to get men to cooperate in facing issues of daily survival, such as water, housing, and sanitation.

Mobilization in Mining Towns and Commercial Centers

Two issues of most concern to women on the outskirts of Huancayo, where I was living in 1974, were the pollution of the stream that ran through the neighborhood and the violence faced by those who walked home in the dark at night. Women were often robbed by gangs of delinquents. Individual efforts to pressure politicians and church or municipal officials to deal with these problems were ineffective. Public officials much preferred constructing a public building that would serve as a monument to themselves to making available waste disposal or street lighting in the neighborhoods of the poor. The men were divided on such issues, but the women were clear about the priorities.

A similar situation existed in the mountain town of Cerro de Pasco, several hours' drive from Huancayo, where most adult men were employed by CENTROMIN. CENTROMIN, one of Peru's largest mining companies, was expropriated by the government in 1974. The government now owned the land on which miners' families had built their houses years ago. Even before the expropriation, the company had begun to evict people from the land so that it could be mined. Families had been promised space for new housing, with water and electricity installed, but as the evictions began, a site for new housing had not even been selected. Miners' families were living as refugees, sometimes ten families to one dwelling. Meanwhile, a main street had become a canal for the disposal of toxic and radioactive wastes. "We don't even know what streets are here," said one mother. "We used to have streets, but the main one has become a cesspool for the company's waste-water."[13]

Seven children had fallen into the canal over a period of time, and all had become seriously ill. Despite numerous delegations that had gone to speak to the government officials who were running the mine, nothing had been done about the problem. Then, in 1980, a child died. When this happened, mothers were ready to lynch the officials. They had been protesting about the wastewater for a long time. The union had never taken up the issues of most concern to women. Several *comités de damas* had been formed, however, and these women decided to mete out justice on their own. "All our lives we've heard promises, nothing else. Actually, many years have passed and the company has never lived up to its promises. We can't expect anything from the *prefecto* (government officials of the locality) either, because they always do simply whatever the company wants."[14]

In an effort to mediate this encounter between angry women and mine managers, male community leaders invited the company officials to come to the area to investigate and provided protection from the women. At the same time, families affected began to take over land that had not yet been designated for housing construction in order to get away from the encroaching mining operations.

These struggles by miner's families, led primarily by women, were labeled "ultra-lefetist" by mine union leaders. Although union officials gave formal support to the land takeovers and protests, they didn't give them the kind of support the barriada organizers needed. *Amas de casa* had to call on former union leaders for help rather than seek support from those presently active in the mines. They felt they needed men to represent them before the government and CENTROMIN, but they knew they had to rely on their own forces to push their struggles forward. In spite of the ready admission by everyone that women were more persistent than men, and more committed than men to political struggle at the neighborhood level, women's organizations were never recognized for purposes of negotiation.

The weak support union men have given to community struggles led by women contrasts markedly with the support miners' wives have given consistently to their husbands in strikes against the companies. Each time miners have gone on strike over issues of wages and work conditions, women have joined them in marches and demonstrations. Sometimes wives have declared hunger strikes to get miners out of jail. They have often accompanied them on long walks *(marchas de sacrificio)* from the mountains to the capital, camping out for weeks and months at a time with their husbands and children to call attention to miners' demands.

When striking miners and their families arrive in the capital, women often lead the protest activities and spend hours every day collecting donations on buses to buy food for the *olla común*. One woman told me she and other miners' wives had taken one company's public relations official aside during a strike and removed all his clothes in order to humiliate and punish him for the lies he had told reporters. She, like many miners' wives, worked for the company herself, scavenging for metal left among discarded rocks. Yet her political activity during that time was dedicated completely to issues defined by men in a union that did not have any female members.

Women and Political Parties of the Left

The political parties of the Left could play an important role in making unions and other popular organizations responsive to women's concerns. However, they have generally not done so, and are only beginning to do so as women demonstrate their own collective power outside the parties. One woman who is seasoned

Families, having walked halfway across the country, protest the closing of mines, demanding back pay. Women take charge of public demonstrations and solicit support for the olla común *(Marta Serra)*

in popular struggles told me the problem was with those who were vying for personal power in these organizations. Men who were in positions of leadership lacked confidence in women's loyalty to party principles. This was true especially in neighborhood struggles. Most women involved in popular neighborhood organizations were not members of political parties, although they were usually sympathizers with one or another of the groups on the Left. They were more likely than men to be on speaking terms with neighbors who were close to political parties of the Right, and even worked with conservative women in Mothers' Clubs or other organizations started by the government.

In Lima one of the political organizations of the Left that was important in the formation in 1979 of the barriada federation, Federación Departamental de Pueblos Jovenes y Urbanizaciones Populares, was the Unidad Democrático Popular, a coalition of five party-type organizations. The UDP was prominent among the groups that initiated the centralization of the barriada movement throughout the country. It was through struggles the women had waged within the UDP that the Secretariat of Women's Affairs of the federation came into being. The women who planned the Mother's Day protests in 1980 and 1981 were active in both the FEDEPJUP and the UDP. There had been a process of attrition of female members of some of the political organizations that made up the UDP. These women had left their organizations because they were frustrated in their attempts to be taken seriously as women and to place women's concerns on the agendas of their organizations. Later, those whose ties to the organizations through marriage or long-term association gave them less choice about leaving met together to formulate and circulate demands for an autonomous organization of women. The parties never responded formally, but the women had enough support by then to go ahead and form their own groups and coordinate with feminists outside their organizations in drawing up programs for women. One of the outcomes of this process was the establishment of a Women's Commission within the UDP.[15]

The Unidad Democrático Popular had been formed in response to the military's promise of elections. Its member organizations did not have ties to governments outside the country or to an international center. The UDP was therefore not firmly tied to ideologies that circumscribed women's efforts to define their own revolutionary programs. Perhaps for this reason most feminists who had former ties with political organizations of the Left felt some affinity with the UDP, even if they had come from organizations outside the coalition. Women who were committed to the UDP were sympathetic to feminists who had chosen to separate themselves from party-type organizations. The UDP Women's Commission sought to reincorporate independent feminists in a Left coalition that would not limit their development as feminists. The commission held its first public meeting in Lima in July 1981.

I participated as an observer in both the planning and coordinating of the first UDP women's meetings. There was a nervousness in the organizing committee about what would happen when hundreds of women leaders having different party sympathies met together out of loyalty to their own consciences as women and revolutionaries. But the committee purposely organized the meeting to allow for a genuine grass-roots process. Ninety percent of the voting delegates were mothers from Lima's shantytowns, elected by their bases. Feminist groups, unions, and women's cultural organizations were also invited to send one representative each. Those who planned the commission meeting formulated guiding principles that came out of their grass-roots experiences working with women: (1) don't work on women's problems with the intention of recruiting women into your party; (2) don't tell women their problems will all be solved as soon as the working class gains state power; (3) do coordinate with feminist groups whether or not they are linked with party-type organizations.

Attendance at the commission meetings was limited to two hundred women, which included only a small number of observers from outside Lima. One man attended, the brother of Rosa Alarco, to whose memory the meeting was dedicated because she had been a founder of the UDP.[16]

The meeting of the UDP women in Lima was most impressive to participants for the solidarity felt in spite of party-line differences that existed among them. There were a number of women from Left parties outside the UDP; they had been chosen to represent union or cultural groups in which other parties had strong bases. Although a public meeting of feminists had been held six months earlier in Lima, and had been attended by nearly all of those who were working full time on behalf of women's rights in the capital, the UDP meeting was entirely different. The feminists were, for the most part, college-educated and belonged to tightly knit groups of twelve to fifteen members each. The vast majority of those in attendance at the UDP meeting had little formal education, but they had years of experience as community organizers. Most of them had not thought of themselves as feminists, but they came to the meeting out of a shared conviction that women needed to unite to formulate their own programs and confront their own political parties on women's issues. They also wanted women on the central committee of the UDP, not as representatives of a *gremial* (special interest group)—a token woman representing the commission—but as regular members of the organization's executive body, where their opinions on all subjects would carry the same weight as men's.

During the meeting working groups were formed to draw up proposals around the questions the organizing committee thought were of most urgent concern to women: (1) experiences in the organization of women, (2) women and political parties of the Left, (3) political struggle and national crisis, and (4) mass communications and ideology. Most of the issues addressed at the UDP meeting were of specific concern to women of the barriadas. Neighborhood organizers spoke with authority as representatives of their communities, in spite of the fact that they had not participated at the higher levels of barriada organizations. It became clear to me that the barriada was one of the major social forces to be contended with in Peru precisely because its main organized base was composed of women who had specific views of what changes were needed in Peruvian society, even though they had had little opportunity to articulate these views. The first UDP Women's Commission meeting in Lima gave many women an opportunity to explore issues which they had never before discussed publicly, and which they could not have discussed freely in the presence of men.

The seventeen-point Revolutionary Program for Women published as a result of this meeting reflected urban women's developing consciousness of their oppression as women in dependent capitalist society, and the necessity of struggle for their own rights:

1. We are against the economic, ideological, political, and social oppression of Peruvian women.
2. We are against the super exploitation of working women.
3. We are for the organization of women as a social force and their active intervention in the transformation of capitalist society, recognizing the right of women to autonomous organization.
4. We are for the recognition of maternity as a social function.
5. We are for the implementation of an hour off daily for nursing mothers.
6. We are for generalization of the practice of paid time off for nursing.
7. We are for the equal distribution of work opportunities, and an end to piecework pay.
8. We are for the creation of child-care facilities at public expense.
9. We are for the creation and generalization of free medical care for mothers and children.
10. We are for equality in the court system.
11. We are for the establishment of social security for women.[17]
12. We are for the promotion of literacy for all women.
13. We are for the right of women to control of their bodies—voluntary motherhood and legal abortion.
14. We are against the ideological repression of women's sexuality.
15. We are for an end to the degrading role in which women are portrayed in mass communications, both as sexual objects and consumers
16. We are for the promotion of women in mass communications as active subjects rather than objects.
17. We are against the bourgeois imperialist institutions that try to use women through economic blackmail [organizations such as CARITAS, OFASA, and Cooperación Popular].

The Problem with Food Relief

The final point in the UDP women's Revolutionary Program refers to church and government efforts to manipulate women by providing food relief only to those who cooperate with the government. The working group I attended at the UDP women's meeting had as its task the formulation of a strategy for combatting the efforts of relief agencies to undermine women's organizing activities in the barriadas. Before attending the meeting, I had been traveling in different parts of the country, meeting with feminist groups in the provinces, and I had heard the same story over and over. "We had a good thing going before the women started getting divided by CARITAS and OFASA. Really, we don't know what to do now." I intended to bring these concerns back to feminists in Lima, and had encouraged women in the provinces to write about their experiences and to seek contact with other women who were having the same problems, rather than to be defeated by them. It was tremendously exciting to me to learn that the UDP Women's Commission would provide a forum for sharing experiences of U.S. food relief programs and that the groundwork had already been laid for the meeting in Lima.

UDP women were unanimous in condemning the manipulative aspects of food relief, whether through the Catholic Church in CARITAS (see Chapter Two) or through the Seventh Day Adventists in OFASA.[18] In Lima, OFASA was identified with the government party, Acción Popular. Barriada women complained that one must be sympathetic with the AP or with APRA in order to be accepted in the program. The Mothers' Clubs sponsored by CARITAS were easier to join, but there was a three-month probationary period during which troublemakers could be weeded out. Since over two thirds of the income of shantytown dwellers goes for food, it's easy to become dependent on relief provisions and to go along with the political requirements the sponsors impose. Seventy-five percent of the deaths in the barriadas are those of children, and most of these are related to malnutrition. So short-term relief is an absolute necessity, but long term solutions to the problems of survival require political action, and that is prohibited by those who administer relief.

The OFASA program gives women surplus food commodities from the United States, paid for by the Peruvian government in local currency. However, to receive the food, women must put in many hours of work, four to six hours daily, in a job program. The jobs include building parks and schools and houses, but the overwhelming majority of the women at work for OFASA are engaged in removing garbage from the streets of their neighborhoods, garbage that should have been picked up by government sanitation services. Garbage dumps are full of rats, and the women are not provided with any kind of protection from the diseases bred in the dumps. Children often accompany their mothers while they are cleaning up refuse.

The value of the food received through OFASA gives women a "salary" approximately half the minimum wage, as established by the Peruvian government, without any benefits. Women still have to find other ways of earning money and getting their housework done, which leaves them no time at all for community organizing. In fact, keeping the women "busy" so they have no time for organizing seems to be one of the aims of the program, according to many of its critics. It is one more way the government is applying the policy of "do-it-yourself" in shantytowns, making pobladores feel they should be grateful for any form of assistance.

In one barriada, a women's organization that was attempting to get the cooperation of the Ministry of Health in bringing preventive health care to their neighborhood found that OFASA served to isolate women from such efforts:

OFASA brings mothers together to work, not for salaries but for food. In this way the mothers are isolated from reality. Once we invited those who work for OFASA to discuss problems having to do with the neighborhood clinic. The leaders of OFASA appeared and told the women that if they were going to come to our meeting, they wouldn't get their food allotments. Since there's a lot of hunger and misery, and no jobs, these mothers have to work for OFASA. We can't give them food, nor wages, because we're poor, too. All we can share with them are our own thoughts. For the leaders of OFASA, to talk about the clinic is to "get involved in politics"; according to them, everything we do is "communism." All they want is to use people for their religion, Adventism, and keep the mothers subservient, not let them form their own opinions.

We're organized mainly to do something about healthcare. Right now we're working to equip the neighborhood clinic, which is totally empty. We want laboratory services, gynecological services. We sent papers to the Ministry of Health asking for immunizations. Every day we have cases of whooping cough, typhoid, tuberculosis. In every neighborhood there are three or four families affected by TB.[19]

While barriada activists are united in condemning the administration of food relief programs, they are also united in not condemning women who participate in such programs. The comment of one community leader is typical: "Of course, we know that aid comes from the *yánqui gringos* in order to take even more advantage of other American countries, but we also know that we're hungry. People are dying of hunger and we need food. In order to organize a *comité de damas,* we need food . . . so we have to use aid to increase the consciousness of the people so they'll understand little by little that this food isn't everything, that oatmeal and milk aren't the only thing that's important, that what's really important is the organization of women."[20]

The strategy most successfully employed to overcome the manipulation of public assistance programs such as CARITAS and OFASA, and to promote the independent organization of women, was the utilization of assistance while simultaneously developing ways women could promote solidarity among themselves to confront public officials. The first noteworthy success occurred in Comas.

AFEDEPROM and the People's Kitchens in Comas

During the upsurge of feminist activity in the barriadas of Lima, women in Comas, with the cooperation of several Catholic nuns and members of left-wing student and cultural organizations, organized the Asociación Femenina en Defensa y Promoción de la Mujer (Women's Association for the Defense and Promotion of Women's Interest). AFEDEPROM's major accomplishment was the establishment of many peoples' kitchens.

Over ninety peoples' kitchens existed in Comas when I visited there in 1982, and AFEDEPROM had more than one thousand members. Each peoples' kitchen was composed of twenty families, and every week each family contributed a sum of money that was considerably less than what it would spend for food if it cooked at home. Families also contributed such utensils as cooking pots, large spoons, kerosene burners, and funnels. Housewives met weekly to decide who would go to the market, in whose home food would be cooked, and so on. Parents and children brought their own plates and utensils to the kitchen and usually returned to their own homes to eat.

The women who belonged to AFEDEPROM invited women from such organizations as the Academia Micaela Bastidas, a neighborhood cultural club with a feminist orientation, to give them *charlas* or informal talks. One woman explained the importance of these meetings: "With these discussions we understand clearly, for example, why our children are undernourished, why there is so much unemployment in our barrio, and why we have to work together. We all know there is not enough money, that we have health problems, problems of transportation and water, but what we need is to know what we are fighting for, what are our ultimate goals."[21]

Bringing women together for such discussions on a regular basis is possible only when they are also engaged in an activity that helps assure their collective survival on a daily basis. Through participation in discussions, women develop new capacities and insights, and the strength to resist outside pressure against their organizations: "We want the women to get over their fears of saying what they think in public meetings. It doesn't make any difference if they don't say things right the first time—the second time it'll go a little better. But for the women to participate we have to overcome a whole series of obstacles, one being the husbands. Many husbands are *machistas*, reactionaries. They say that since they bring money to the house they're the only ones who have a right to give their opinions. We try to help mothers see that it's wrong to accept this. We think it's urgent that the mothers develop their own ideas, not only for their own sakes but for their children's."[22]

Women learn through organizations such as AFEDEPROM that the problems they face are common to poor women everywhere, and that they are not insoluble. A widely distributed cartoon pamphlet, published in Peru, gives the personal testimony of Domitilia de Chungara, a miner's wife who organized housewives in Bolivia. She tells other women how to overcome the problems of organizing. Domitilia describes her campaign to get

Families in Cerro de Pasco, protesting the disposal of toxic wastes in the streets by mining companies, camp out on company property after eviction from their homes. (Ernesto Jimenez)

her husband to stop accusing her of "not doing anything." She says she decided to stop doing one thing—washing diapers. She cut up his trousers and shirts, curtains and tablecloths, to use as diapers, terribly afraid that her husband would "assassinate" her. He did order her out of the house. But through patient and persistent struggle, she was finally able to gain his support and confidence so she could continue attending meetings and organizing.[23]

The testimony of Peruvian housewives who have successfully broken away from the duties of the home to attend classes or to participate in neighborhood organizing is full of stories like Domitila's, although not all of them end so successfully. By sharing these stories, women are encouraged to take risks in their battles to gain the respect of their husbands. In cases where a break is inevitable, women usually express relief at having been able to escape from men who are unloving and unable to change their ways. While many women are still resigned to male abuse, those who stand up to their husbands are gaining support. I was told that in one neighborhood in Comas women blow whistles to call for the help of other women when their husbands are abusive. It is not unheard of for a woman who is married to say, "I'd give anything to live alone with my children and help them forget the treatment he's given them."[24]

As women discuss such questions in barriada women's meetings—and Comas is not the only place where this has occurred—their views have come to be reflected in the popular press of the barriadas. One woman testified in a barriada publication:

Why do we organize in the barrio? In the first place, so we can carry on our struggles at home to make our husbands understand our situation. They always say, "I'm the provider," and we explain what we know from having seen what life is like for the wife of the bosses. "She pays a cook: I cook for you and save you 40,000 soles a month. She has someone to take care of her children. I don't pay for a cook, nor a washer-woman, nor for someone to sew clothes, because I do all these jobs for you and for our children. And when you were single, what other expenses did you have? Didn't you go to hotels or brothels? And now, for love, I save you this money, too." We go on adding up accounts to show how much our work is worth, even if neither they nor the system recognize it. This is why we are organized in women's committees, so we can learn to stop being timid, to have courage to say what we think and what we need, to contribute to our own development and that of our children. We need more child-care centers and peoples' kitchens, and we need to set up workshops to produce things. We need parks, musical groups, games, and art classes. . . .[25]

One of the topics discussed in AFEDEPROM was Women and Religion, a critical look at how religion affects women. Basic literacy courses, and courses in women's health, were also offered. These educational activities were markedly different from those offered by the Mothers' Clubs established by church and public assistance officials.

As the women of Comas demonstrated their capacity for effective independent organization, they were able to take over from the churches the distribution of relief food. In other places, where independent organization was not so advanced, and especially in the provinces, small groups of women who demanded that the churches relinquish control of food distribution to them were met with immediate repression. The relief organizations withheld food from the neighborhood or from the women involved in protesting the abuse of public programs. Church officials said "directions from Lima" did not permit collective use of relief commodities.

A popular organization may win the right to receive U.S. food shipments directly from the government, but that does not constitute an unqualified victory in the popular struggle against imperialism. The food must be accounted for; records must be kept. These requirements can compromise the independence and integrity of popular organizations, especially when government repression is increasing. When community organizing is made illegal, neighborhood networks that have become known to the government can easily be wiped out. With the implementation of "antiterrorist" laws in 1982 and 1983, the residents of Comas became the first in the city to suffer massive arrests and violent reprisal.

The March to the Government Palace

The emergence of women's organizations as an independent political force in the barriadas of the capital happened as the Belaúnde government was delegating to municipal authorities the responsibility for providing public services and assigning land titles to familes. Formerly as *pueblos jovenes,* the category assigned to these settlements by the military government, the barriadas had been eligible for public assistance. The *pueblos jovenes* had given rise to neighborhood organizations that eventually challenged the methods and priorities of the central government. The government then had to negotiate directly with pobladores who were represented by barriada organizations federated at the district level. And these federations had even come together in congresses held at the national level. Now, under the Belaúnde program, instead of being represented by community organizations, each family had to negotiate separately with the municipal government to establish its title to property and to pay in advance for the installation of water and electricity. Authorities had to spend their time settling land disputes between familes, weakening their ability to negotiate with the central government on behalf of the entire community. The government had given this system the dubious name, Cooperación Popular, sayng that the pobladores would be forced to "cooperate among themselves to develop self-reliance." But with emphasis on individualism built into the system, cooperation was actually discouraged. To receive services, each family had to deposit money in banks (where it was left for years without accruing interest) while the government blamed inflation for the delay in delivering promised services. Since land claimants had to present marriage certificates to legalize property rights, mass public weddings were held in the barriadas. Families resorted to bribing public officials in order to procure special favors. This made it even more difficult for municipal representatives to take the place of popular organizations as the peoples' advocates.

In spite of these divisionist tactics by the government, a strong coalition of popular forces enabled pobladores in some barriadas to prevail upon municipal government to confront Belaúnde's Cooperación Popular. In Comas, residents protested

the government's budgeting of services for 160 cases of tuberculosis when there were actually more than 2,000 cases needing
such services. They complained of new rules requiring the payment of three separate bus fares to get to work, and the discontin-
uance of several bus lines. They questioned the taxation of
residents for water, especially since the water was unavailable to
them because of broken pumps. They were paying high prices for
polluted water sold to them by the barrel from trucks. Delegations
were repeatedly rebuffed when they carried these concerns to the
municipal government, but because the community was well organized, it carried the struggle to even higher levels.

In February 1982, fifteen thousand residents of the Comas
district, representing hundreds of grass-roots organizations,
marched for three hours to the government palace in downtown
Lima, demanding money for the repair and construction of water
pumps and for other urgent necessities. The mayor of the district
was nominated head of the combined *comité de lucha,* and walked at
the head of the march. President Belaúnde refused to meet with
the pobladores, saying he had never heard of the organization
sponsoring the march. However, he promised to come to the
district within fifteen days, at which time he would meet with the
mayor.

The march on the government palace by the residents of
Comas was one of the largest challenges to the Belaúnde government up to that time. Women represented the vast majority of
those who marched. They were an even higher percentage of those
who had first confronted the mayor with the pobladores' demands. Their efforts were partially successful. Neighborhood
clinics did receive funding, and attention was given to several
other long-neglected concerns, including the problem of water.
More than anything else, the women came to understand that their
personal survival depended on their own capacity for community
organization.

In the past, the philanthropic organizations that provided
limited funding for specific projects had done little to develop
general solutions to the needs of pobladores. Their "pilot projects"
offered no means to spread services from the models to an entire
community: the construction of one classroom through special

funding could drain away the energy required to satisfy the need for many schools among an expanding population. Things were left half-finished, and the inhabitants of the barriada demobilized.

In contrast, where barriadas are already well-organized and politically advanced, specially funded projects can be incorporated into overall struggles. Project administrators live in the barriada, help publicize marches and demonstrations, and participate in community meetings. When this happens, as it did in Comas, project personnel are punished by the government, and support is likely to be withdrawn by churches or other funding agencies. Nevertheless, everyone's political awareness is increased, the unity of pobladores is made evident, and popular organizations expand their bases.

No victories are gained without cost, and nothing can be achieved without understanding the limitations inherent in the specific stages of struggle. The possibility that project personnel will be coopted, drawn away from popular struggle to participation in funded projects that serve to demobilize communities, is always present when outside help is solicited. However, through accumulated experience, popular forces can minimize this danger, and defend community organizers more effectively when repression occurs.

As more and more Peruvian women became involved in developing political power in their communities, they learned that their efforts were only a modest beginning in a protracted, dangerous, and extremely revolutionary undertaking. The personal growth and freedom of individual women was no small part of that revolution.

5 : *Working Women and "Development"*

Industrial Growth and the Peripheral Economy

IN SOCIETIES undergoing "modernization," a man and a woman cannot live a stable life together with their children. The ideal marriage becomes attainable only among the well-to-do. Often men cannot depend on regular work in industry; women are systematically excluded from such work. Nevertheless, women's and men's cooperative work roles in traditional sectors of the economy are undermined through competition with industry. The result is that most women and men working in sectors of the industrial economy are marginally productive and barely remunerated. They are officially classified "underemployed," and much of the work they do is considered illegal. Under such circumstances, health and happiness in family life is nearly impossible.

Whenever Peruvian women attempt to gain a foothold in production or service jobs that are covered by social benefits and remunerated at minimum wage or better, they are perceived to be competing with men. Ironically, young women without children are better able to do this than women who are struggling to support families. Women who retain indigenous cultural traits in language and dress are considered totally ineligible for such jobs.

For all these reasons, the percentage of women who are considered "economically active" in Peru has declined with the acceleration of "industrial progress." Yet masses of women are selling personal services that are demeaning or degrading. Even more are selling commodities in the streets, legally or illegally, or contracting to work day and night as pieceworkers in a growing underground economy.

During the past decade, real wages for Peruvian workers have been cut in half as the currency has been devalued by more than 400%. Since most women neither receive cost-of-living salary adjustments nor enjoy the right to collective bargaining, their situations are much worse than these harsh statistics would indicate. Women's marginalization in the work force is advantageous to business because it helps to keep wages low in the industrial sector and provides a ready source of labor in times of industrial expansion. Marginal workers are a creation of the "international division of labor" in which low-overhead, low-skill work can be done on contract, and services to those who work for multinational companies can be provided cheaply. Thus, work that may appear to be "pre-capitalist" is in fact an integral part of the capitalist system.

Among the segments of the female work force caught in this process of marginalization are laundresses, prostitutes, household workers, vendors, pieceworkers, assemblers, and women who seek to establish family or cooperative industries in their homes or neighborhoods. Some of these women are self-employed. A growing number work through middlemen or on contract. All are part of the peripheral economy and suffer the hazards of repression whenever they seek better opportunities or improvements in their work-lives.

It has been extremely difficult for women to organize to demand the right to work for wages because unemployment is so high for both men and women and because women's time is so occupied with daily survival and the care of children. Furthermore, there is little likelihood that the crisis in Peru's economy can be overcome so long as the economy is tied to international financial arrangements and markets over which Peruvians have little control. Considering these realities, the dramatic struggles Peruvian women have waged to secure viable alternatives for themselves in the industrial economy are remarkable achievements. The gains from these struggles must be measured, however, not so much in the concrete benefits won, but in the confidence and insight women have gained.

Factory Takeovers

Among the reforms won by Peru's workers during the period of military rule in the 1970s was a law permitting the establishment of cooperatives in factories that were threatened with illegal closure or lockouts by management.[1] The formation of cooperatives in such circumstances became more difficult as the military government became more repressive. As the number of factory closures increased because of economic recession, workers' militancy in defending their right to work also increased. Those factories most vulnerable to closure were the very ones where women were trying to improve work conditions and form unions to bring salaries in line with inflation. By the time military rule ended, more than forty-six companies had been taken over by workers. Half of these were managed by women, and the head of the umbrella organization to which cooperative members belonged was a woman.

By 1978, it was already clear that the government did not favor the transfer of businesses from individual to cooperative ownership. Even when workers won rulings in their favor, businesses were able to act with impunity to prevent implementation of the law.

A major test of government policy came in August of 1978 when 380 employees in a Lima underwear factory, LOLAS, found upon entering the factory building that most of the machines had disappeared. A "new" company was functioning out of one wing of the building, contracting out piecework for women to do at home. The factory owner had declared bankruptcy, hoping to nullify women's right to collective bargaining and work benefits. He had already accomplished this in another factory. Three hundred women formed a reconstituted union and voted to seize the factory that same day. Two weeks later, the women occupying the factory were attacked during the night by several hundred private thugs, while police cars and tanks "patrolled" the area. Fifty-two women were injured during the ensuing battle. However, women were able to hold on to the part of the factory from which the machinery had been removed.

Interviews with participants in these events reveal the fear the workers felt as women, as mothers, and as youth threatened with assault and disfigurement by the attackers. Some women were trapped alone by henchmen and had to be rescued by others. Police did nothing to stop the attack or to protect those inside the factory. Instead, they yelled at the women to go home and tend to their cooking. One woman said: "There were more than two hundred henchmen. All of them were masked, and all had on combat boots and gloves. They were armed with knives, acid, with ropes which had metal balls attached to the ends, and with chains which whistled through the air. Everybody grabbed sticks and ran. They came after us with everything. They even had gasoline and burned down the outside door. We fought for three hours. The children who were accompanying us were put inside the factory to keep away from these men who were attacking us. Despite this, some of the children received burns on their face and on their feet from the acid. My fellow worker, Eugenia, had her head cracked. Others had bruises on their hips and on their hands. The armored personnel carrier of the police, instead of helping us, gave free rein to the attackers. The police were accomplices of everything that happened that night. They even threw tear-gas bombs at us."[2]

When the battle was over, the number of workers who stayed on to occupy the factory was reduced, but their commitment to struggle was intensified. Public support grew, while personal support was often lacking. One worker explained: "The struggle we women have is tremendous. We have to leave our homes, leave our little children alone, leave our responsibilities in the home, and furthermore, we are economically very much affected. Some of our male co-workers don't understand our situation and do not permit their wives to fulfill their responsibility as workers. These men don't understand what it is to defend our rights. I, in my case, I think that if I didn't have the husband I have, I surely would have abandoned the struggle no matter how much of a strong will I would have had."[3]

Some husbands abandoned their wives or divorced them during the fight to keep the factory open. Some women left their husbands because of lack of support. One woman described how her husband literally dragged her from the workplace. On arriving at home, she said to him: "Look, *hijito* [sonny boy], this is where our life together ends. If you had spoken to me in a different way, perhaps we could have come to an understanding. But you have used the most ineffective means. So this is it, you go your way and I continue . . . I'm going back to my *compañeras* [companions, comrades]. My life is defined."[4]

Battles raged off and on at LOLAS for over a year before the women were eventually evicted by government troops. By the time the struggle at LOLAS ended in defeat, others were under-way. They attracted the attention of feminist organizations in Lima. Feminists helped to secure more union support for women and international support to put pressure on the Peruvian government. A worker from CONEL (Consorcio Electronico), where women assembled radio and television parts, was invited to Europe by feminist organizations in Holland, and workers at CONEL inspired the formation of a coordinating body for feminist activity in Lima.

The occupation of CONEL began in 1979 when the factory management attempted to gain a competitive advantage by sending the work force on a forced vacation in order to replace them with cheaper temporary help. Most of those who decided to occupy the factory had been working at CONEL for more than six years. On returning from their "vacation," and finding their places taken by contract workers, they pried the gates of the factory open and reclaimed their positions. They themselves had trained male engineers who were hired to supervise production. They felt confident of their ability, and they continued production on their own. While the women and their children occupied the factory, a petition was filed before the government to form a cooperative. At 2:00 a.m. December 18, one week before Christmas, fifty men who were hired by the company stormed the factory premises. Women fought back successfully against the knife-wielding *matones* (thugs, killers). Workers at CONEL eventually gained the right to take over production, but their forces were depleted during the nearly two years of struggle, and a number of women were fined and given jail sentences.

The women at CONEL were able to join forces with workers in the children's clothing factory, LUCY, to gain public support for women's right to work. At LUCY several women had been fired when employees attempted to form a union. The others were punished by giving out easy work to temporary contracted employees and assigning such difficult work to regulars that they had to take clothing home to finish sewing at night. A spokesperson for the workers recalled succeeding events: "The campaign against us was stepped up with the arrival of *la patrona* [owner] in April of 1979. She locked the door of the workplace with a key while we were inside, pushed the sewing machines against the wall and ordered us not to say a word of conversation to each other. In January, we had presented our first list of demands—a raise in salary, better work conditions, aprons, building repairs, and a lunch table. On May 7 Luisa Bustinza, defense secretary of our union, was fired, supposedly for organizing a work stoppage. On the ninth of May, *la patrona* tried to remove the sewing machines and was stopped by various workers who stood in the doorway of the factory. From then on, we've been sleeping here in order to make sure the machines aren't taken away."[5]

Another woman describes the occupation more graphically, explaining how the workers prevented the removal of machinery from the factory premises: "We told the truck driver, 'You get out of here immediately or we'll burn your truck. We're defending our social rights.' For the next two days we worked all day and at night we stood guard out in the street, without sleeping, just sitting on newspapers."[6]

On June 11 the factory was officially closed by the owners, and the women inside sent a complaint to the Ministry of Labor. Later they petitioned to form a cooperative. By September 25, the women had won their right to assume control of production.

In the cases of both LUCY and CONEL, the government reversed itself several times, responding to political pressure generated by publicity. The eventual outcome was hailed as a victory for women in their struggle for the right to work. However, the political and economic climate in Peru is so unsupportive of

A moment of joy as the workers at CONEL electronic parts factory receive papers legalizing the takeover of the factory after nearly two years of struggle. (Ernesto Jimenez)

women's efforts to run small businesses that new factory takeovers are unlikely.[7] What the women gained from these struggles was an understanding of the kind of organization and discipline needed to make their demands felt by government and to make the public aware of women's situation. Workers' experiences in learning to maintain internal unity and discipline during factory occupations were shared with others. One woman explained to a reporter:

We learned to organize ourselves. Every Saturday in the evening we had a meeting to discuss the week's work: Places we had to visit to get support, who was going to stay in the factory each day and night and who was responsible for meals.

I remember one Saturday when we organized to do propaganda in the buses, entering them to distribute leaflets. Everybody knew who had taken on this responsibility. When the time came for them to give a report, there was a long silence, no one said anything. Finally, at the insistence of the woman who directed the assembly, someone spoke. The *compañeras* had arrived at the bus stops, but were too embarrassed to get in. That made everyone think. The struggle we had begun was so hard for us, we had so many problems, problems that male workers don't have when they decide to wage a struggle. Then we said, "Why were we so embarrassed?" Because women were fighting—because women were talking about a strike—because women were distribution leaflets? The decision to sleep in the factory five months ago had created a hard life for us and we had been courageous. Why were we ashamed to enter the bus?

With this conversation, we decided once again to enter the buses. The next Saturday, the *compañeras* reported at the meeting that they had talked to people, given them leaflets, and collected money in the buses.[8]

Workers also shared with other women the problems they were having with husbands. One woman said: "They haven't understood our struggle. . . . It was different when we first began working and bringing home a salary. They didn't tell us then, 'Your family and your children come first.' They said, *Anda a trabajar!'* [get to work]." Another worker summarized women's experiences: "With respect to the women workers, the case of LOLAS, CONEL, and LUCY has provided a forum for defending our right to work, to earn money, to eat, but it also served to defend the potential of women—marches in the streets, meetings at the gates of parliament, integration in hunger strikes."[9]

Following the example of women who took over the factories, women workers in other sectors took over churches to call attention to demands for maternity leaves, child-care centers at their workplaces, and other benefits accorded them by law. Demonstrations and pickets denounced rape and harrassment of women by managers and bosses, demanded equal pay for equal work, and equality for women workers in general. Women who belonged to male-dominated unions took increasingly important roles during extended strikes, pushing for attention to non-economic issues in public health services, government offices, and factories. Even in areas where women had in the past hoped to attain or maintain "respectability" by refusing to become involved in workplace disputes, worsening economic conditions and the increasing visibility of politically active women drew women workers into the struggle.

Strategies for Survival in "the Peripheral Sector"

Inability to secure stable work opportunities, adequate salaries, child care, and other conditions that would permit their incorporation into the wage labor force alongside men has forced more and more Peruvian women to work out of their homes. The first thing women usually think of when they are forced out of the paid work force is the manufacture of clothing at home, and the experience women have in factories often leads them to attempt to set up their own workshops together with neighbors and friends. However, their efforts often lead to more dead ends. As one woman explains: "In the clothing industry it's almost impossible to compete with the huge factories. They have large amounts of capital to invest, so they can buy and stock raw materials in bulk at very low cost—we can't! These factories also have a high level of technology and we only have our old sewing machines. So the factory owners contract jobs out to third parties at infinitesimal prices. By contracting work, the bosses can keep production costs very low. They don't have to pay payroll benefits, of course—and they earn up to 100 percent or more in profits!"[10] Women often attempt to sell their products to their own friends and family because they can't compete on the general market. But with economic crisis, most of the poor can't afford to buy new clothing. So women give up the effort to set up their own businesses and end up taking piecework from contractors instead.

Most piecework involves sewing together pieces of ready-cut cloth into trousers or shirts or other articles of clothing, averaging about thirty items per week. Even when women work ten to twelve hours daily seven days a week, piecework can't provide subsistence for families. Older children are often recruited to help and are always expected to take over other housework and the care of younger children. They have little time to study or play. Families who do sewing at home suffer from illnesses caused by inhaling fiber. Among the complaints most often made by piece-workers, however, is that those who contract work out to women get so much more for the product than what workers or sellers receive. Contractors have practically no overhead expenses. Women own their own machines, or else they rent machines privately. Delays in repair can cause extended crises for families dependent on income from piecework.

Women doing piecework in their homes in the barriadas are not immune from the radical currents of thought sometimes thought by intellectuals to be the exclusive domain of factory workers. They are not "grateful" to their contractors for the small amount of money they receive after many hours of hard labor. And they are not isolated from the great social movements that have occurred during the past decade. The situation of the piece-worker in the economy was summed up by a participant in a working women's meeting held a number of years ago in Lima: "Contracted work endangers the woman worker and the entire working class, lowering salaries, worsening work conditions, denying work benefits, rights, and conquests, breaking our struggle and dividing our organizations—in a word, beating down the proletariat." Since that meeting there has been only scattered

A woman peels garlic cloves to sell in plastic bags. Unable to afford an investment in their own operations, such women work for middlemen or on contract to fulfill quotas set by commissioners. (Lynn Murray)

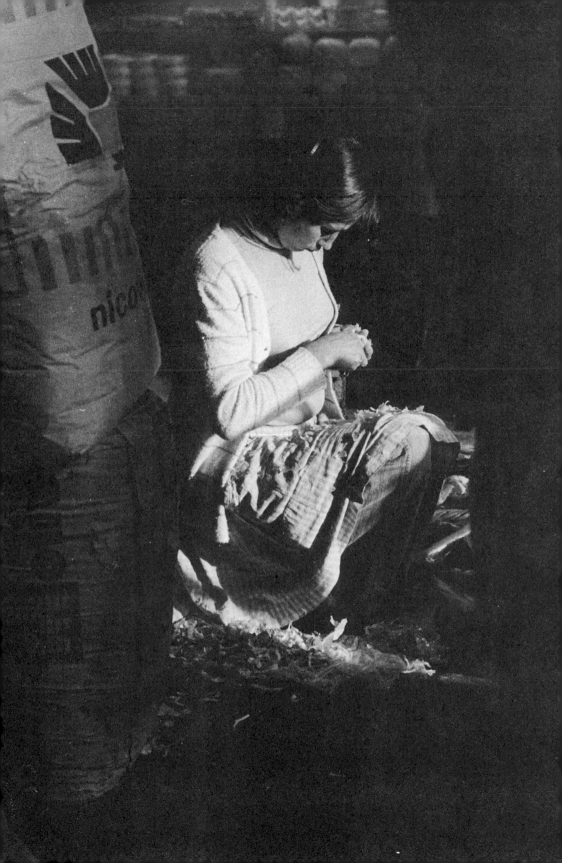

success in organizing contract workers and the unemployed. However, women have been more consistent than men in recognizing the need for contract workers to become part of the struggles of the proletariat. They have insisted that contract workers be included in meetings of workers usually reserved for union members having regular jobs in established industries.

Among the least organized of those who work out of their homes in Peru are the women who take in laundry. Women who do this are often recent migrants to the city, and in the provinces most of those who do laundry for others speaks very little Spanish. Nearly all those who have worked for a number of years washing clothes all day long in the river have lost at least one child to respiratory diseases. The women themselves often succumb to tuberculosis, rheumatism, or pneumonia. Those who wash clothes in the home of clients have to suffer the humiliation of *patronas* who feel they are doing a woman a favor by letting her wash the family's laundry for an amount of money so small it does not even allow her to eat three meals a day, let alone support her own family or return occasionally to visit her relatives outside the city. And those who work for contractors are given no assistance whatsoever in making the conditions of their work conducive to the health and well-being of themselves and their children.

Women's search for ways to escape from the periphery of an industrial economy has led them to take jobs in the service sector from which male workers have been fired for waging struggles to improve working conditions. A recent situation of this sort occurred in 1982 when thousands of municipal workers were fired after a year-long strike. Newspaper ads offering street-sweeping jobs brought responses mainly from women. One thirty-two-year-old woman testified about her life as a street sweeper in Lima: "I have to leave my house at 4:00 in the morning. I'm accustomed by now to sleeping only a few hours. By 10:00 we get a lunch break and I buy a bowl of soup and a glass of milk, which reduces my pay to less than two thousand soles, and that's not counting bus fare. My older children cook, wash, and take care of the little ones. I kept having more [children] thinking that if I did my husband wouldn't leave me, but that was a big mistake because when a man's head is turned around it doesn't make any difference if he has a hundred children. . . . When we first came to work people were happy to see us because nobody wanted to do this work. It was hard because we didn't have anything to work with. Thank God they finally gave us face masks and gloves and carts."[11]

Street sweepers often become ill with infections or lung diseases or have to quit working because of exhaustion. Early in 1983, three hundred women who work as sweepers in Lima—most of them single mothers—formed a commission to represent themselves before the municipal government. They knew the government would not recognize a union, but they also knew they had to have some kind of representation. The members of the commission were immediately fired, and the women turned to feminist organizations to aid their cause through publicity. Because feminists had been waging a constant battle with newspapers to get coverage for issues of concern to women, and because women themselves had developed skills as writers and interviewers, the situation of the street sweepers could be brought to public attention.

On International Women's Day, March 8, 1983, the Left daily *El Diario Marka* carried a special supplement with feature articles on the plight of Lima's street sweepers, and on rape and prostitution in Lima. An unmistakable implication of the material presented was that personal denigration is the price women are paying for their attempt to secure paid work in a society where money is necessary to survival. This is indicated in an increase in the incidence of violence toward women, an increase in the abandonment of women by working-class men, and a loss of chivalry among men of the middle and upper classes. The articles, all written by women, were accompanied by women's poetry and photographs taken by women, but they were prefaced by a full-cover page of a nude young woman posing seductively and a poem, written by a man, extolling a distinctly male version of free love. The entire supplement was edited by a man and contained an editorial expressing satisfaction that the day of "rabid feminism" was over, even as the era of "rabid machismo" was approaching its end. The dramatic increase in rape in Lima during recent years, which seemed to have escaped the attention of the editorial writer, was nevertheless documented in the articles written by the women, who said that 90 percent of reported rapes go unprosecuted. Usually only when minors or virgins are raped do offenders receive punishment. There is no recourse for pregnancies resulting from rape—even in the case of incest—and women are regularly raped by government counterinsurgency squads *(sinchis).*

The Growth of Prostitution

Foreign publications have designated Peru "one of the world's biggest centers of prostitution." Tourist agencies even include *tours de placer* (pleasure tours). By 1983, Cuzco and Iquitos were drawing women from surrounding areas to compete with Lima as centers of both drug traffic and prostitution. The biggest profiters were the state, which taxes and licenses prostitutes, the "mafias," who schemed to build prostitution into big business, and government authorities, who profited from the payoffs connected with clandestine prostitution by minors. One member of parliament introduced legislation that would allow port cities to finance public works through state-sponsored prostitution. In Iquitos women were contracted directly by oil companies to provide sexual services to workers. Young girls from the jungle were sometimes introduced to prostitution by being raffled off in bingo games.

Twenty years ago there were fewer than five thousand registered prostitutes in the entire country. Today there are between fifty and one hundred thousand.[12] This does not include those who are engaged in prostitution clandestinely. Since the state requires licensed prostitutes to carry identification certifying that they have paid their fees and submitted to regular health examinations, many of those who earn money through prostitution, even those who can meet age and health requirements, choose to risk prosecution rather than operate legally. By operating unofficially, they can also avoid having over half of their fees utilized for payment to intermediaries and rental of space. Women must pay higher licensing fees to offer "luxury" and "first class" service and to work in establishments that offer such services. Those who are taken to jail for violating the laws regulating prostitution complain of being housed in overcrowded rooms lacking furniture or sanitary facilities and of being subjected to constant abuse by police.

The main illnesses of prostitutes, besides venereal diseases, are cancer of the uterus, respiratory ailments, including tuberculosis, and severe psychological stress. Many women quit working as prostitutes more than once, but return when they cannot find other work or because they must do so temporarily to pay medical bills or keep other family members alive. Ninety percent of the registered prostitutes are single mothers. Some families encourage their daughters to prostitute themselves so that they can purchase television sets or other luxuries which would otherwise be completely unobtainable.

An ex-prostitute in an advanced stage of syphilis once sat down opposite my husband and me at a restaurant and began eating from our plates. She bared her bosom seductively, then began telling us her life story. She said her lifelong desire was to have someone "stay with me after making love, put his arms around me and hold me, just a little while." She said her father had surprised her in bed with her boy friend when they were both teenagers. Her friend jumped out the window and was killed. She ran away from home and eventually began working as a prostitute. Now she could no longer work because she was incurably sick.

When we left the restaurant, she followed us home. On reaching our doorstep, she said, "You think I'm going inside your house with you, but I'm not." Then she sat down on the ground and sang a song, in Quechua, that translates as follows:

You took me to have a bath because you thought I was dirty.
    What a fool I was!
You took me to church and I thought it was time for mass.
    What a fool I was!
The band played and I thought it must be your birthday.
    What a fool I was!
When we lit the candles, I thought it was because it was dark.
    What a fool I was!
When the rice fell on my head, I thought it was hailing.
    What a fool I was!
When your house was filled with people, I thought it was my birthday.
    What a fool I was!

"Women have a right to say no." Feminist organizations in Lima protest rape and domestic violence. Urban culture has brought denigration to women; prostitution, rape, and pornography have spread throughout the country. *(Ernesto Jimenez)*

When we got into bed, I thought it was because I was afraid and you were
    comforting me.
    What a fool I was![13]

The song most likely refers to occasions when feudal landowners forced young couples to wed after the woman became
pregnant at the hands of the landowner or one of his sons. I had
heard the song before, always sung sadly and accompanied by
weeping. It seems to express the universal condition of women
who are forced into sex without love. The longing for closeness is
frustrated not only by male dominance, but also by economic
exploitation and disease, which destroys community life, separates
women and men, and consumes the energies of the poor.

Like their counterparts throughout the world, Peruvian
women neither escape moral judgment by engaging in prostitution nor become prostitutes out of whim. However, it seems to me
that the element of prostitution concealed in all forms of commercial exploitation is well understood by many Peruvian women,
especially those who have not become fully incorporated into
consumer society. To use one's body as a commodity is only one of
many sources of alienation in a society that promises personal
fulfillment through the acquisition of things. At the farm-workers'
convention in Lima (see Chapter Three), one young woman was
asked what she thought of the Miss Universe contest that was
going on in the city. She replied: "Indian women sell themselves,
too, but not because they want to. They sell themselves because of
hunger."

While prostitutes are not a leading force of the women's
movements in Peru, they do have a capacity for organization as a
group, because they are hired and regulated by government and
business, and they are not untouched by the political events
around them. Prostitutes have gone on strike in Lima to protest
the worst abuses to which they are subjected. They have lobbied
the Peruvian government successfully to permit refusal of services
to clients who are drunk, and they have tried to get legislation
requiring health cards of clients. The refusal of services to drunks
could undoubtedly be won, because it helps the owners of establishments where the prostitutes work avoid situations of disorder

and severe sanitation problems. Requiring men to submit to health examinations could be another source of much-needed government revenue. One can only conclude that failure to have this demand taken seriously by lawmakers is a matter of men protecting their own prerogative to engage the services of prostitutes without bringing any attention or reprobation to themselves.

Repression of Street Vendors

While prostitution proliferates with the cooperation of authorities, those who sell food or hot meals in the street, prepared out of their own homes, are practically regarded as outlaws by the government. By far the largest percentage of "underemployed" in Peru are those who sell food or clothing in the streets. These vendors are usually called *ambulantes* because they must keep on the move to avoid repression. Especially in the provinces, most of them are women.

Women have traditionally bartered or sold their own products in marketplaces, especially on the *feria* days, which occur once a week in small towns. But the proliferation of vendors today has very little to do with this tradition. Women who sell in the streets very often secure products on credit from middlemen and pay for them after they've been sold. Vendors are restricted by government as to where they can sell, and they are charged fees for permission to sell as well as rent for occupying public space. Prices are set for the sale of many products sold in the street, and vendors must pay fines when they violate rules and regulations.

In many cases, street vendors spend half of their time cooking or otherwise transforming the products they sell. As the economy worsens, perishable foods, which is what most female vendors sell, are more and more likely to be left unsold. Losses are sustained by the seller, not by the intermediary from whom the vendor purchased the farm products that went into the meal. Children who are old enough to help their mothers sell sometimes get desperate enough to pick pockets when sales are bad. They hope to escape their mother's wrath by bringing in a little extra money, but often they only compound her problems.

The government periodically launches campaigns against street vendors in an effort to "prevent crime," "protect public health," and "lower the price of food."[14] The proliferation of vendors is an embarrassment to public officials; the health and welfare of the vendors and their families is of little concern to officials. Street vendors become defensive, cantankerous, and combative in the face of the onslaught against them. One observer explained: "The places where they sell their products are generally uncomfortable, insecure, unhealthy, and often temporary. It's notorious how their conduct changes; they become aggressive and well able to defend themselves against attacks and competition, which differentiates them greatly from the peaceful, almost familial, conduct of women in the *ferias comunales campesinas*."[15]

The campaigns against the street vendors are seen by vendors themselves as an effort to divert attention from the real causes of the economic crisis. Vendors know that their ability to provide a simple living for themselves and their families by cooking and selling in the streets is helping to keep the economy going and preventing starvation among the unemployed. They are resentful of being used as scapegoats in campaigns to "reduce inflation" and to promote *la limpieza* and *el orden público* (cleanliness and public order). The vendors, especially, are in a permanent state of combat with municipal authorities.

To a certain extent, government policy stimulates competitive attitudes among vendors to prevent effective organization. Those who have regular stalls in the markets are relatively privileged, as are those who get commissions for selling. The least privileged are those who operate on their own in temporary locations. Campaigns launched by the government are directed mainly against *ambulantes*. But the marketers and *ambulantes* are united in their hostility toward public officials who come around to collect fees and fines. They cooperate among themselves in the transportation of products, warding off robbers, helping each other out in times of illness or hardship, watching each other's stalls, and lending each other money. Most marketers have been street vendors at one time or another. Vendors and marketers have also organized unions in which their common interests are emphasized to insure that their rights are respected.

A street vendor cries out during a mass march of ambulantes *in Lima. Under-employment forces women into the streets, where they develop solidarity in the struggle against official repression. (Marta Serra)*

Health measures introduced by the government are seen by sellers as repressive devices and excuses for exploitation rather than as legitimate controls. The charging of fees for required medical exams, and even for the use of latrines, discourages the use of these services and facilities. Government efforts to "help" street vendors by locating them in special areas set aside for selling are also seen as repressive measures because the sites provided have not usually attracted enough buyers. Besides, once vendors are permanently located in a market, additional fees and regulations are instituted.

In June 1981 the government began a massive relocation of street vendors in Lima. To accomplish the relocation, military force was necessary. Subsequently, thousands of street vendors marched in protest, and government troops were called to disperse the demonstration. A permanent police presence was employed afterwards to assure that the "public nuisance" of *ambulantes* in Lima's plush downtown areas did not return.

All of the repressive measures used by the government against those who sell in Peru's markets and streets have not succeeded in demobilizing vendors, whose numbers continue to grow daily. Some members of the "middle classes" may be won over through government propaganda that describes vendors as a threat to the public welfare. But even this effort contributes to the political awareness of the vendors themselves. In becoming a "social problem," street vendors have also become a social force. Those who sell in the streets are gaining respect from others for their combativeness and for their tenacity in working to support their families in spite of constant harassment and condemnation. By organizing to oppose government repression, they are gaining an understanding of their situation in the economy and they are finding out who are their allies and who are their enemies.

Women marketers have usually chosen male leaders to represent them in negotiations with the government, perhaps because they think government officials will be more likely to recognize their unions that way. However, in base organizing and in spontaneous actions women have shown their capacity for leadership and their ability to articulate demands. In Huancayo, women who serve meals to the public in the market and in the streets united with housewives in a militant demonstration to demand that kerosene be supplied to the region more regularly, "requisitioning" vehicles to transport fuel and blocking the highway to call attention to their problem. When I was living in Huancayo, market women also protected students who were being chased by police after being dispersed during a demonstration. The women refused to let police enter the market area where the students were hiding.

Organization of Household Workers

Of all the popular struggles waged by women workers in Peru, that of the household workers is probably least understood by the public. College-educated feminists and leftists are often as insensitive as others to the plight of household workers because many of them have at one time or another utilized the services of such workers in their homes. Yet the resolution of the contradiction between household workers and their *patronas,* or employers, is a decisive element in the struggle for women's liberation.

Domestic servants, or household workers, are the largest single grouping of women in the "economically active population" of the country. They compose one fifth of the legally recognized female work force. Most household workers are young. Over half are legal minors. Nearly all are Indians who have migrated from the countryside. Household work, often performed in the homes of relatives who have moved to the city, is usually the first experience a rural woman has in attempting to support herself outside her native community.

Peruvian law requires that household workers not be prevented from attending school, but it also requires that household workers be given "at least" eight hours off each day. This means that they can be made to work sixteen hours. Usually employers promise the young women who come to work in their homes that they will be able to attend school at night and prepare themselves for better jobs. But the pressure of work, the lack of money for transportation and books, the patronizing attitudes of many teachers, lack of time for study, and lack of cooperation by employers prevent most young women from completing classes. Those who do attend school say that teachers often insult them, don't understand the problems they have in attending classes regularly and completing assignments, or try to explain away their problems with *patronas* by pointing to their own weaknesses. Those who quit school because of such experiences are often rewarded by their employers for giving up.

The fear of being without work, far from home, and without friends or relatives to whom they can turn for help increases the dependence of household workers on their employers. Employers often resent the young women who work for them, interpreting as ignorance, incompetence, and stubbornness the very real problems rural women have in relating to urban and mestizo or foreign life-styles. Employers complain to each other that it's "impossible to find good help," that young women are "uppity," prone to steal, slack off on the job, and gossip. Many rationalize to themselves that they are doing their *empleadas,* or employees, a favor by introducing them to city life and providing them with food and shelter.

Resistance to learning foreign ways is one way the employees defend themselves against their employers, engendering mutual hostility and distrust on the part of employers. Alienation is another common defense, evidenced by the incorporation of values which negate one's own sense of identity and self-worth. Watching soap operas on television is one way Indian women are drawn into "mainstream culture," and this sometimes brings them closer to their employers, who also watch such programs. But cameraderie between employer and employee based on such experiences is superficial. There is little the household worker gains from it, other than personal degradation.

The sexual exploitation of household workers by members of their employer's household causes trauma for both the *patrona* and *empleada,* and frequently results in pregnancy and loss of employment. Young women's emotional isolation also causes them to be vulnerable to the sexual advances of young men they meet on their days off, causing endless problems with which they are unprepared to cope. Few survive city life without falling prey to influences of urban culture in one way or another, making return to their home communities in the countryside difficult if not impossible.

There have been numerous attempts to organize household

workers in Peru, none of them very successful. By the end of the 1970s, approximately 5 percent of household workers belonged to unions. Only in Cuzco had the union of household workers gained legal recognition. Since employers do not have to hire out of union halls, those who do so are likely to be progressive people who would honor household workers' legal rights in any case. Unions have been useful in pushing for better legislation, however, and in providing advocacy services and promoting popular education about the household workers' cause. They have also been useful in providing a national forum for household workers who have come together from various parts of the country to discuss tactics and strategy and to learn how their struggles relate to those of other workers and to the economic and political situation of the country as a whole.

In household workers' unions leadership is entirely female. This has not prevented internal power struggles, however, based on party sectarianism as well as real political differences. Women who participate in recently established native organizations have been critical of the tendency of some union leaders to emphasize issues such as pensions and economic security for household workers rather than to provide leadership to bring an end to servile relationships through the revolutionary transformation of society. Since women in native movements criticize the small or nuclear household unit as the basis of the economy, advocating a reinforcement or strengthening of communitarian arrangements, household workers who are leaders in these movements feel they are in a better position than are orthodox leftists to bring a revolutionary perspective to the household workers' movements.[16]

One of the constituents of the native movement in Peru is the Comunidad Femenina Micaela Bastidas, which had fought for nearly a decade to keep a common residence for household workers in downtown Lima. The members of this community have been outspoken in challenging the system of servile relations to which household workers are subject. The community also challenges family systems that put the burden of child-rearing on individual mothers. Members of the community have publicly criticized those feminists and leftists who expect household servants to care for their children while they "go off to demonstrate for human rights." There has been little public response to these criticisms, but individual feminists are struggling to come to terms with the challenge posed by indigenous women, who are also becoming involved in barriada movements in the cities. The struggle between urban feminists and household workers is a crucial part of the emerging dialogue between mestizos and indigenous peoples in general.

Before their eviction by the Convent of Santo Domingo (see Prologue) in November 1982, members of the Comunidad Femenina Micaela Bastidas occupied a building that was nearly in ruins. Each bedroom contained four to eight beds, with no space for tables, chairs, or storage of personal belongings. Everything the women owned was stored under their beds or hung on the wall. Children slept with their mothers, and women sometimes doubled up to accommodate new members until they were able to acquire an additional bed. No one who lived in the community claimed that it was an ideal life-style. Yet the alternative for most of them was to live at their place of employment, a situation that members of the community wished to avoid at any cost.

The community originated as a church project for the protection and guidance of young women who came to the city seeking work. Early in the formation of the household, women quarreled with a nun who had been living with them, and subsequently gained independence from church control. The break with the Church, and the inclusion of older women and children in the community, made possible a radical transformation of the household. It was changed from a temporary shelter to a nucleus for collective living in the city; it could serve as an example for the masses of women whose traditional places in society no longer existed and who wanted to have some say about their own future.

I had known about the community almost since its inception in 1975 and had written about it in feminist publications in North America. During my visit to Peru in 1982, I found the members of the community in crisis over the threatened eviction, which they had managed to postpone temporarily through publicity and the mobilization of support from friends of the community.

I was invited to stay in the community during this struggle, and lived there for nearly a month. I was impressed by the way members of the community were able to help each other with personal problems and share what little each had in order to defend their way of life. The women ranged in age from fifteen to forty-five. They came from many different parts of the country. Some had children, and some did not. There were no elaborate schemes for housecleaning or child care, hauling water, or Sunday cooking at the community. Most women ate weekday meals at their places of work. I never saw children spanked or even severely reprimanded, a commonplace in barriada families, where community support is not readily available to parents. Women taught each other skills such as sewing and basketmaking, and took turns attending cultural or political functions, drawing on a common fund established for that purpose. They invited outsiders to give talks and teach them songs and help them with theater and folk-dance productions. All of the young women were able to attend school at night. Those who were temporarily unemployed were able to sustain themselves with the help of others.

Men were included in the cultural activities of the community, usually conducted on Sundays. But men who abused their welcome in any way were pressured to stay away. A male musical group—its members were special friends of some of the community's leaders—began practicing regularly in the large interior parlor, but it was asked to stop when its presence began to dominate the household. Women who attached themselves to men through whom they were able to gain some special privileges were severely criticized or ostracized from the group, while those who were in love were able to share their happiness with each other and invite their boy friends to visit with them any time in the household's front hallway. Members of the community were free to move out to live with boy friends or marry, but they were also free to return if things didn't work out.

In the long legal battle preceding the eviction of the community from its residence, members defended their right to occupancy of the building by citing the Church's usurpation of the property after the War of Independence. Nevertheless, the women continued paying rent to a bank in order to insure their status as legal inhabitants. The Dominican priests who claimed title to the property cut off the water supply to the building. They accused the women of "loose morals" while at the same time renting the adjoining building to a noisy canteen which was open day and night. The women had to carry water from a welding shop across the street. Several members of the household became sick with typhoid fever during the years of struggle with the Church.

In defending their community publicly against the Church's attacks, women spoke on a radio program, a Sunday morning women's hour inspired by feminist organizations in Lima. The community's representatives called on other women to form their own households, saying: "How else can we women organize to emancipate ourselves? We don't want to aspire to be like the people we work for. We don't want to forget where we came from. We think it's our obligation to live in community, like our ancestors did."

One of the leaders of the household told me: "Most of the women would like to live with men—I would, too—but we know men are alienated by the kind of society we're living in. We're better off in a women's community, defining our own conditions for relating to men."

Lawyers hired by the priests who evicted the women tried to intimidate the members of the community by calling them "street women." This infuriated the women, who told me that if anyone had tried to corrupt their morals, it was the priests themselves. Eventually, priests and lawyers were able to utilize divisions among the women caused in part by the influence of the various political organizations that became involved in the struggle. Eviction came at a time when most of the women were at work; they were not well enough organized to mobilize full occupation of the premises twenty-four hours of the day. Nevertheless, because of the eviction, the community gained publicity for the cause of women's emancipation. A core group of members began actively organizing to create new collective households and develop their political understanding to prepare for higher levels of struggle.

The leaders of the Comunidad Femenina Micaela Bastidas criticize those feminists who call for a united front of all women regardless of social class, and those leftists who think the problems

Household workers of the Comunidad Femenina Micaela Bastidas are evicted by the Convent of Santo Domingo. Members sought to live communally and protect their right to education and personal freedom. (Marta Serra)

Telephone workers take over a cathedral in Huancayo during a national strike. (Ernesto Jimenez)

of women are secondary or "psychological." Rich women, they say, are complicit with rich men: they "form a mafia together with the government and the church to rob the workers of the product of their work . . . They enrich themselves at the cost of the rest of us—the Indians." Of middle-class women: "They dream of being in the upper class and try to please their bosses to see if they can be invited into their midst. Failing this, they get terrible complexes which they unleash against us, their household workers, distancing themselves as much as possible from us, and treating us with total contempt." Writing about love and marriage, a spokesperson for the community said: "A frivolous woman only seeks a solvent man to whom she can submit herself in the hope that her economic problems will be solved. By means of this 'contract' she assures herself of 'having a man' and thereby becomes his private property."[17] Not surprisingly, the Dominican fathers who evicted the community call the woman who made these comments *la diabla* (the little devil).

The idea of women as "private property" is a predominant theme in literature published by the household workers' movement. A *historieta* ("comic book" or cartoon pamphlet) published in Cuzco describes household workers as the private property of their *patronas*. A middle-class woman in the city is shown telling her sister, who teaches in a village: *Traeme pues a una chica de empleada, y también traeme carnecita. ¿Ya?"* [Bring me a girl from the country next time you come, and bring me a side of meat, too. O.K.?]. The *historieta* concludes simply: "This small domestic economy has to change."[18]

Popular theater and *fotonovelas*[19] produced by household workers ridicule bourgeois society, showing what it does to deform even the individuals who are considered successful. Contrasting daily life in the homes of the rich, or those who are aspiring to be rich, with the lives of their own families, household workers gain an awareness of what is happening to themselves and to their society. They seem to be in a better position than many to envision the changes that are necessary to build a society where material prosperity will be available to everyone without the sacrifice of human dignity.

Women and Economic Development

Overall, Peruvian women's attempts to gain a place of equality for themselves within the "modern" sector of the economy have not resulted in notable successes. Dependent capitalism continues to produce larger and larger reserves of unemployed or marginal workers. Among these, women continue to be the most prominent. The fact that many men have been unable or unwilling to fulfill the cultural expectation of providing consistent economic support for women and children under conditions of "modern life" has forced women to explore ways to achieve economic independence from men. Women's efforts to secure access to jobs and gain work benefits, assistance with child care, and enough money to survive in a cash economy have contributed to their organization and political awareness, both as workers and as women. At the same time, domestic conflict has increased, and men's hostility toward women has grown. Men fear women's independence even as they flee from family responsibility.

When bourgeois academicians address the problems of women in what they call "developing economies," they tend to assume that through "enlightenment" women will win a place for themselves in the industrial order. Feminists have sometimes accepted such perspectives. Educational activities, especially those conducted under the auspices of bourgeois institutions, do not always address the underlying causes of women's problems. Forums and academic conferences can cause women to avoid discussing avenues of political struggle that are not acceptable to sponsoring agencies.

It is not surprising that financial support for initiatives of groups like the Comunidad Feminina Micaela Bastidas has not been readily available. The community as a political organization addresses the central problems of child care, cultural alienation, and survival in ways that are not compatible with the objectives of "developmentalists."[20] While reformists posit women's gradual incorporation into an industrial economy without altering basic economic structures, the community calls for an end to servile relationships in home and workplace. Its vision is more radical than that espoused by many feminist organizations, and more radical than the objectives declared by unions and most popular organizations of the Left.

Often in the drive to attain security and comfort as individuals in bourgeois society, workers lose sight of the sense of community that is essential to psychological well-being. Women's struggles to overcome marginalization as workers and to find ways to rear children in a community—even where traditional family and community relations have been broken—promises to reveal the potential that human beings have for real social transformation. Demands for child care at workplaces are of little significance when transportation to work is expensive and highly unreliable. Family networks that help to provide working women with support in child care often disappear when women need time away from their children for political organizing. Women's organizing efforts too often must be split between workplace and neighborhood, while their problems are not so conveniently split. Through efforts to unite these struggles—to build the collective strength of women both as mothers and as producers of goods and services in capitalist society—women alter the meaning of politics. This process can provide the "missing link" in the worldwide struggle for socialism.

6 : *Native Revival and Revolution*

AT THE EXTREME periphery of Peru's economy are the native peoples of the tropical rain forests and the most inaccessible mountain areas. The battle against profiteers who covet their territory or demand their allegiance is forcing these people to end the isolation which has protected their way of life. In such circumstances, emerging struggles between women and men are tempered by the threat of genocide and by the increasing responsibilities of women in subsistence economies. Women's historical resistance to mestizo, male-dominant culture is accompanied by a great desire to secure men's cooperation in the all-out struggle for survival.

Women's efforts to resist the colonization of the jungle have been blunted by the penetration of Protestant missionaries during this century. However, a recent resurgence of nativism is helping women to assert themselves as leaders. In the cold dry puna,[1] the high mountain areas of central Peru that border the hot, wet jungle, women's efforts to defend Indian communities and to preserve communal values is increasingly focused in guerilla campaigns that have brought nationwide and worldwide attention to the revolutionary potential of Peru's most oppressed peoples. Women have deliberately assumed military leadership in the widening guerrilla war.

Religion and Tradition in the Receding Rain Forests of the Peruvian Amazon

Until very recently, information about the daily lives, aspirations, and world views of the native peoples of the South American jungle was conveyed to outsiders only through entrepreneurs and missionaries, who regarded natives as objects of manipulation, exploitation, or conquest, or by male anthropologists whose bias has been so pronounced as to make many of their findings suspect.[2] In addition, native culture has been so powerfully affected by outside influences during the past centuries that we cannot expect ever to know with certainty what it was like before.

The enslavement of the native peoples of Peru has at times threatened to destroy their communities altogether, as the following account illustrates: "During the first decade of the twentieth century, 80 percent of the native population of the Putumayo River was annihilated. At the same time, of the 28,000 rubber workers of the Loreto jungle, approximately 22,000 belonged to native groups. The human losses produced by mistreatment, epidemics and forced labor were replaced by raids during which members of tribal societies were captured."[3]

Despite rapid encroachment by outsiders who have introduced mining, large-scale cultivation, lumbering, grazing, and other extractive economic activities that have led to the disappearance of game, fish, natural vegetation, and native peoples themselves, the South American jungle is still the largest area in the world where hunting and gathering societies exist. The temporary cultivation of manioc on small plots and the domestication of chickens and pigs have helped to keep subsistence economies alive in the tropical rain forest and led to a settled, if precarious, life for hunting and gathering peoples. The struggle for survival is also a struggle against men's domination of women because, in spite of instances of extreme antagonism between the sexes, native culture is, in many respects, "prepatriarchal." If feminists are ever to know to what extent women have enjoyed equality with men in our historical past, and to comprehend how patriarchy comes into existence, we are likely to learn much from our sisters in the South American selva. Fortunately for us, and for them, native women are beginning to speak for themselves, collectively, about what they want to preserve or regain from their own past and what they would like to achieve in the future.

Accounts of the lives of men and women in the areas of the Peruvian selva that were relatively isolated from missionary and commercial influence show that aborigines are born into loosely connected social groupings. These groupings are not really villages, for families do not necessarily live in close proximity; neither are they really tribes, as membership is not defined by kinship so much as it is by social and economic ties. In general, men hunt and fish to provide for their family's daily consumption, while women gather and plant. However, on occasion, women participate in fishing parties, and sometimes men go out in groups for special hunts. Men usually clear the ground before women plant. Women beguile men into hunting and try to attach themselves to those men who are good hunters. It is more common for women to fight over men than for men to fight over women. Fathers may also try to recruit as lovers for their daughters men who will be good hunting partners for themselves. But women are the final arbiters of sexual relations, either temporary or long-term. Lifetime pairing is rare, although stable relations are common and are signified by a man's putting up his hammock in the household of his mate. It isn't always certain by whom children have been fathered. Names given children are not related to lineage. In some communities, temporary sexual liaisons are accompanied by great efforts at secrecy; elsewhere the need for secrecy hardly exists at all, especially among children, who engage in sexual play free of adult sanction. Since sisters usually continue to live together throughout life, they also help each other in daily work and nurse each other's children.

Among households living in close proximity in the jungle, people are not called by their given names but by their social relationships—sister, aunt, etc. Relationships have to do with rights and obligations, which includes adult sexual prohibitions, such as incest, and prohibitions against certain kinds of hospitality to people from outside one's own group.

As both game and fish have become scarce due to encroachment on native territory, traditional sharing among friends has been replaced by a certain amount of secretiveness and deception about what one has acquired through hard work. Objects acquired from outsiders or bought with money are not freely shared, because they are also scarce. Family life is affected by the constant temptation to seek paid work in service to traders, missionaries, or companies that come to the jungle to extract natural resources. Contact with outsiders weakens the ability to fulfill traditional obligations at home, and often leads to abandonment of native communities. Depending on the kind of labor sought by outsiders, out-migration may affect either men or women, but it always leaves native communities with sexual conflict.

There is confusion among the inhabitants of the selva about clothing. Outsiders look down on painting of bodies, which traditionally has to do with rituals of seduction and hunting. Traditional robes, beads, and feathers have a dollar value for tourists, making them "scarce," and thus limiting the likelihood that natives will wear them on a regular basis. People who interact with outsiders usually wear clothing resembling that of urban dwellers or mestizos. Men wear trousers and shirts and women wear simple cotton skirts and blouses or dresses. Regardless of their dress, the natives of the selva do not show bodily shame so long as they are in the familiar surroundings of home. There are no partitions or walls in most houses, and everyone bathes outdoors in the river.

The native religions of the tropical rain forest peoples of Peru are similar to the early religions of the entire Andean region of South America. These have to do with the sun and moon, water and earth, and plant and animal life. There are also "sister" and "brother" deities, the protectors and teachers of particular peoples, who reside in sacred places in close proximity to them on earth. The spirits of animals and of ancestors are held to be sacred, as are the sustenance-giving plants that can be used ritually to invoke inspiration and good feelings among people. At community gatherings women and men consume a fermented drink made mainly of manioc root (called *yuca* in Peru). The drink, called *masata,* is prepared by the women, who chew raw sweet potato and mix it with cooked *yuca* in a wooden vessel which, for a large gathering, might be a canoe. When the mixture has begun to ferment, it is combined with fresh river water and strained through a basket.

The drinking of *masata* at community gatherings is accompanied by all-night dancing under the full moon. Old people lead the dancing, winding around in patterns imitating a snake crawling on the ground. Women sing in screeching voices that sould like those of a bird, but the screeches represent words and have to do with natural and human events. Old men blow on panpipes or beat drums slowly and monotonously so as not to overpower the singing. Young people and children follow the older women and men, forming lines of their own and echoing the women's voices. The experience is more awe-inspiring than sensuous. On the occasion I was invited to be present, the celebration invoked in me neither joyfulness nor sadness, but a powerful sense of unity with nature.

A Yanesha elder (called Amuesha by anthropologists) describes the native celebrations of his people in the following terms: "We hold large celebrations where we present different kinds of dances and music, such as drum dances, women's dances, panpipe dances, and men's dances. There is much happiness among us; we share roast meat, manioc beer, and coca leaves. In this way we demonstrate friendship and good friendly relations among our people." A missionary, writing about the Yanesha in 1924, said: "They are accustomed to celebrating on the full moon. . . . They sing extremely dull songs, dance to the sound of the drum and flute which barely has one or two notes, and drink manioc beer until they are completely drunk. The dance is extremely monotonous and dull. Afterwards, they remain stretched out there under the dominion of Bacchus, the god which they have honored with that wild and monstrous orgy."[4] These contrasting views are symptomatic of the clash between the sense of community of native peoples and the contempt with which they have been regarded by those who wish to "save their souls" or exploit their riches.

Foreign encroachment in jungle areas has threatened communal life by disturbing the already fragile relations between women and men. Money is increasingly needed for survival, and women have less access to it than men. One-sided dependency and uncertainty with regard to rights and obligations replaces customary reciprocity between the sexes, and severe repercussions are bound to occur.[5] Instances of extreme male domination exist, and in some places women are even forbidden to take the drugs that are used traditionally to stimulate dreams and visions.

As natives become aware of the acute dangers brought by those who come to tempt them with promises of easy wealth and excitement, or to frighten them with the prospect of hell, they resort to sorcery to ward them off. In times of distress, women turn to the snake as a symbol of revolt and revolution, for the snake represents natural forces that erupt when things are out of balance. To outsiders and to native men who fear that women's powers will be turned against them, women have come to be identified with the uncontrollable. It is believed that they must be conquered and punished to appease the gods of money and male domination.

For all these reasons, native women of the selva do not resemble the powerful Amazons described by conquistadores in the sixteenth century. Yet they are far from submissive. There is no reason to doubt that warrior women existed in the past. The only basis I can find for discounting stories that women of the selva were leaders in battle at the time of the Spanish conquest is the assertion by one male anthropologist that the Spanish may have mistaken men for women because men wore skirts and had long hair. Such an assertion is a doubtful basis for turning credible social facts into "legends," especially as it comes from one who also declared: "Peruvian women are 'lovable' in that they still occupy that proper domestic sphere from which their Northern sisters seem desirous to emancipate themselves, and to which the latter will have some day to return."[6]

Certainly many of the stories of Amazons are legendary. But it is clear that female warriors existed in both North and South America, as well as on the Caribbean Islands. "The assumption that Amazons were present in America did more than merely help male Europeans to comprehend the customs and practices of Native American cultures. It immensely magnified the lure of the

New World by extending a challenge of sexual conquest which hitherto existed only in fantasy."[7]

The Beginnings of Reform and the Intensified Colonization of the Jungle

Centuries of open hostility between inhabitants of the jungle areas immediately to the east of the Peruvian Andes and the missionaries and colonists who attempted to establish outposts there ended about the middle of the nineteenth century. At that time, a yellow fever epidemic threatened to wipe out the Indians. One historian relates how the Yanesha, one of the largest groups in the area, surrendered to outsiders: ". . .oral history informs us that a leader among them decreed that the Peruvian colonists had sent the disease as a new weapon and that their only chance for survival was to lay down their arms, burn their magical plants for war, and allow the whites to enter their valley. A series of gift exchanges took place with some residents of Huancabamba, until finally, as the Amuesha tell it, they amassed on the bank of the Chorobamba river opposite the hacienda 'Carolina.' One by one they crossed the river, shaking with fear, and walked into the arms of the Peruvian residents."[8]

Hacienda owners sought help from the Catholic Church to complete the conquest of the valleys inhabited by the Yanesha (Amuesha). German colonists were also invited to settle there and help in the "civilization" of the Indians. The Church acquired title to vast expanses of land from the Peruvian government, ostensibly to protect the rights of indigenous peoples, in whose name the titles were offered. The Yanesha, however, were never informed of the terms of the agreement, and were subsequently required to work several days a week for the Church in payment for their right to occupy their own lands. In the 1940s, lumber companies entered the area and were able to buy land from the Church. Yanesha leaders who objected to business deals between the companies and the Church were jailed, and years of litigation ensued. Although court cases over this dispute, as well as many others between natives and colonizers, usually ended up in favor of the natives, the government never did anything to insure implementation of these decisions. More and more land was seized violently by outsiders; those who resisted and tried to preserve the territory for native use were violently repressed. Coffee plantations and lumber operations flourished, and North American Protestant missionaries established a large settlement in the region to "save" those Indians who had not been adequately "civilized" by Catholics. Many Yanesha came to regard themselves and their culture with shame and to see their native religious practices as superstitious. The poverty and severe exploitations of natives were, however, a source of renewed conflict with outsiders, and came to be an embarrassment and threat to the government. By the time General Velasco seized power in Lima, in 1968, the pacification of the Amazon region had become a priority of government.

Under the military regime, provisions of agrarian reform established boundaries in disputed areas, giving natives certain areas where their rights were to be at least temporarily protected, while giving colonizers title to other areas. Velasco's policies permitted the continued colonization of the area, but under government supervision. Natives were required to entitle *comunidades nativas,* the counterpart to the *comunidades campesinas* of the sierra. In addition, they were promised government assistance to help them develop the means to integrate themselves into the Peruvian economy without becoming servants and peons to foreigners.

Like earlier attempts to recognize the existence of natives in areas that were considered to be frontiers for conquest by those who were seeking quick profits, agrarian reform under the military regime failed to provide the Indians adequate means for economic survival in a territory that was constantly shrinking. It gave them no way at all to defend themselves militarily.

As in the rest of the country, reform programs recognized only male "heads of households" as representatives of the people, disregarding the historic roles of women in economic and political life. Also, as in other places, churches were given power to distribute relief commodities in times of severe hardship. In the jungle, hardship was caused mainly by flooding and other disasters brought on by destruction of the regional ecology. Native

women were enrolled in Mothers' Clubs, where they were encouraged to behave as "proper wives," which meant subordinating themselves to men and cooperating with colonizers.

Missionaries of the Summer Institute of Linguistics—an extension of the Wycliffe Bible Academy of Oklahoma (U.S.A.)—catalogued native languages and documented the habits and beliefs of the natives, established churches among them, and employed them as servants at their settlement in Pucallpa, but did nothing to provide education or skills that would help the natives to defend themselves against the "march to the jungle" being promoted by government. The institute's identification with the U.S. Central Intelligence Agency and with government schemes for intensified colonization of the region provoked the hostility of some native leaders, who called for the expulsion of missionaries from the area. The government, under pressure from native organizations, gave the institute four years to complete its linguistic work and prepare to leave.

In 1980, the civilian regime of Belaúnde extended the missionaries' stay to ten years, slowed down or blocked the process of giving legal recognition to native communities, and invited Catholics and evangelical Protestants not connected with the SIL to extend their influence in the area. The Belaúnde government also invited U.S. AID to help plan and finance the construction of roads and a model city that would make possible the extraction of raw materials from the jungle by multinationals. With increasing privatization of "development" of the region, the "clandestine" cultivation, refinement, and export of cocaine grew to scandalous proportions. Campaigns to wipe out cocaine plants hurt natives and small-scale cultivators more than speculators and dealers, serving as an excuse to further dislocate natives. The campaign against the cocaine trade also made it easy to isolate and jail the defenders and allies of natives by arresting them on phony drug charges.

Schoolgirls performing for their parents in Satipo. Integration into national life occurs at the expense of native pride and prosperity. (Monika Lupescher)

Natives were increasingly forced to choose sides among contenders for power in the region near each river, or within each political organization. Some groups with long histories of opposition to imperialist schemes were given special favors in return for nominal support for government and business designs on the region. Among the Yanesha, however, native leadership was able to bring about the federation of some thirty-six communities in solid opposition to further foreign penetration and economic development under multinational control.

Federation of Indians in the Pichis-Palcazú River Area (Chanchamaya and Oxapampa)

In July 1982 I was a guest at a week-long congress of Yanesha Indians held at Puerto Amistad, in Oxapampa province, Cerro de Pasco. I had met the young *cornesha* (political or religious leader) and other members of the Federación de Comunidades Nativas Yanesha when they visited Lima to present a series of complaints to the government. They had offered support to the Comunidad Feminina Micaela Bastidas, where I was staying, during the community's struggle against eviction.

The Yanesha congress was not held in secret. During the first days, uninvited representatives of the Summer Institute of Linguistics and of the U.S. AID project being promoted in the region were in attendance. But as the congress proceeded, it became clear that the outcome would be the consolidation of opposition to foreign plans for the Amazon region and the denial of Yanesha cooperation in these plans. Another outcome of the meetings—one that had probably not been foreseen by most of its organizers—was the emergence of female leadership in an organization that had been entirely male. The congress was the first public manifestation of female rebellion against the manipulation of women by church and state. The process of subordinating women to men was one in which native men had been complicit, and was not likely to be challenged without strong and determined leadership by Yanesha women.

On the first day of the congress, a young woman who was head of agricultural production in her community was elected to the federation's four-member *directiva*. She was one of only two or three Yanesha women who had come to the congress. For many of the nearly two hundred who attended, the congress had meant traveling for days or weeks along jungle trails or rivers and streams. I learned that in Yanesha communities there are women *jefas* (elders or leaders) as well as male *jefes,* and that women's assemblies meet traditionally to discuss issues of concern to women. When I asked several people why *jefas* had not served as delegates from their communities, I was told, "The boat wasn't big enough." Probing further, I learned that most women had young children who would have to accompany them, taking up valuable space, and that women couldn't leave their agricultural work for such a long time. No one gave as a reason for the preponderance of men at the congress the fact that government structures set up by the reform programs to define *comunidades nativas* did not recognize the parallel leadership of women and men. This did come up, however, at one of the commission meetings, where the formation of a Women's Secretariat for the federation was proposed. The secretariat's task was to be the assessment of women's situation in each community, and the preparation of a program of action for women.

A Secretariat of Youth was also proposed in order to educate and mobilize young people to stay in their communities and join in the struggle for the renovation of cultural life among natives. Young men and women had begun to seek stimulation elsewhere, leading them to involvement in drug trafficking and prostitution. The Secretariat of Youth was also intended to provide material support for all the children of the community, many of whom were being reared by single mothers who could not adequately provide for them. The fear of annihilation through malnutrition and disease forced the men to accept the idea of responsibility for other than their own kin, a step toward renewal of reciprocal agreements that had been broken with the "civilization" of native communities.

Teresa, the young woman who had been elected to the *directiva* on the first day of the congress, had introduced the proposals

Yanesha federation meets in Puerto Amistad. Women are reclaiming their places alongside men in the organized defense of native territory and native culture. (Ernesto Jimenez)

for a Women's Secretariat and a Secretariat of Youth, and she presented them to the congress, speaking assertively but without rancor of the terrible oppression of Yanesha women and of women's need to speak out about their own problems and to organize to act in their own interests. She said women desperately needed the help of the entire community in rearing their children and that they needed to join in the worldwide struggle for women's liberation in order to bring about equality between women and men. "We are just as intelligent as men and we work harder than men. We deserve to be treated with respect and to fight against the missionary clubs that give us little gifts while at the same time they try to deform our minds." Later she told a reporter: "I'm a single mother and I have one daughter. Part of my time is spent working and the rest visiting in the communities, educating others. My little girl gets sacrificed to my work because I have to leave her with my mother or someone else. I do this so her life will be better than mine. It's not easy to live alone with children as so many of us do. It's an honor for me and a matter of pride for our federation that I'm involved in its leadership. It's necessary because it's obvious that with the colonization of our territory there are many dangers. We have to prepare ourselves so we won't be taken advantage of like so many have been. One way to start is to support our *compañeras,* to support the women who want to learn, so they can all be part of the struggle. Don't you agree?"9

Teresa's intervention in the Yanesha congress took place without fanfare, and her proposals were accepted without debate. A number of women who lived in the vicinity of Puerto Amistad, where the congress was held, sat on the ground or stood under trees with babies in arms watching the proceedings. They listened soberly to Teresa's words, and one refused to leave when her husband ordered her to return to where the women were preparing meals, but it seemed to me the audience as a whole had failed to sense the importance of her words. I remarked about this to one of the male leaders of the federation when he asked my impressions of the congress, and that evening he recited to the gathering a poem he had composed in order to give special emphasis to the things Teresa had said and to encourage delegates to bring many women to the federation's next congress. I felt that the burden of making that happen would inevitably fall on Teresa, however, since most of the men did not seem to understand the radical implications of what was taking place. This was borne out in the days that followed. A confrontation with the U.S. AID representative made necessary the formation of a special commission that was to go to Lima after the congress to insist on his expulsion from the jungle. Twelve men made up this commission, and there was no discussion of sending any women.

Important decisions were taken in Lima, where the Yanesha men, dressed in their native robes, made public their united opposition to the government's refusal to recognize the federation and its leadership. No doubt the men were convinced that government officials would be more likely to recognize them if no women were present. They were, however, refused a hearing both in Peruvian government offices and in the offices of U.S. AID.

As reports of open conflict in the jungle began to be heard in the capital, government counterinsurgency forces called for the arrest of a number of native leaders, who were forced to keep continually on the move to avoid detention. The political mobilization of women, already underway, was hastened by the need to confront new dangers facing the long-suffering inhabitants of the selva.

Cultural Revival in the Jungle

Among the resolutions adopted at the Yanesha congress was one calling for all the communities in the river basins occupied by the *Yanesha* to assume control of the cultural center set up in the jungle by foreign anthropologists. This was felt to be necessary so that the center would not create divisions among them or provide special privileges for paid staff who had begun to behave as if they

felt superior to others. Another resolution called on the communities to revive the practice of native religion and give up ad-
herence to Christian doctrines which demeaned them and divided
them as a people. The leader who presented the last motion had
himself come under missionary influence at one time and was not
dressed in native garb as were the young members of the *directiva*.
He was a former leader of the federation, and his willingness to
serve as a spokesperson for the cause of cultural revival made it
easier to achieve unity among delegates.

While the vote on the resolution regarding religion was unanimous, it was obvious that some Yanesha would not so easily give
up habitual denigration of their own native culture. At night,
when the old men and their young protégés[10] began beating
drums and blowing panpipes under bright moonlight, and the old
women began screeching their words of native wisdom, women
and children came from the surroundinng forest, where they had
been sleeping, to join in the dancing. Pockets of young men
avoided the native celebration and listened instead to taped *huaynos*
(music of the sierra) and *cumbias* (music of the coast) in secluded
places. The houses of Puerto Amistad had been built to facilitate
community gatherings and were filled only when people left their
huts in surrounding areas to come together for meetings and
celebrations. On the night when the dancing began, it was not
clear at first that many delegates to the congress intended to
participate. Not until the women and children came out of their
huts did the others begin to join, some of them for the first time in
their lives.

When the congress was over, I was invited, along with several
others, to visit Huacamayo, where a Protestant evangelical sect
had begun to invade native territory. The purpose of our visit was
to witness the invasion in order to help in the natives' defense. By
the time we arrived, the household where we stayed had already
heard about the decisions taken at the congress. Six families lived
together under one roof in a clearing in the forest. None of the
women had attended the congress, but one of them was extremely
knowledgeable about the issues that had been discussed. She was
excited about the decision taken regarding religion and had already
painted her face to celebrate it. She said she didn't know any of the

songs the older women knew and wanted to tape them so she could learn them. She told me the history of the community, how they had been robbed of land they hoped to cultivate communally so they could gain money to improve the health and education of their children. According to natives, government officials had sent a priest around to get signatures from them through deception. Now they were being invaded again, by Peruvians armed with machetes and guns who were fleeing drought-stricken areas in the sierra in search of "the promised land." Complaints to the government had brought a parliamentary delegation to the area, but the parliamentarians spoke only with the invaders, ignoring those who had made the complaints. Then they recommended the formation of a commission to "improve communications" between the parties in the dispute.

The Peruvian government does not recognize the ecological limitations of the tropical rain forest, which cannot tolerate either continual cultivation or grazing. Once the forest is removed, the land becomes dry and infertile within a few years. Those colonists who have learned from natives to let the land revert periodically to forest, planting in each cleared plot for only a short time, are also threatened with the loss of their land to newcomers. The land is taken from them by newcomers on the pretext that it is being "neglected." The government wants to assure that Peru's borders will be protected from neighboring countries because of the valuable resources the region contains—especially petroleum. Colonization of the jungle is also seen as a way to reduce unemployment and counteract the effects of natural devastation in other parts of the country, problems that have occurred because of a lack of planning and regulation during the process of "development." Though the colonists who move into the area and cooperate with the multinationals may be faced with starvation when the natural resources of the jungle are depleted, they are preferred by government officials to the natives and earlier settlers, who have already become hostile to the government.

Cultural conflict between the natives and the new immigrant Protestants is bound to compound the difficulties of survival for both groups. Of special interest to me were the differences in how the women of the two groups regarded themselves and were regarded by men. The newly arrived Protestants were Indians, but they wore headcoverings and dressed "modestly" to indicate their subordination to men. They are probably more sexually restricted than any other group of women in Peru, while the native women of the selva are among the least affected by bodily shame.

The rejection of Protestant religion by the Yanesha was, I think, seen by native women as an assertion of their right to continue enjoying their own sexuality, something evangelicals have tried to deny them, as did representatives of the Catholic Church during earlier periods. At the same time that natives have been threatened with sexual exploitation by mestizos or foreigners, they have been told by missionaries that they must protect themselves by covering their bodies and denying their own sexual appetites, by becoming "decent" or "civilized." Some native women of the selva realize that when they defend themselves against such ideas, they gain a victory for women everywhere.

On my last visit to Peru, I became acquainted with several Shipiba women who live outside Pucallpa, where they have organized a cooperative for making and selling traditional jewelry and clothing. Shipibas, unlike their husbands, wear native clothing when they come to Lima to market their wares. As I was about to leave the country, my friend removed the beautifully made knife that had been hanging loosely from a cord around her neck and handed it to me with a broad smile. She had told me that Shipibas traditionally fought with each other over men, using knives such as the one she carried with her. By giving me her knife, she was making it a symbol of our friendship, but I think she also meant to send with me a complex message to other women, a message of respect for her own culture as well as a sense of sisterhood in the struggle to solve shared problems.

Traditional Life in the Andes

In the Andean mountain regions bordering the Peruvian jungle, the regions least affected by mestizo or foreign influence, the balance between men and women in complementary work roles can be seen in its purest form. The harmony or balance of power that is necessary in work and family life is expressed in the concept of *chachawarmi* (in the Aymará language) or *ayni* (in Quechua). Wife-beating is a violation of *chachawarmi,* and men who are abusive of women in any way are considered unmasculine.

Included in the concept of *ayni* or *chachawarmi* is a division of labor which makes community members dependent on each other.[11] Both men and women weave, but they make different kinds of cloth. Men, for instance, make the stuff of clothing, and women make blankets and ponchos. Jobs that are sex-typed because of physical aptitude are least rigid, and most can be exchanged when necessary, so that complementarity is based more on culture than on biology (and so that community members can survive without their spouses). Property "belongs" to whoever commonly uses it. Decisions about birth control and the distribution of agricultural products are traditionally made by women.

Andean communities have ritualized ways of maintaining a balance between women and men. Groups of men and women often sit on a hillside in the evening singing improvised *huaynos* that are half-joking insults passed between them. Women have license to throw rocks at men who have offended them or who persist in begging them for sex when they are not in the mood. Men joke about the burden of keeping their mates satisfied sexually, as if that were the only reason for their insistence on making love. Women and men spit at each other when fighting in private, and women publicly berate their husbands on certain fiesta days, when drinking by both men and women is customary.

All of these ritualized ways of preserving a balance of power in relationships between women and men are forgotten or put aside when people of the sierra migrate to the city. There, a man who submits to a woman's demands is quickly labeled *"varon dominado," "pisado,"* or *saco largo"* (dominated man, one who is stepped on).[12] Wives complain that the attention and helpfulness of husbands during the early months of their lives together give way to sulkiness and refusal of friendship as children appear and economic difficulties mount. These tendencies are also evident in the mountains wherever mestizo culture has penetrated.

The music of the mountains reflects the struggles women

have had in retaining friendships with men. One woman who has been collecting and translating *huaynos* for thirty years told me: "The *huayno* in pure Quechua is innocent, profound . . . the *huayno* expressed in a mixture of Quechua and Spanish shows malice, offense, and insult; when it's stylized, it becomes gross and offensive to women." Most *huaynos* in Quechua address themselves to flowers or animals, mountains or rocks, though the theme is often one of love or sorrow. Songs may be sung by either a man or a woman without distinction, while those in Spanish are more often addressed either to a man or to a woman. Women sing Spanish songs about husbands who drink *("entre licuor y licuor")* and about suicide ("While you'll be eating at the *fiesta,* the worms will be eating me in my grave . . ."). Some *huaynos* compare men's treatment of wives to the way meat is pounded for cooking or to the way animals are dragged by ropes to slaughter. One ends with the refrain, "Better I should throw myself into the river than marry," while another, which recounts the suffering of married women as well as the unsatisfying experience of the single woman who is "eaten like an apple and then tossed to the ground," ends with the refrain, "So I'd like to marry you—but just for tonight!"

In spite of the strong tradition of partnership between women and men in the sierra (or perhaps because of it?) women have deliberately separated themselves from men when they could not maintain equality and respect—or when men succumbed too rapidly to foreign ways. In the puna, where women pasture animals seven or eight months of every year, many continue to practice ancient religious rituals in an effort to restore balance to their lives by communication with the spirits of animals and ancestors. Some have even taken on the roles of men in communicating with male ancestors. Such women are accused of witchcraft by church authorities, although accusations of witchcraft are ludicrous, because concepts of "good" and "evil" are not part of indigenous religion.

I was told in the Department of Puno that many Indian dances are inspired by confrontation with Europeans. These dances ridicule the Spanish for their superstitious beliefs. In one of these, a woman who is identifiable as "European" by her short skirt, her

Huaynos, *the music of the sierra, often express the sadness or outrage of forced marriage or the loneliness of lovers forced to separate. Composing humorous* huaynos *helps couples contend with the problems of married life. (Jean-Pierre Perpoil)*

Women make costumes for native celebrations mocking the conquistadores. *The doll represents the Christ child. (Jean-Pierre Perpoil)*

angel's wings, and her knight's headdress, blows a whistle as she high-steps around the dance area, commandeering elaborately costumed devils in wild escapades.

After hundreds of years of nominal Catholicism in the sierra, the principal deity is still Pachamama, the embodiment of all natural phenomena: "Everything that exists is part of her or comes from her. The past generates the present, and is the present, just as the present generates the future, and is the future. . . . Those who die were born of Pachamama and return to her, thus returning to life. Pachamama contains all those who will be born in the future, and cares lovingly for all those who are presently living on earth. Since the entire universe contains the life-giving force of Pachamama, in her is concentrated all space, all being, and all time."[13] In the Department of Junín, where many men work in mining towns and many women are engaged in commerce out of necessity (though they continue to conduct agricultural work with little help from men), celebrations regularly honor the "goddesses" of the moon, corn, water, and potatoes. The moon is particularly important because the planting and harvesting of crops are traditionally done by lunar calendar. The Catholic saints are sometimes the embodiment of such native or natural deities.

I discovered on a recent visit to Junín that priests in the Mantaro Valley had been instructed to remove the statues of the saints from the chapels of the churches and store them in the basement. Parishioners were told they had erringly used the saints to practice idolatry instead of worshipping "God the Father." Even the Virgin Mary was controversial because she was identified with the moon, Mamaquilla, and with the pleasures of unmarried love. In another part of Junín, comuneros who were in conflict with the government over control of the land phrased their protest in religious terms, promising to give their lives for Mother Earth if necessary: "In Otocsaico, all the *ondoriños,* with the faith and confidence of old, swore never to abandon their mother, whom they have been seeking for so long. They must be prepared to give their lives for her, by reinforcing their *guardias campesinas* and *comités de damas.*"[14]

Defense of the land and defense of language, religion, and culture are inextricably connected. Peruvian women have been more consistent than men in understanding these connections. Yet the survival of the women and their families today depends on mastery of communication skills and technical knowledge that comes from foreigners. Those women who wear braids and *bolas* (full skirts) and who carry babies and bundles on their backs also want access to trains, telephones, and tractors. Many are hungry for education and look to outsiders to help them, but they want interaction with outsiders to take place on their own terms.

The women of the high sierra, like the women of the tropical rain forest, have never had anyone they could trust to represent their interests in the Peruvian government. Most of them would not be able to speak to government officials directly even if they were invited to do so, because they do not speak the same language. In conversations among themselves, they speak of "Peruvians" as foreigners, as people of "another world," but one that affects them more and more. The campesino union, which recently began to recognize the rural women's right to a voice in deciding their own future, did so only after many women of the sierra had begun to turn to open insurrection against the state. In the central provinces of Ayacucho and Apurimac, it was the guerrillas of Sendero Luminoso who began, in the 1980s, to provide a dramatic outlet for women's frustration and anger against the powerful men who controlled their destinies.

The Guerrillas

It was in the Department of Ayacucho that the last battle against the Spanish was fought in South America. Hundreds of years earlier, according to *ayacuchanos,* their ancestors fought against Inca domination, thus inheriting the name, Aya-cucho, which means, in Quechua, "corner of the dead." Stories of these battles always note that women fought ferociously alongside men.

Some women of Ayacucho and Apurimac participated actively in the guerrilla movements of the 1960s, which were centered in nearby Cuzco. Women also joined men in rebelling against the military government of Juan Alvarado Velasco when disappointed in the advance of promised reforms. In June 1969, forty *ayacuchanos* died in one day's fighting against the rule of hacendados in the countryside; three days later, the government promulgated agrarian reform. Within a year a group of mothers and secondary school students were protesting a new law that would have required a special fee of students who reentered school after having been temporarily absent. They succeeded in having the law revoked. However, during the struggle over this issue, twelve students died. The streets of Ayacucho bear their names, and they are honored as martyrs throughout the region.

The Universidad de San Cristóbal de Huamanga, located in the city of Ayacucho, was for many years an intellectual and cultural center that attracted from all over the world people who were interested in the history and philosophy of the Andean people. It was at this university that a social movement was born in the early 1970s, and it was to become the greatest challenge to the Peruvian government since the revolt against the Spanish crown in the early 1800s. A split in the Communist Party of Peru (PCP), led by a philosophy teacher at the university, resulted in the formation of a student organization, Federación Estudiantil Revolucionaria, por el Camino del Sendero Luminoso de Mariátegui (FER, "for the shining path of Mariátegui").

The name the students chose for the organization honored José Carlos Mariátegui, founder in 1924 of what later became the Communist Party of Peru. Although Mariátegui lived to be only thirty-five, his activities in editing, writing, and coordinating workers' struggles and indigenous movements in Peru made him the *amauta,* or teacher, of all Peruvian revolutionaries. Many barriadas, bookstores, publications, and popular organizations throughout the country bear his name. Among the first publications of the senderistas, as they came to be called, were a booklet about the feminism of Mariátegui and a reprint of Alexandra Kollontai's essay, *Love in a Communist Society.*[15] Mariátegui had written an essay in the 1920s describing feminism as a progressive movement that should be wholeheartedly embraced by communists. He made distinctions, however, among expressions of feminism which he called bourgeois, petty-bourgeois, and proletarian.[16] The senderistas picked up on the ideas of Mariátegui and organized a Movimiento Femenino Popular. They began working among miner's wives to help establish cottage industries so that women could improve the conditions of their lives in the mining towns. They emphasized the problems women faced because of economic dependence on men. Members of the movement engaged in public debates challenging other Maoists who insisted that the "woman question" did not merit the attention the senderistas were giving it. As early as 1973, the senderistas published a program on women's rights. Later, they organized a National Student Conference on the Emancipation of Women. In 1975, they held a National Convention of Working Women; it was the first event of its kind in the country.

After these first years of activism among students and women, the wing of the Communist Party of Peru which was centered in Ayacucho itself came to be known as Sendero Luminoso. The student movement had suffered severe repression when government troops took over the university, and the party was temporarily disoriented by the deterioration of the economic and political situation in the country and by changes that occurred in China after the death of Mao.[17] Many of its members returned to their home communities to live as campesinos or sought other work in rural areas. They shared the poverty, the language, and the customs of the people, who were without doubt the most destitute in Peru.

Frustrated by the failure of reforms promulgated in Lima and by the stagnation of an economy directed by banking interests outside the country, a majority of the senderistas decided that a return to civilian government would not signify any improvement in the situation. They decided to boycott the elections of 1980 that the military government was organizing. In part, the senderistas refused to participate in the elections because it would have forced them to form an alliance with Left parties led almost exclusively by mestizos and, in some cases, linked ideologically with governments they considered to be bureaucratic or "revisionist," including both China and the Soviet Union. At the same time, they decided to give less attention to the education and organization of women workers in order to dedicate themselves to preparations for armed struggle. The PCP-Sendero Luminoso became a tightly disciplined clandestine organization, but it never abandoned its

Ashaninkas live in constant fear of incursions by speculators and the abuse of soldiers. Their territory is coveted by foreign profiteers and colonizers who hope to displace the natives by terror. (Monika Lupescher)

A young girl in Vincos, Ayacucho, inherits an indigenous culture little influenced by foreign domination. The survival of Ayacucho children into adulthood depends on the outcome of civil war. Whole villages have been massacred because the inhabitants supported guerrillas or because they did not vote in elections or refused to move to military control zones. (Lynn Murray)

commitment to sexual equality within the party. Some women abandoned the organization at this time because they thought the militarization of the party was a retreat from feminism, which they felt could only be advanced if internal struggle against male domination was backed up by a conscious mass movement of women. At any rate, since that time, the thousands of military actions initiated by Sendero Luminoso indicate that they are preparing for a prolonged war, surrounding the cities militarily while weakening them from within. Anticipating outside intervention against them by both the Soviet Union and the United States, they say their goal is to attain state power definitively by the year 2000.

Escalation of Military Encounters

The predominance of women in the desolate mountain region where the Sendero Luminoso movement first flourished helped to guarantee that the organization would not be dominated by men. While the principal founder was a man, and the movement attracted other men who were campesino union leaders from Andahuaylas (Apurimac), the outstanding military commanders have been women. The organization recruits mainly from secondary schools, conducting *escuelas populares* (peoples' schools) in which the large majority of students are reportedly female.

The military operations of Sendero Luminoso began in Chuschi, a small town in the Department of Ayacucho, where election urns were burned on May 18, 1980, and senderistas took control of municipal offices. Chuschi has been noted by anthropologists as a place where last names, even more than first names, are given according to the sex of the child. In other words, there are certain surnames given only to women and others given only to men. In Chuschi, as in most of Ayacucho and Apurimac, women who pasture animals live alone with their young children in huts made of straw, where they also occupy themselves with making ponchos and growing whatever crops will survive in the puna. Men bring provisions from the communities below, where they live with the older children, who attend school and occupy themselves mostly with agriculture.

Families come together frequently or infrequently, depending on accessibility and the demands of work. During the months when agricultural activity is most demanding, women come down from the puna to live with the men. According to anthropologists who grew up in the region, unmarried women who live in the puna organize parties whenever possible, calling on a certain number of young men to climb uphill to join them in dancing and singing and engaging in erotic games which end in temporary mating. Marriages which take place later are, however, not necessarily related to these events. In any case, women seem to appreciate men at the same time that they enjoy a certain independence from them, both economically and socially.

During my most recent visit to Peru, in 1984, I met four sisters from the city of Abancay (Apurimac) who appeared at a communal work event in the indigenous community where they grew up. They hoped meet their mother, whom they had not seen since they descended from the puna four years earlier. They had been angry with her because she had taken on a new lover after rejecting their own father for drinking too much. Her new companion was also a heavy drinker. As the daughters were growing older themselves and having their own problems with men, they wanted to reconnect with their mother, but were not ready to go looking for her on the high mountaintops. They were also worried about her because of drought that was devastating the region. By coming to the workday event, they could at least count on receiving news of her from other women. When I asked some of the women from the puna how often they saw their husbands, other than during harvest time and communal workdays, they told me that they generally got together on Sundays when their husbands came to help them work in the *chacras* where they raised corn. They said that fiestas were only celebrated twice a year, that young people had very little opportunity to know each other before pairing, but that few mated permanently in any case. In other communities I was told that men are "scarce" not only because many leave their communities to seek paid work, but also because those who remain have begun to die young from drinking.

These conversations helped me to understand why guerrilla women are able to gain the respect and support of many com-

uneros in spite of the demands they make on them. When guerrillas enter a village to carry out *"justicia popular"* against those
who are buying up the land of poor campesinos, threatening a
return of the hacendado system, they address villagers from a
rooftop in the village square, talk to them for hours about their
reasons for making war on the government, and call on others to
join them. Sometimes, after forcing those who do not support
them to resign their positions in the village government, and after
redistributing the land and goods of the community and canceling
debts owed by poor campesinos, senderistas party with the villagers. When they depart, they disappear while climbing up
mountain pathways to the high regions where they can protect
themselves from government troops, the same regions where
many of them would live out their lives whether a war was going
on or not.

After gaining effective control of the area surrounding
Chuschi, the senderistas initiated a campaign to restrict imports
and exports from the region; their aim was to establish a self-
sufficient economy as a base for future actions. Businessmen and
their families took their possessions and left the area. The guerrillas organized villagers to control petty crime and prostitution in
the areas under their control. In March 1982 Sendero Luminoso
attacked the state prison in Ayacucho, freeing 360 prisoners, many
of whom were political prisoners. The action demonstrated the
government's impotence before the guerrillas, since none of those
freed were ever located by government officials. It also demonstrated the confidence of the guerrilla organization in its women
leaders, since the action was led by a woman. During the rest of
that year, senderistas carried out hundreds of attacks on government installations, using dynamite hurled by homemade
slingshots. Dynamite was stolen from the mines, and automatic
weapons were stolen from the police—sometimes by young
women who lured them away from their posts and then disarmed
them.

By the end of 1982 the guerrillas had a large part of the central
sierra under their control. Even when the government was able to
capture some of the guerrilla leaders, they were unable to keep
them in prison. This was the case with Edith Lagos, a woman of

nineteen who had led the assault on the prison in Ayacucho as well as many other guerrilla activities. The government tried to imprison her several times, unsuccessfully. However, in September 1982 she was captured, and she was later declared dead by the authorities. Her family suspected that she had not been killed in battle, as government officials had said, but that she had been tortured and assassinated after being detained. Their suspicions were confirmed when they reclaimed her body. When they brought her body from Andahuaylas to Ayacucho, crowds met them all along the way, paying tribute to her. According to a *Wall Street Journal* article recapitulating the events: "More than 30,000 people attended Edith's funeral, a number equivalent to half the population of Ayacucho and more than double the number of tourists and local people who used to flock to the city's famous Holy Week processions."[18] In spite of the state of siege that existed in the province, Edith's body was clothed for burial in her green guerrilla uniform and red beret, her poetry was read aloud by her sister, the local radio station was taken over to denounce government actions, and members of the municipal council who had been partisans of Acción Popular, the party of President Belaúnde, resigned their posts and their membership in the party.

One of the poems read by Edith's sister at her funeral ends with the following words, which expresses the unity of the people of the sierra, in life and death, with the wildflowers, the sky, the mountains, and the rocks:

> Yerba silvestre, aroma puro
> Te ruego accompañarme en mi camino
> Serás mi aroma y mi gloria
> Serás mi amiga cuando crezcas sobre mi tumba
> Allí, que la montaña me cobije
> Que el cielo me responda
> Y en la piedra lápida todo quedará grabado.[19]

Faced with the popularity of Sendero Luminoso in the region, the government was reluctant to send the army to the central sierra. Disputes between the local Guardia Civil and the Guardia Republicana had already developed. The Guardia Republicana was

Wall posters support the takeover of factories by women workers and promote the Movimiento Feminino Popular. *(Lynn Murray)*

Edith Lagos, who led the attack on the Ayacucho prison in March 1982, died under torture after her detention. Her funeral was the occasion for popular takeover of the city. (Naomi Walsh)

Edith Lagos

accused of attacking the civilian population and attributing their actions to guerrillas. However, under pressure from the United States government, which also provided military assistance and equipment, thousands of soldiers began pouring into the area in January 1983. They threatened death to anyone who betrayed sympathy for the guerrillas, and even to those who obeyed senderistas out of fear.

After the Peruvian army entered the area, atrocities and massacres were reported on both sides, including the murder of eight journalists who were attempting to investigate the credibility of government reports. Given the government's embarrassment over the death of the journalists, and rising protests all over the country about the abusiveness of the military toward civilians, the *sinchis,* or counterinsurgency forces, were withdrawn temporarily in June 1983.[20] However, the entire country was declared in a state of emergency, and counterinsurgency forces were later increased.

In spite of the freedom given government troops to use whatever force was needed to wipe out the guerrillas and their supporters, armed struggle did not cease. Instead, it spread to every region of Peru. Many people fled central Andean towns to avoid being caught in the cross fire. But new recruits to the guerrilla movement became active in other parts of the country, including both the department and the city of Lima.

The repression of the guerrillas, and the declaration of a state of emergency, were intended to bring all public organizing against the government to a halt. Civil liberties, including the right to assembly, were suspended. The Left Unity electoral coalition and other popular organizations entered into intense internal debate about the significance of the political crisis created by the standoff between the guerrillas and the government. Restrictions on public meetings and demonstrations were openly defied throughout the country. Strikes in copper mines that began in July 1983 were backed up by **extended** strikes in other sectors of the work force, including campesinos. United States aid to Peruvian counterinsurgency programs jumped from $3.5 million in 1983 to over $9 million in 1984. Yet the situation appeared to be one the government of Fernando Belaúnde Terry would be unable to control.

7 : *Feminism and Popular Struggle*

Increase in Anti-Government
and Popular Struggle

FEMINIST ORGANIZATIONS in Peru were among the first to come to the defense of prisoners arrested under the "antiterrorist law" the Belaúnde government decreed after the assault on the Ayacucho prison. Feminists denouced the systematic use of torture and rape by government officials. While many leaders of left-wing electoral coalitions were joining government officials in denouncing armed struggle as "terrorism," feminists were declaring: "Apart from the political positions that each of these women may represent . . . we believe that they represent the surfacing of the economic crisis and social discontent that all women in our country are experiencing."[1]

Within a few weeks of Edith Lagos' funeral, a woman who had directed one of Edith's earlier escapes from prision was said to have replaced her as the leading figure among guerrillas in the Ayacucho region. Carla Carlota Tutti soon became a folk heroine throughout the country. News stories about her capture by officials were regularly followed by evidence that she was still alive. Her *compañero* was said to have died during the prison attack in which both participated; after that, rumors began to circulate about her giving birth to a baby in the midst of a big celebration in the high puna where guerrilla bases were located.

The names of other women said to be leading guerrilla actions in various parts of the country began to appear in Lima newspapers almost daily. In July 1984, a woman arrested in Lima was identified by the government as the principal leader of the Communist Party of Peru—Sendero Luminoso in the capital. She was a former schoolteacher named Laura Zambrano. Her arrest came after a series of guerrilla actions had jolted the city, following the government's refusal to negotiate with striking schoolteachers, students, and state employees. The leadership of the teachers' union in Lima and in several provincial towns had by this time been assumed by women.

The state employees' union, the Confederación Intersectorial de Trabajadores Estatales (CITE), had been formed in 1979. The national strike whch began in June 1984 was its first such action. The union represented over half a million state employees, those who worked in the ministries of the central government as well as state hospital employees and other workers in public institutions, the majority of whom were women. Hundreds of thousands of women were brought into a high level of political struggle for the first time in their lives through their involvement in CITE. Some of those who organized the union, however, brought years of experience in political struggle to their work. In 1984, the union took a position of open opposition to government policies, calling for annulment of the government's pact with the International Monetary Fund, repudiation of the foreign debt, and the nationalization of large businesses and banks. In its national congress, held in August 1984, CITE also called for discussion at the local level of international questions involving Central America, Afghanistan, and Poland.

When the government refused to negotiate with the striking teachers and state employees, denouncing union activity as an attack on the government itself, strikers and their supporters did not retreat. Instead, they displayed huge banners which read: "Bring down the government!" They continued to march in the streets in defiance of a government ban on meetings and demonstrations. Government officials, in spite of repeated declarations that they would not capitulate to strikers, finally met some of their demands, and strikers returned to work. Soon afterwards, however, in a three-day military operation during which civil rights were suspended throughout the country, police forces, aided by the army, reportedly arrested more than twenty thousand people.

These extraordinary measures did not stem popular revolt. Within a few weeks, guerrillas expanded their territory dramatically, forcing the government to transfer counterinsurgency forces stationed in Ayacucho to other parts of the country, including the jungle.[2] CITE began organizing for another strike to begin in October.

It was during these days that the arrest of Laura Zambrano took place. Her detention was followed by reports that she was being tortured barbarically. When she was brought to court for a hearing, the judge was forced to suspend it because of the state of her health. Public protests forced a medical review of the case, which asserted that Laura had a broken nose and other facial wounds, bruises all over her body, and cuts in her vagina and rectum. The fate of other women prisoners was largely unknown, since the government suspended family visitation on the grounds that subversive literature had been encountered inside the women's prison. Young men who were seen by police at night painting grafitti on walls in support of Laura were gunned down. At the same time, banners announcing the birth of new guerrilla organizations began to appear in the streets of Lima.[3]

Even those Peruvians who were hostile to the guerrillas appeared to be impressed by the success of guerrilla attacks reportedly led by women. The attention to women's participation in revolutionary activity stimulated a flurry of publicity for women in the armed forces of Peru, who were depicted as gallant defenders of the country's honor. There was speculation that President Belaúnde, whose party had suffered an enormous defeat at the polls in the municipal elections of 1983, and whose candidacy in the 1985 presidential elections was prohibited by law in any case, would encourage his wife to run for the office.

Some of those who opposed the spread of armed struggle in

The standoff between people and government is symbolized by a young girl already accustomed to political struggle. She and her compatriots demonstrate in defiance of a state of emergency declared by President Belaunde. (Marta Serra)

Peru did so because they felt it was ill-timed, in view of popular gains at the polls in literally all the country's major cities during the municipal elections. It was generally admitted, however, that the challenge of the guerrillas had forced the electoral Left to mobilize and unite its forces. Some leftists felt that guerrillas were too quick to judge who should be punished as exploiters or government collaborators. Whether politically active or not, many felt unjustly caught "in the middle." In some rural areas, union activists organized vigilante groups to oppose both government terrorism and guerrillas who entered their villages. In others, the government stepped up its organization of paramilitary forces among campesinos, forcing them at gunpoint to cooperate or to move to areas under military control.

Traditional hostilities among certain indigenous communities reportedly played into the government's hands, as did the government's offer of economic aid to those who cooperated with it. Nevertheless, most Peruvians were much more frightened of the *sinchis* than of the guerrillas. Campesinos and political activists of all kinds had no assurances that their legal rights would be protected by authorities, even though the government continued to maintain that it represented "democratic" rule. Thousands of people detained in the central provinces were never to be seen again. By July 1984 only one percent of those whom the government formally acknowledged detaining under the "antiterrorist law" had been brought to trial. The government was seeking the death penalty and exclusive military jurisdiction for prisoners accused of "subversion." Even without gaining such authority from parliament, military forces acted on their own with impunity. Reporters who attempted to investigate the treatment of prisoners or discover the whereabouts of disappeared persons were themselves fearful of detention, brutalization, and assassination. Almost a year after the fact, the government was forced to admit that its troops had massacred an entire village whose members had refused to participate in municipal elections. The massacre had previously been attributed to Sendero Luminoso.

In spite of the government's attempt to blame guerrillas for the wanton violence in the central sierras, it became clear over time that government terrorism was responsible for most of the deaths and disappearances there. By August 1984, the mutilated bodies of those arrested or kidnapped by government troops began to be found lying in gullies or in fields outside the towns and cities where military operations were underway. Mass graves of the disappeared were also uncovered. The minister of interior protected himself by declaring before parliament that military leaders had "exceeded their authority," but the general who was directing military operations in Ayacucho was fired when he suggested that the problems in Ayacucho stemmed from a lack of government attention to the economic problems of the people. Foreign reporters stationed in Peru quoted "counterinsurgency experts" as saying that security forces had a double purpose in leaving bodies on public display: "This raises doubt about who did it and intimidates and dissuades people. The idea is to reduce the terrorists to their hard core by using greater terror." Among the strategies adopted by the military was a decree forbidding the use of ponchos in Ayacucho. This was an open declaration of war on poor campesinos, who had no other protection against the cold. Military and police sources also acknowledged openly that the spreading of false reports or "disinformation" was part of their strategy against the guerrillas.[4]

I was in Peru just as these events were beginning to unfold. Many people were confused by conflicting reports regarding repression, insurgency, and counterinsurgency. Within family circles, there were heated debates and, at times, disquieting attempts to joke about the macabre reality.[5] However, there was little disagreement about the source of the problem. Most people knew that Peru owed well over $13 billion to foreign banks. And for several years, inflation had been running at nearly 130 percent annually. Foreign creditors continued to demand periodic devaluation of the Peruvian currency, while the Peruvian peoples' demands for higher wages continued to be labelled "subversive." Protective tariffs imposed on textiles, steel, and minerals in the United States had almost brought these industries to a halt in Peru. As major industries closed out their operations, smaller industries were forced into bankruptcy. Public investment in agriculture, the sector most severely hit by economic crisis, constituted only one percent of the national budget.

The inability of the Belaúnde government to deal with political and economic crises had caused Acción Popular to be swept from power in the municipal elections of November 1983, and now it aggravated the already tense situation existing between the central government and the dependent municipalities. The municipalities under the control of the opposition were being pressured to make things easier for the people. However, there was little that these elected officials could do to challenge the central government. Massive strikes and demonstrations following Left victories at the polls forced members of Belaúnde's cabinet to resign, but policies did not change.

In Lima the Left Unity coalition, calling on aid from international sources, was successful in establishing a network of neighborhood organizations for the distribution of milk to children and nursing mothers. It hoped to utilize this network to build a base for the 1985 presidential campaign of Lima's mayor, Alfonso Barrantes.[6] But many of Barrantes's own supporters were frustrated by his conciliatory overtures to capitalist interests and his inability to stop repression against street vendors, striking workers, students, and barriada organizations. In Huancayo the Left Unity mayor was killed by unknown assailants. In Ayacucho, where a female mayor had been elected on an independent ticket, a call for a truce between the government and the guerrillas did not reduce tensions, and conditions of life did not improve. There was no way to reconcile the needs of the Peruvian government and those of the people, who were suffering the effects of economic crisis. Everywhere prostitution, delinquency, illness, infant mortality, and early death through malnutrition and poverty increased. The "informal sector" of the economy grew, as greater numbers of Peruvians lived by extorting bribes from others who avoided taxation and government regulations in order to carry on businesses outside state control.

Testing of Women's Organizations with the Spread of Natural and Economic Disaster

In towns such as the port of Callao, prostitution became the primary source of municipal funds, either through mumicipal licensing and taxing policies or through their open operation of the brothels.[7] This additional burden on women was simply one more indication that those who directed public life could not be trusted. In Callao, the women in the fishing industry and the women in the brothels waged a joint struggle to improve their working conditions. Among their demands was the conversion of brothels into cooperatives so that prostitutes would not be exploited by middlemen. The abolition of prostitution itself would have to await more propitious times, but at least one feminist organization emerged to provide support to prostitutes who were seeking alternatives, both personal and political. Several temporary shelters *(refugios)* were established for women who were forced into desperate choices because of their physical abuse by men to whom they had submitted out of fear or need. Diminishing work opportunities for both women and men contributed to the passage of a new law that freed men from legal responsibility for the maintenance of children if the mother earned more than the father. While this law was promoted as a step toward the emanicpation of women, its immediate effect was to place an even greater burden on mothers and create even more stress within families. The law also removed restrictions on the legal adoption of Peruvian children by other Peruvians in order to reduce the selling of children to foreigners.[8]

The working women of Chimbote suffered a severe blow as the fishing industry once again fell victim to problems in the international market. The canning factories, which hired approximately nine thousand women at the end of 1982, were hiring less than one thousand by the end of 1984. The decline of the industry was produced largely by competition from Chile, Japan, and South Africa, not by a disappearance of fish. And fishmeal, once again the primary export from Chimbote, was increasingly produced with the use of machines. Most of those employed were men. Women who sought work in the fishing industries of Chimbote were forced more and more to submit to the sexual advances of employers in order to obtain work. Once hired, they were worn down through speed-up techniques that the companies were continually perfecting. Of those laid off work, 90 percent were women.

Increasing numbers of women in Chimbote could be seen

selling contraband clothing, house to house—on credit—but they had little success. The barriadas of Chimbote expanded as overall conditions in the area worsened. Floods which inundated the entire northern coast of Peru in 1983 ruined agriculture and brought death and disease to the people. Water supplies were so disrupted that, a year later, even the affluent of the cities had only irregular access to potable water. Transportation was made more difficult than before as roads went unrepaired. Corruption in the administration of relief programs increased the already formidable battle of the people against government bureaucracies.

Relief agencies in Chimbote were reactivated as church and government leaders split over the monitoring of popular unrest. Seventh Day Adventists took over the administration of relief in many barriadas, combining the distribution of food through OFASA with the promotion of birth control. Mother's Clubs connected with CARITAS were encouraged to establish *comedores infantiles*—soup kitchens for children—patterned after those initiated and staffed by nuns as early as 1976. However, those who gained control of the soup kitchens were accused of wielding dictatorial power in their communities, and grass-roots community organizations sprang up to challenge this power. More than twenty thousand children were fed daily through such relief programs.

Feminists in Chimbote attempted to centralize women's organizations, hoping thereby to give them some independence from outside institutions. At the time of my visit to Chimbote in June 1984, seventy-six women's organizations in the Santa Valley had united and were meeting regularly, without either church or government support, although some of the principal organizers were members of progressive church organizations or former members of the city council.[9]

In Lima, women who were involved in Catholic Church programs in the barriadas met to form a feminist organization within the Church. Part of the impetus was a series of advances and reverses in AFEDEPROM and other programs involving collective meal preparation. The idea of peoples' kitchens had spread to nearly all the barriadas of the city, partly because of increasing need and partly because the kitchens or *comedores popu-*

lares were increasingly seen as a focal point for struggle over the control of political direction in the barriadas.

On the one hand, the government itself became directly involved in setting up large peoples' kitchens in those barriadas where popular pressure was greatest, such as Villa El Salvador. On the other hand, *comedores* organized by people at the grass roots found it more and more difficult to obtain supplies from CARITAS or other outside sources. Increasingly, groups found ways to utilize their own resources to offer meals at low prices to neighborhood people. Occasionally, men became involved along with women. In cases where participation in organization was widespread, free meals were provided for those who could not pay anything, and sliding scales were established for the others. In some cases, those who worked full time at cooking and planning meals received free meals for themselves and members of their families. Formal membership or family association was not always required, as it was in the beginning stages.

In the barriada where I lived for a time in June and July 1984, the peoples' kitchen was turned over to any group that wanted to work there on weekends; they could sell meals to earn money for their own sustenance or to raise funds for a cause they wanted to support. On weekdays, the women of the organization (Comité de Damas Aurora Vivar) that had set up the kitchen sold nutritious but inexpensive meals. They took turns working or provided a member of their family periodically, but they elected one woman to be permanent head of the operation. I attended some meetings of the organization and was impressed by how much more aggressively the women were involved than they had been several years earlier, when I had first observed them discussing other issues. The experience they had gained through working to solve problems in the operation of the *comedor* had brought them closer together and had, at the same time, made them more vigilant toward each other in assuring that no one reaped unfair advantage by her participation. They apologized to me for exposing differences through their arguments. However, I was amazed at their perseverance in searching for ways to improve the structure of their organization so that everyone would feel satisfied the operation was fair. The first kitchens I had seen were in the homes of

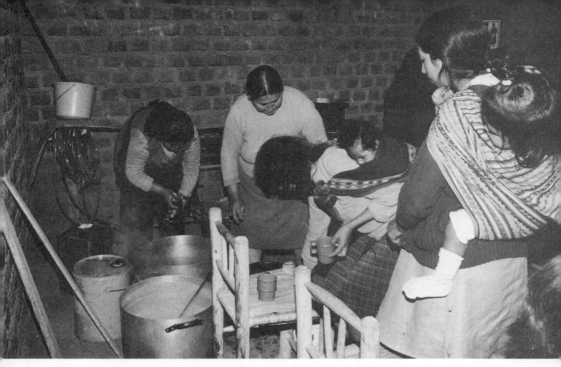

A people's kitchen in the barriada El Planeta. Women arriving from the provinces to visit family members in prison receive shelter and food here.

Health workers and state employees join in national strikes demanding the resignation of government officials and the reversal of government policies. (Ernesto Jimenez)

socios, or participants. By 1984, it was becoming more common for neighborhood groups to attain a permanent *locale,* even if this meant taking over part of a church or a school or a clinic. This transformation seemed to be important in helping the kitchens serve as centers for the expansion and development of political work in the community.

Some feminist organizations in Lima began in 1984 to train and assist women in setting up neighborhood child care in their own homes. The women I talked with said they were doing this because of the difficulties of securing building space and maintaining standards for large-scale operations. However, I wondered if the politicizing of peoples' kitchens had not influenced funding agencies to promote home-care programs. In any case, the experiences of women in the *comedores populares* served to make them aware of the problems they might encounter in other endeavors, and of the advantages to be gained through the continual evaluation and control of these endeavors by a collective body.

Regrouping of Feminists

The issues of organizational structure and control of programs that affect women in Peru surfaced primarily as a conflict between women who had been able to obtain financing for feminist projects and those who had no resources that would permit them to be "professional feminists." These issues also surfaced as a conflict between those who left political parties—even in some cases after having attained positions on the central committees of the parties—and those who lived in the barriadas, where to leave a political party would also mean separating themselves from their bases. Women who stayed within parties to struggle with men and try to involve men in neighborhood causes such as clinics and comedores felt abandoned by those who offered their "professional services" as feminists only under conditions that met the approval of financing agencies. The funding of forums, conferences, documentation centers, resource centers, and leadership training programs and publications brought "qualified" women into the feminist movement, primarily in Lima, but these women were not necessarily

more available to the poor. They invited poor women to participate in funded projects instead of providing help to those poor
women who were initiating their own organizations. When poor
women did not respond exactly as they expected, feminists sometimes turned instead to providing personal assistance to women in
careers or legal problems, and to supporting each other in their
personal struggles for sexual fulfillment and independence from
men. Several feminist activists declared their intention to run for
parliament as independent members of the Left Unity coalition.

As feminism spread through the middle class, and as early
revolutionary feminist publications began to be replaced by
"slicker" publications aimed at "broadening the base" of feminism, middle-class feminists became more and more isolated from
women in rural areas and in the shantytowns.[10] Feminism came to
be identified as the province of those who could afford to be
"pure" in their opposition to men as exploiters and who were
dedicated to pursuing goals separated from ongoing neighborhood and community struggles. When interviewed by journalists about the issues that divided poor women and women of
the middle class, the representatives of funded organizations constantly asserted that poor women had the same problems as other
women but that they suffered even more severely from them.
There was little if any recognition of the qualitatively different
experience of mestizas and indias, or of the conflicts that would be
necessary to bring about greater solidarity among women in the
fight against male domination.

The crisis of feminist leadership which brought such issues to
the surface was reflected in the opportunity middle-class women
had to host the Second Latin American and Caribbean Feminist
Meeting. This meeting, convened in Peru in July 1983, attracted
nearly six hundred women and was held in an atmosphere of
excitement and cameraderie. The most widely attended sessions at
the first meeting, which had been held in Bogotá, Colombia, two
years earlier,[11] had discussed relations between feminists and political parties. The conference in Peru met in a luxurious hotel, partly
as a precautionary measure—the country was in a state of emergency because of political conflict—and partly as a result of divisions among feminists. The most widely attended session was that

A young mother of Ayacucho joins other relatives of "the disappeared"—over 1,500 in 1983 alone—demanding that authorities answer their questions: "Julio C. Laurente Cisneros. Where is he?" (Ernesto Jimenez) having to do with sexual preference or lesbianism.[12] Women dressed in native clothing were conspicuously absent from this conference, and they had not been invited to see movies that middle-class feminists had made about them. A group of women who were critical of the meeting's organizers succeeded in getting a resolution passed condemning aggression in Central America and proclaiming solidarity with the women of Nicaragua, but they did not succeed in bringing to the conference local women whose advancement in organization had been most outstanding. Some feminists defended themselves by arguing that, although rural and barriada women in Peru were increasingly powerful and many were well organized, they were not "real feminists." Dissidents accused such spokeswomen of distorting the meaning of feminism to suit their own purposes.

Months later, some of the Peruvian women who had sided with the dissidents at the international meeting formed a new organization, inviting barriada women in Lima and some rural organizers who were meeting in the city to join them in an International Women's Day march. *"Feminismo Popular!"* the unofficial slogan for the march, was chanted enthusiastically by thousands of participants. At the end of the march, and after the planned rally was over, a group of women on the platform began spontaneously to sing traditional *huaynos* to express the feelings they were sharing.

At the time of my latest visit to Peru, several months after the 1984 International Women's Day event, its organizers remained an *ad hoc* grouping. The slogan *Feminismo Popular!* had not come into common usage among the masses of women whom it was meant to inspire. Yet among those who had participated in the march, a new concept had been born and a new spirit of combativeness had emerged, allowing them to wage battles internal to the movement with greater clarity and force.

Some women were disheartened by the barriers which existed among feminists. Others were angry, even as they rejoiced that the impact of feminism on Peruvian society was beginning to be felt. Eventually representatives of feminist organizations agreed to confront issues of financing and class privilege openly. A series of meetings was planned to allow women who were recipients of financing to hear the views of others and to discuss among themselves the impact funding had had on feminist organization. Issues such as racism and class privilege were sure to surface and to make women even more uncomfortable with each other than they had been. But the challenge of political and economic crisis in the country was likely to force an outcome that would move feminist organization in more radical directions.

One of the preludes to these events was an Encuentro Feminino that had been held in the city of Puno in October 1982. Similar conferences were held later in other regions of the country, but the campesinas of Puno had the longest history of organization and were therefore in a position to lead the way in articulating the concerns of rural women. In 1981 they already had a membership of sixteen hundred women from sixteen indigenous communities. They had called on others in the following terms: "The problem that we confront in organizing has little to do with learning to cook, caring for our children, or acting as 'good wives.' It has everything to do with understanding why the system we are living in tries to maintain the people divided, weakened, quarreling, frustrated, and distrustful of each other. What we need is to gain self-respect and strength as women, so that as equals with men we can transform our society into a society that is good for all of us."[13] In the publication resulting from their more recent meeting, the Puno women said: "To the extent that our communities are weakened and changes are brought about by the gradual penetration of capitalism where we live, we women don't have any power of decision in the activities we have to carry on. We're just cheap labor, without any value of our own. We are kept outside of everything, without education, without ways of producing efficiently, and that causes us to have little confidence in ourselves and in the organizations that affect us. This is also a problem for our husbands and all the comuneros who resist organization."[14]

Women from the Department of Puno recalled how they had participated in land takeovers in 1979 because of the corruption in agrarian reform. They recalled how they had been helped by several nuns in forming a group to produce handicrafts for sale and how, in coming together, they began to question things, including the Church itself. Then the Aymaras established links with the

Quechuas and had all-day meetings. But these meetings made many women impatient: "We get tired of listening to speeches. We don't like to waste our time." So they decided to confront the big companies and even the church people who were telling them what to do and how to do it—seemingly for the good of campesinas—while all the time looking for ways to exploit them. In the end, the women concluded, they had been forced to import food and machinery and other products that brought them nothing but sickness and misery, not to mention new forms of abuse by men. In an evaluation of the 1982 *encuentro,* the Puno women criticized those women from the coast who had been invited to the conference. They felt invitees should have participated more actively. "Perhaps a more comfortable meeting place and resolutions more distinctively feminist were what some of our *compañeras* who came from the capital wanted."

If the women of the Department of Puno were dissatisfied with their relationship with feminists from the capital city, they should not have been surprised that women who were not linked with the campesino union, nor with the large enterprises established through agrarian reform, felt uncomfortable with them. The emergence of a competing women's organization in the Department of Puno represented the growth of the native movement during 1984 and the struggles of women from some fifteen indigenous communities that were a part of the movement. Some of these women had participated in the activities of the "8 de Marzo" organization of Aymará and Quechua women. But differences had emerged during the campaigns for municipal offices in 1983. Women of the CCP were accused of becoming too much involved in electoral issues of the Left organizations that were represented in their union, issues which others felt didn't concern them directly. What the new organization emphasized was the rebuilding of indigenous communities and the development of self-reliance, which they felt would require stronger regional organization and less allegiance to "party lines" dictated from Lima.

The native movement had some fifty organizations throughout Peru by 1984. Some of these were student organizations in Lima.[15] The movement was itself divided into different tendencies. I talked with members of the Comunidad Femininia

Micaela Bastidas, about these tendencies.[16] According to them, native organizers who received financing from the United States government sources were fanatically nationalist. "These people represent no real threat to capitalists," they said, and serve to effectively divide the various oppressed sectors of the population by race or nationality. Native organizations which receive money from anthropologists and from certain segments of the Church and European governments interested in creating a sphere of influence in South America tend to emphasize *indigenismo*. They promote the preservation or creation of "special rights and privileges" for particular native groups, seeking legislative reform within a framework of social democracy. The view of most traditional leftists is to uphold "self-determination" for natives while actually favoring their assimilation in industrial society.

Apart from all these tendencies which weaken native movements, according to the leaders of Micaela Bastidas, is the position of *"indianistas,"* who have a harder time finding sources of outside financial support. *Indianistas* believe that Indian cultures are superior to "Western" culture. In order to ensure the survival of the planet, they say, it will be necessary for both Indians and non-Indians to reclaim preindustrial values of community and reciprocity, while utilizing those aspects of technical knowledge that can serve to enhance natural life, whether this knowledge is ancient or modern. Political structures which subordinate natives to international market systems leave them powerless before the destructive tendencies of Western individualism and superpower rivalry.

Unfortunately, the conquest of machismo, which native leaders claim is a distinctively modern or European cultural pattern, has not advanced in most native organizations any more easily than in other political groupings. Nevertheless, at a conference on *"Poder Indio"* (Indian power) held in Lima at the end of June 1984, organized by a dissident native leader, nearly 90 percent of those in attendance were women. The conference had been hastily organized simply by sending letters to barriada organizations. Several hundred people came. The strength of women was evident not only in their numbers but also in the assertiveness and radicalism of those who spoke. A sixteen-year-old who had taken refuge in the women's shelter in the barriada where I was staying, and who had come to Lima from the jungle when her mother died, was so inspired that she volunteered to head the Cultural Commission. She had no previous political experience other than participation in the meetings of those who lived in the shelter and attendance at local cultural and political events.

The "Indian Power" event, whether or not it represents a significant step in the organization of native women, illustrates the potential that exists for such organization. Women have defended native communities for hundreds of years in Peru. A native movement without strong female leadership is a movement that is still waiting to be born.

The Development of Theory and Practice in an Atmosphere of Crisis and Hope

The intellectual women who formed the first feminist organizations in Lima in the early 1970s were already ideologically in advance of most of their counterparts in North America and Europe. They had no illusions that women's emancipation was just around the corner. For most of them the personal rewards had to do with psychological empowerment rather than material benefits. As economic crisis overwhelmed their ability to win concessions from the government, these women suffered setbacks. They were both discomfited and gratified by the emergence of new feminist movements outside their circle of influence. One of the founders of ALIMUPER (Acción para la Liberación de la Mujer Peruana), from which a number of organizations and activities grew, wrote recently: "Why do I say feminism is subversive? Because it attacks one of the fundamental pillars of the system, the traditional family, center, essence and transmission cord of authoritarian societies. . . . It also attacks the powerful ideological base that defines all sexist cultures: monogamous marriage, the ideology of maternity, education in different roles according to gender, exclusive heterosexuality, recognition of masculinity as the foundation of everything positive and of femininity as the sphere of the irrational. Not long ago we witnessed the phenomenon that feminism was an 'arm of imperialism,' since it was born in North America. That's like saying that since Marxism was born and grew in capitalist countries, it's 'imperialist.' Next, people accused the feminist movement of 'dividing the working-class struggle,' saying that it wasn't valid for women to have a separate politics. This kind of ideological threat had its effect in the first stage, especially among the elite of women in the parties. Now things are very different."[17]

A feminist scholar who is perhaps closer to the traditional Left than to the feminism of ALIMUPER, expressed a view that I think is representative of most intellectual feminists in Peru today: "A dependent capitalist economy, Peru's relation to the world economy is reproduced at the national level where internal colonialism characterizes the relation of the coast to the Andean area. Relations of dependency can be traced to the local level, where campesinos are dominated by mestizos. Finally, women may be viewed as the last link in the chain of dependency, since their dependence on men is increasing with the spread of capitalist relations."[18]

This view can be misleading if "dependency" is taken to mean that the oppressed are without power. Profiteers are dependent on the hard work and acquiescence of those whose resources they are interested in exploiting. As the pages of this book have shown, acquiescence can no longer be taken for granted. Therefore, neither of the above statements may adequately represent the positions that will be taken by women in Peru when those who are now in most intense struggle for survival have had a chance to formulate their views. However, it is interesting and instructive to note that the experience and struggle of the poorest women in Peru has already influenced legislation that goes into effect in 1985. The new civil code stipulates that there will no longer be any legal discrimination against children born out of wedlock, nor will the relationship of parents be noted on birth certificates. Furthermore, practices of trial marriage or *sirvinacuy* (also called *pantanacu, huarnichacu, palomay,* and *uqtasiña*) will be recognized, as will divorce for either party who desires it after one year of separation. The responsibilities of women and men who are parents will no longer be defined by gender, and married women will not be required to add their husband's names to their own when applying for electoral cards, a practice that has been especially repugnant to native women.

The government official who has been in charge of formulating the new law admitted when interviewed by the press that he himself had grave concerns about its "moral implications" but that the commission was forced to take into account the reality in which people are living. While the law is controversial in Peru, it was being hailed by some as the "most advanced in the world."

Legislation in Peru is enforced according to executive discretion, and there is no reason to believe that the new civil code will alleviate women's burdens or free them from exploitation and abuse by men. However, any legislation that calls attention to the crisis in the family system must be seen as favorable to women's struggles. Labor legislation decreed under the military government is now under attack, as is agrarian reform. Yet these were concessions made to the people. The controversies surrounding them, controversies having to do with implementation as well as conceptualization, have positively advanced popular organization.

Peruvians may experience bitter defeats in their struggles for democracy, socialism, and communism, but it is through these struggles that popular wisdom matures. What many Peruvian feminists are learning through political activity is that although their major antagonist at present is the state, insistence on attention to women's problems is not misplaced. Antagonisms between women and men of the popular classes must be recognized and dealt with in order for the struggle against the state to succeed— but the struggle against the state must succeed in order to make possible the full realization of the human potential of both women and men.

Few wealthy women in Peru are interested in feminist issues. Those who are must give up their identification as members of the social elite in order to become active politically as feminists. This is so because the emancipation of women requires a complete overhaul of the economic and family structures that keep ruling elites in power. The present political situation in Peru is one of extreme polarization. Imperialism and the struggle for survival cause issues of patriarchy to surface. However, the struggle against

A long legacy of suffering in Peru is reflected in the eyes of children already wise beyond their years. The new society envisioned by revolutionaries can give them hope, but its attainment will cost many lives and many years. (Jean-Pierre Perpoil)

patriarchy cannot advance unless women and men cooperate in overthrowing the state.

Each time women unite with men in order to advance the cause of social revolution, they also gain power as women. Each time these same women separate themselves from men in order to strengthen their organization as women, they gain power as well. This is not true when women make concessions to the state in order to defend their class privileges. Because poor women are locked in a terrible battle against the state in Peru, while at the same time making conscious efforts to improve their own situation relative to that of men, they are in a position to push forward the cause of all women more effectively than are women of the more privileged classes. This is true even when feminist goals are not clearly defined. Intellectuals often fail to realize the importance of the victories won by women of the popular classes which enable them to come together politically, the ways they increase the power of all women by constantly confronting men and supporting each other, regardless of the issues around which they are organized. When called upon for assistance, intellectual women sometimes retreat, either because their involvement is not valued consistently or because they feel guilty about exposing their own weaknesses before women whose experiences of oppression are so extreme.

From my own experience, I feel that the way to resolve these contradictions is not to make a virtue of poverty, but to remain clear about priorities. Until women of the popular classes have attained a sense of power equal to the social contributions they are making, they will not really be free to express their hopes for a better life. Rather than attempt to speak for them, we need to give them all-out support and the respect they deserve as political leaders.

Repression forces people to come together in new ways which can either help them break down social barriers or create new ones. The testimony of a woman from the Department of Apurimac who regularly visits a relative who is a political prisoner in Callao illustrates what can happen even in the most adverse circumstances when women are conscious of their historical destinies. Speaking of the women she visits in prison, she says:

"These women have linked with each other so tightly that they're like a family. . ... All of them are politically conscious. Those who weren't at first have become that way because of living with each other in community. It's beautiful to see them sing. . . . Those of us who are spectators, so to speak, can't help but feel they are a highly privileged group in our society—privileged in the sense that they are a vanguard of the new society."

There are, of course, those who know of the "new society" only because they fear it, or because they are afraid of losing what little they have in the fierce struggle for power now occurring in Peru. It was an old women who evidently showed her opposition to the guerrilla movement by cooperating with the military authorities in announcing the arrival of the group of journalists who came to her village in January 1983 in search of information about paramilitary actions in the area. The journalists were killed. Mario Vargas Llosa, a well-known conservative writer who headed the governmental commission that conducted a hearing into the case, described seeing, as he and his group were leaving, a woman dancing and tapping her legs gently with the tangled branches of a small tree: "Was she cursing us because we belonged to the strangers—senderistas, 'reporters,' *sinchis*—who had brought new reasons for anguish to their lives? Was she exorcising us? . . . That frail, tiny woman had undoubtedly been one of the mob who threw rocks and swung sticks, for the Iquichano women are famous for being as warlike as the men."[19]

Photographs of the hearing held in the high sierras show the all-male government commission seated in a half-circle facing the men of the village, whose explanations of the assault on the journalists are being recorded on tape. Vargas Llosa apparently felt more comfortable questioning rhetorically the meaning of a small woman's dance than asking her directly what had motivated her to kill.[20]

Ultimately, those who at first appear most "backward" may also have much to say about the future. The experiences of women in Ayacucho, in Chimbote, in Comas, in Puno, in Jauja, and in the tropical rain forest are becoming part of the experience of Peruvian women in general. Their experiences in daily work, in conceiving and giving birth to children, and in fighting against oppression can be used as a guide in the creation and re-creation of womanhood and of humanity.

In Peru, as in many other places where patriarchal authority is closely identified with imperialism,[21] with the restriction of communal democracy in favor of production for the private benefit of nonproducers, women can reclaim their humanity with the full knowledge that they are defending not only themselves as women, but also their sons and daughters. It will not be the first time in history that people engaged in battle have felt they represented the interests of the entire species, but it may be the first time they have done so with so much justification.

Notes and References

Chapter 1: A Look at Women's History

1. Elinor Burkett, "Indian Women and White Society: The Case of Six-teenth-Century Peru," p. 105.

2. While the term *mestizo* literally means "of mixed parentage," in Peru it refers more specifically to the adoption of non-Indian culture and status; it is more a class difference than a racial difference.

3. For details on the many aspects of women's loss of power under Spanish rule, see Irene Silverblatt, "Andean Women in the Inca Empire," pp. 37–61; and "Andean Women under Spanish Rule," pp. 149–85. The religious persecution of women (discussed briefly in Chapter Six) is also revealed in her studies, and is mentioned by Elinor C. Burkett, op. cit. Burkett, however, focuses on the advantages women gained through knowledge of Spanish culture as marketers, mistresses, and so on. Male commoners were restricted to work that kept them isolated from Spanish family and business life.

4. Scholars who argue that the *incanato* was not an empire or a society based on conquest describe ritual wars in which both men and women participated. The small arms preserved from that period are thought to be symbolic, unusable in actual combat. A special corps of women is said to have separated combatants forcibly when the fights became too aggressive and threatened the well-being of communities.

5. The Spanish deliberately destroyed technologies associated with fine weaving in Peru, ostensibly to protect Indian women from the abuses of the *obraje,* a system in which they were forced to weave cloth for export to Europe. Most historians agree that the real reason for laws against *obraje* was to protect the European textile industry.

6. According to Donald Lathrap, early migrations of Andean people into the jungle show that they were familiar with agriculture and animal husbandry techniques in the sierra before they became nonsedentary horticulturists, hunters, and gathers in the jungle. This contradicts commonly held assumptions about the evolution of technological development, and lends credence to native claims that

their life-style is appropriate to the ecological demands of their environment. See Lathrap, "The 'Hunting' Economics of the Tropical Forest Zone in South America: An Attempt at Historical Perspective."

7. This process, mentioned parenthetically by anthropologists, is still going on in the selva, according to present inhabitants of the region.

8. United States investments in Peru and U.S. relations with the successive governments of Peru in this century are discussed in Virgilio Roel, *Esquema de la evolución económica;* Anibal Quijano, *Nationalism and Capitalism in Peru;* and William Bollinger, "The Bourgeois Revolution in Peru: A Conception of Peruvian History," pp. 18–56.

9. This quotation from Hugo Neira, *Los Andes: Tierra o muerte* (Madrid: Editorial ZYC, 1968), was cited by Christina Girón in an unpublished International Labor Organization study, "Participación social y política de la mujer rural en un contexto de reforma agraria" (Cuzco, 1981).

10. A subject outside the scope of this book, but of such importance that it needs to be mentioned here, is the danger presented by the loss of one of the world's most important sources of oxygen through the destruction of the Amazonian jungle.

11. In Ataura, a Huanca Indian village near Jauja, where I was married to a descendent of the community, we were required to produce evidence of at least nine months of successful cohabitation. My husband's mother came from Lima to oversee the marriage procedure, a tradition she insisted on carrying out though she and I were the same age and both had grown children. She hoped that our marriage in Ataura would help to re-establish her use-rights to land in the community.

12. Florence Babb, *Men and Women in Vicos, Peru: A Case of Unequal Development,* p. 13. This paper is a valuable source for understanding the impact of recent agricultural reforms on women, since the Vicos project served as a model for subsequent government programs. The official report on the Vicos project is Henry Dobyns, Paul Doughty, and Harold Lasswell, eds., *Peasants, Power, and Applied Social Change: Vicos as a Model* (Beverly Hills, Calif.: Sage Publications, 1971). Names used in the quotation have been changed.

13. Juana Larco, "Se abre camino al andar," *Mujer Levántate* 1, no. 2 (June 1981), p. 7.

14. *Mujeres del Cuzco: Trabajo y vida cotidiana,* Serie: Mujer, no. 1 (Cuzco: Asociación Amauta, February 1982).

15. For a very different view, see Heinz Dieterich, "Some Technical and Methodological Observations about the Inca Empire and the Asiatic Mode of Production." See also Manuel Burga and Alberto Flores-Galindo, *La utopia andina.*

16. Virgilio Roel, *Los sabios y grandiosos fundamentos de la indianidad,* pp. 8–9.

17. Gaul Carnero Medina, *Los dioses comunistas,* p. 24.

18. See especially William Bollinger, "Peru Today: The Roots of Labor Militancy"; and Barbara Stallings, "Privatization and the Public Debt: U.S. Banks in Peru."

19. César Pezo, Eduardo Ballón, and Luis Peirano, *El magisterio y sus luchas: 1885–1978* (Lima: Centro de Estudios y Promoción del Desarrollo, 1981), pp. 241–42.

20. I. Osono, *El Diario Marka* (Lima), November 30, 1978, p. 23.

21. Ibid.

22. *El Diario Marka,* September 20, 1979, p. 5.
23. Ana María Portugal, "Hacia una comprensión del feminismo en el Perú."
24. Alternation of military and civilian rule has a long history in Peru. As the popular press puts it: "The failure of civilian government opens the door to military government. The wearing down of the military brings about the reinstatement of civilian government."
25. The history of women's suffrage and early political party participation is not dealt with in this book. Feminist organizations originated within literary circles in the 1880s, and again in the 1920s and 1930s; see Linda Lema, "Las mujeres del '90: Primer instante lúcido de la condición femenina en el Perú." Women received the vote in 1956, but apparently never succeeded in markedly influencing elections or party positions; see Ana María Portugal, "Realidad de las mujeres: Un desafío a los partidos políticos"; and Elsa Chaney, "Women in Latin American Politics: The Case of Peru and Chile."
26. Quoted in Gustavo Riofrío and Alfredo Rodríguez, *De invasores a invadados: Diez años de autodesarrollo en una barriada* (Lima: Centro de Estudios y la Promoción del Desarrollo, 1980), p. 74.

REFERENCES TO CHAPTER I

Babb, Florence, E. *Women and Men in Vicos, Peru: A Case of Unequal Development.* Michigan Occasional Paper, no. 11. Ann Arbor, Mich., Winter 1980.
Bollinger, William. "The Bourgeois Revolution in Peru: A Conception of Peruvian History." *Latin American Perspectives* 4, no. 3 (Summer 1977): 18–56.
———. "Peru Today: The Roots of Labor Militancy." *NACLA Report on the Americas* 14, no. 6 (November–December 1980).
Burga, Manuel, and Alberto Flores-Galindo. "La utopia andina." Pontificia Universidad Católica del Perú, May 1982.
Burkett, Elinor C. "Indian Women and White Society: The Case of Sixteenth-Century Peru." In *Latin American Women: Historical Perspectives.* Edited by Asunción Lavrín, pp. 101–28. Westport, Conn.: Greenwood Press, 1978.
Carnero Medina, Gaul. *Los dioses comunistas.* Cuadernos Indios, no. 4. Lima, 1982.
Chaney, Elsa. "Women in Latin American Politics: The Case of Peru and Chile." In *Female and Male in Latin America,* edited by Ann Pescatello, pp. 103–39. Pittsburgh: University of Pittsburgh Press, 1973.
Deere, Carmen Diana. "Changing Social Relations of Production and Peruvian Peasant Women's Work." *Latin American Perspectives* 4, nos. 1 and 2 (Winter and Spring, 1977): 48–69.
Dieterich, Heinz. "Some Theoretical and Methodological Observations about the Inca Empire and the Asiatic Mode of Production." *Latin American Perspectives* 4, no. 4 (Fall 1982): 111–32.
Dole, Gertrude. "The Marriages of Pacho: A Woman's Life among the Amahuaca." In *Many Sisters: Women in Cross-Cultural Perspective,* edited by C. J. Mathiasson, pp. 10–11. New York: Macmillan Free Press, 1974.
Dore, Elizabeth, and John Weeks. "The Intensification of the Assault Against the Working Class in 'Revolutionary Peru.'" *Latin American Perspectives* 3, no. 2 (Spring 1976): 55–82.
Dorregaray, Elvira. "Importancia de la participación de la mujer en el desarrollo." Huancayo: Sistema Nacional de Apoyo a la Movilización Social, 1972.

Historia de los Cajamarquinos. Lima: Centro de Estudios y Publicacions, March 1982.

Kapsoli, Wilfredo. *Las Luchas Obreras en el Perú,* 1900–1919. Lima: Delva Editores, 1976.

Kleinbaum, Abby Wettan. *The War Against the Amazons.* New York: McGraw-Hill, 1983.

Lathrap, Donald. "The 'Hunting' Economies of the Tropical Forest Zone of South America: An Attempt at Historical Perspective." In *Peoples and Cultures of Native South America,* edited by Daniel R. Gross, pp. 83–95. Garden City, N.Y.: Doubleday, 1973.

Lema, Linda. "Las mujeres del '90: Primer instante lúcido de la condición femenina en el Perú." *Mujer y Sociedad* 1, no. 3 (June 1981): 3–9.

Maira, Luis, and Carlos Rico F. "La política latinoamericana de la administración Carter: Materiales para un primer recuento." Mimeographed, n.p., n.d.

Mariátegui, José Carlos. *Siete ensayos de interpretación de la realidad peruana.* Lima: Empresa Editora Amauta, 1975.

Portugal, Ana María. "Hacia una comprensión del feminismo en el Perú." Publicaciones ALIMUPER, no. 1, Lima, April 1978.

———. "Realidad de las mujeres: Un desafío a los partidos políticos." Publicaciones ALIMUPER, no. 2, Lima, 1980.

Quesada, Miro. "La mujer en el sistema capitalista." *Analisis-Cuadernos de Investigación* no. 10 (January–April 1982): 27–41.

Quijano, Anibal. *Nationalism and Capitalism in Peru.* New York and London: Monthly Review Press, 1971.

Roel, Virgilio. *Esquema de la evolución económica.* Lima: Biblioteca Amauta, 1971.

———. *Los sabios y grandiosos fundamentos de la indianidad.* Cuadernos Indios, no. 2. Lima, 1980.

Silverblatt, Irene. "Andean Women in the Inca Empire." *Feminist Studies* 4, no. 3 (October 1978): 37–61.

———. "Andean Women under Spanish Rule." In *Women and Colonization: Anthropological Perspectives,* edited by Mona Etienne and Eleanor Leacock, pp. 149–85. New York: Praeger, 1980.

Stallings, Barbara. "Privatization and the Public Debt: U.S. Banks in Peru." *NACLA Report on the Americas* 12, no 4 (July–August 1978): 2–38.

Suskind, Janet. "Tropical Forest Hunters and the Economy of Sex." In *Peoples and Cultures of Native South America,* edited by Daniel R. Gross, pp. 226–40. Garden City, N.Y.: Doubleday, 1973.

Torres, R., Oswaldo. "Participación de la mujer a través de la historia del Perú." Huancayo: Sistema Nacional de Apoyo a la Movilización Social, 1973.

Varese, Stefano. *The Forest Indians in the Present Political Situation in Peru.* International Work Group for Indigenous Affairs, document no. 8. Copenhagen, August 1972.

Chapter 2: Entering the Global Economy

1. *Business Latin America,* March 16, 1983, p. 86.

2. Carmen Tocón, María Rodríguez Atilano, and Carmen Urbina Herrera, "La situación de la mujer en Chimbote, ensayo," p. 44.

3. Roberto López Linares, "Informe: Las conserveras," p. 7.

4. When Peruvians are suffering from the strains of domestic life or the pressures of work, they often say their livers are acting up.

5. In Trujillo, the members of the organization were wives of agricultural workers on the sugar cooperatives.

6. Tocón, Rodríguez, and Urbina, op. cit., p. 44.

7. Ibid., p. 45.

8. Testimony of Magda Portal, in Esther Andradi and Ana María Portugal, *Ser mujer en el Perú,* p. 216.

9. The steel mill in Chimbote, nationalized by the military government, is at this writing about to be reprivatized. Steel is now being imported, and foreign companies are interested in opening up new plants in the south. With reprivatization, contracts with the steelworkers' union can be nullified. The state-owned ELECTROPERU has recently been converted into a *sociedad anónima,* allowing part ownership by private companies. The most profitable areas can then be given over to private hands.

10. Testimony of Nelly Rumrrill, in *Presencia de la mujer en las barriadas,* 2nd ed. (Lima: Centro de Información, Estudios y Documentación, 1981), p. 89.

11. Tocón, Rodríguez, and Urbina, "La situación de la mujer en Chimbote, ensayo," p. 35.

12. Catholic Relief Services, or CARITAS, is one of several organizations empowered to distribute relief food in Peru. CARITAS administers approximately half of the PL 480 credits and surplus-food programs of the United States government.

13. See Chapter Five for a discussion of the origins of the Mother's Day protests.

14. See "Informe sobre la problemática y los últimos acontecimientos en Chimbote," *Faena,* no. 2 (April 1981). Raúl Martinez, in "Salud y intereses del imperialismo," ibid., also documents how the U.S. Central Intelligence Agency used malaria control and other health projects in Peru specifically to gain intelligence and establish a foothold among populations engaged in insurgency, or for other strategic military purposes.

15. Bonnie Mass, *Population Target,* discusses the history of U.S.-sponsored population programs in Peru, criticizing both the theoretical assumptions made about "overpopulation" and the racist and sexist attitudes that have characterized leadership of these programs.

Another example of psychological exploitation by outsiders is the advertising of baby formula. Members of a women's group in the barriada La Primavera in Chimbote told me that many of them thought, before joining the group, that the white powder in cans was "real milk," while the *leche* that flowed from their own breasts was only a poor substitute.

16. The quotations are taken from *Acción* 2, no. 4 (March 1979), p. 5. Approximately 37 percent of the deaths registered in Peru each year are of children under the age of one. The pressure for access to contraception is therefore extremely great. However, because of pressure from the Catholic Church, all state contraceptive services were closed down in 1980. At that time there were an estimated 85,000 abortions in Peru every year. A crisis was created by the large number of women coming to hospitals as a result of complications from abortions, and the withdrawal of contraceptive services only caused the situation to worsen.

17. See López Linares, "Informe," p. 36.
18. Personal communication to the author.
19. The overall development and impact of the Christian "base communities" espousing liberation theology, first articulated by the Peruvian priest Gustavo Gutierrez, is not analyzed in this book. In any case, the role of the Church in promoting revolution appeared to be blunted by the 1980s, as most Church leaders succumbed to pressure from Rome to separate themselves from political parties of the Left.

REFERENCES TO CHAPTER 2

Agua y desague en Chimbote. Serie: Problemática Urbana no. 1. INDES, 1981.
Andradi, Esther, and Ana Marí Portugal. *Ser mujer en el Perú*. Lima: Ediciones Mujer y Autonomía, 1978.
Aramburu, Carlos Eduardo. "Consecuencias socioeconomicas del crecimiento poblacional en el Perú." Lima: Pontificia Universidad Católica del Perú, August 1980.
Caballero, José María. "Sobre el carácter de la reforma agraria peruana." *Latin American Perspectives* 4, no. 3 (Summer 1977): 146–60.
Caravedo Molinari, Baltazar. "The State and the Bourgeoisie in the Peruvian Fishmeal Industry." *Latin American Perspectives* 4, no. 3 (Summer 1977): 103–22.
Carlier, Ana. "La Ciencia:¿Al servicio y en beneficio de la pareja?" *Mujer y Sociedad* l, no. 3 (June 1981): 38–41.
Centro de Educación Familiar. *Amor y sexo. Chimbote, June 1980.*
"Club de madres." La Voz de la Mujer. Boletín, no. 4. Chimbote, August 1981.
Comisión de Justicia Social Prelatura de Chimbote. Boletín, no. 37. Chimbote, 1981.
———. "¡Las trabajadores del hogar también tenemos derechos!" Serie: Derechos Laborales, no. 1. Chimbote, 1981.
Comité Revolucionario de Conserveros. Press release, Coishco (Chimbote), November 6, 1981.
"¿Como hacer un plan de trabajo?" *La Voz de la Mujer*. Boletín, no. 6. Chimbote, May 1982.
Diestra P., Fidel, and Roberto López Linares. "La industria conservera en Chimbote." *Informes Chimbote*, no. 4 (October 1981).
Equipo de Promoción de la Mujer. Concurso literario sobre la mujer de hoy. Chimbote, September 1981.
Federación Sindical Departamental de los Trabajadores de Ancash. Seventh Congress. Motion presented by women fish-cannery workers. Chimbote, March 1982.
"La gran huelga de pescadores." Leaflets and clippings reproduced from October and November 1976.
Grupo de Educación Popular. "Maria despierta—ya es hora de que te levantes." Cuadernos de Reflexión. Chimbote, May 1978.
Huerta, Miguel. "Las cooperativas agrarias en emergencia." *Faena*, nos. 4–5 (1982): 20–21.
"Informe sobre la problemática y los últimos acontecimientos en Chimbote." *Faena*, no. 2 (April 1981).
Llerena, Elizabeth. "Condiciones de trabajo en la industria conservera y sus repercusiones en la salud del obrero." *Faena, nos. 4–5 (1982): 33–39.*

Lópes Linares, Roberto. "Informe: Las conserveras." *Faena,* no. 1 (December 1980): 2–14.

————, and Fidel Diestra P. "Cooperativas del Valle del Santa: Situación y perspectivas." *Informes Chimbote,* no. 6 (January 1982).

Malpica S., Carlos. "La desnacionalización de la flota de PESCAPERU." Lima: Ediciones Labor, 1976.

Mass, Bonnie. *Population Target.* Toronto: Women's Press, 1976.

Montes, Eva. "Polémica: Por el aborto libre y gratuito." *Mujer y Sociedad* 1, no. 1 (July 1980): 24–25.

Movimiento Hacia una Nueva Mujer, Sindicato de Pescadores. "Los derechos laborales de la trabajadora." Chimbote, March 1982.

Muñoz Cabrera, Teresa. "Situación de la mujer en Ancash." Draft study, Instituto Nor Peruano de Desarrollo Economico y Social, February 1982.

Sara-Lafosse, Violeta. "Dinámica de población y derechos humanos." Lima: Pontificia Universidad Católica del Peru, November 1974.

————. "La ley de reforma agraria y sus implicaciones en la estructura familiar." Lima: Pontificia Universidad Católica del Perú, November 1974.

Toćon, Carmen. "Mujer, sexo, y realidad." *Faena,* nos. 4–5 (1982).

————, María Rodríguez Atilano, and Carmen Urbina Herrera. "La situación de la mujer en Chimbote, ensayo." *Informes Chimbote* no. 7 (February 1982).

Villanueva, Victor. "The Petty-Bourgeois Ideology of the Peruvian Aprista Party." *Latin American Perspectives* 4, no. 3 (Summer 1977): 57–76.

Chapter 5. Agricultural Reform in the Mountains

1. "Collective capitalist farm" is a term used by scholars. Government propaganda avoided use of the term "capitalist" when describing reform programs at that time.

2. Since the government has severely cut national expenditures for public health, tuberculosis and typhoid fever have become epidemic. North American companies monopolize the pharmaceutical industry in Peru. Medicines are in short supply and even more expensive than in the United States.

3. While sexual relations among youth in indigenous communities are casual, and marriage is not consolidated until a couple have cohabited for some time, adultery may be severely sanctioned. There have been instances in which women have cut off the noses of transgressing husbands. Divorce is rare in most campesina communities, where ties among comuneros are close. When divorce occurs, both spouses are usually obliged to leave the community. Big regional differences in marriage and courtship practices have been noted by anthropologists. In some places romance is paramount and in others economic considerations predominate. Only in coastal communities, however, is it common for couples to be married because of parental pressure.

4. These meetings were held in 1980 and 1981. In some cases, funding made possible the publication of illustrated pamphlets for nationwide circulation. In other cases, mimeographed reports were prepared for circulation among those who had attended.

5. The government hired pantomime artists to propagandize its programs. Soon, street theater was taken up by popular movements and became a liability for the government. Pantomime survived, very literally, as guerrilla theater, including female as well as male actors. Popular theater depicting land takeovers and other movements of the 1970s flourished in the capital and toured overseas as recently as 1983. However, the same history, when depicted in markets and plazas of rural communities, was severely repressed.

6. Similar events were, of course, happening all over the world at this time. In Lima, apparently as a spin-off of North American movements, and no doubt related as well to government programs, independent feminist organizations began as early as 1973. These brought small groups of educated women together to discuss their own problems and to call public attention to the objectification of women in the mass media, the secondary status of women before the law, and the reproductive issues, such as abortion and contraception. Such groups experienced a decline as economic crisis grew, but women who were active in political organizations that were stimulated by economic recession began at the same time to view their participation in feminist terms. This "second stage" of feminism was characterized by focusing organizing activity in the barriadas and in popular organizations that were formed to protest government policies.

7. As of this writing, state schools have not begun to teach women studies. However, the Catholic University in Lima began offering such courses in 1982.

8. A concerted attack on leftist scholarship in Peru would most likely result in the closing down of social science departments: most social scientists today utilize a Marxist framework for analysis.

9. In another case, comuneros exposed earlier U.S.-sponsored studies of "nutrition" in which orphaned children were used to test starvation diets. These studies had been conducted, the comuneros said, to discover the minimum amount of food needed for survival and for productive output. No follow-up had ever been conducted to see what permanent damage had been done to those who were part of the experiments.

10. The largest of these mines have been expropriated by the government, with compensation; but the exportation of minerals continued, as does environmental destruction. The newer, more lucrative mining operations are foreign-owned.

11. See Oscar Nuñez del Prado, *Kuyo Chico,* for information about the effects of missionary activity in indigenous communities.

12. The planting of forests or the construction of canals, roads, and other projects, once joyous events, became a new form of slave labor. Wealthier members of the community avoided work by paying small fines or by lending the use of a truck. Church or municipal authorities were sometimes able to direct the work for their private advantage. Nevertheless, while I was living in the Mantaro Valley, I noted enthusiasm among older women on communal work days.

13. The CCP was not given official recognition by the Peruvian government. However, the political organizations that were represented in the union in the early 1980s participated in parliament. These were primarily the Unidad Democrático Popular (composed of several Marxist-Leninist organizations) and, to a lesser extent, the Trotskyists. Each of these parties or organizations became involved in organizing rural bases of women. Each has its own internal history of

struggle against sexism and for the autonomy of women. These organizations came to permit and even, in some cases, to encourage the growth of autonomous women's organizations before other political groups of the Left in Peru. I think this had something to do with their support among indigenous peoples whose experiences of parallel power for men and women were not entirely remote.

14. Quotations are taken from *Voz Campesina,* no. 12, 1982.

15. Shouting slogans in this manner is characteristic of political organizations whose cultural origins are in the cities. Although it jarred me a little to see indigenous women pick up on it so easily, I understood it as an expression of unity between the city and the country, and of campesinas' entrance into "national politics." There was certainly no cultural rigidity possible at a meeting attended by women from so many different regions of the country. Among these were a few wearing khakis and U.S.-style baseball caps instead of traditional clothing. They retained long braids, however, and told me they wear traditional clothing, too. None of the campesinas wore make-up, tight blouses or slacks, or high-heeled shoes, all characteristic of "stylish" women in the cities. As we moved from a dirt area to meet on a cement basketball court, the women mumbled that the cement *"trae la pestilencia"* (carries diseases), but they sat down on it anyway.

REFERENCES TO CHAPTER 3

Adams, Richard N. *A Community in the Andes: Problems and Progress in Muquiyauyo.* Seattle and London: University of Washington Press, 1959.

Andreas, Carol. "Rural Women in Peru." *Resources for Feminist Research* 2, no. 1 (March 1982).

Andreas, Joel. *Los condenados Rockefeller: La familia más poderosa del mundo y el imperialismo yánqui.* Lima: Tarea Publication, 1977.

Asociación Amauta. "La situación de la mujer en la región de Cuzco, 1980: Justificación, diagnóstico, plataforma de lucha." December 1981.

Bourque, Susan C., and Kay Barbara Warren. *Women of the Andes: Patriarchy and Social Change in Two Peruvian Towns.* Ann Arbor, Mich.: University of Michigan Press, 1981.

Campaña, Pilar. "Estudio preliminar de la condición y participacion económica de la mujer en el Perú rural." Paper presented at the Research Conference on Women in the Andean Region, Lima, June 1982.

Carlier, Ana. "Por el único camino: Una experiencia de campo." *La práctica del desarrollo rural.* Cuaderno, no. 3. Huancayo: Instituto de Estudios Andinos, 1980.

Carpio, Lourdes. "La mujer campesina: Una alarmante postergación." *Educación* 1, no. 3 (1976): 9–17.

Centro De Asesoria Laboral (CEDAL). *La leche: Transnacionales y consumo popular.* Lima, 1980.

Comunidad Santa Rosa de Yanaque. Almanaque documental. Puno, 1982.

Confederación Campesina del Perú. Agreements and resolutions of the Fourth National Council. January 1982.

———. Motions presented at the Sixth Congress. July 1982.

Democratic Women's Front of Cajamarca and the Women's Association of The Comunidad Campesina Santa Barbara. Organizing Commission. Reports. Huancavelica, 1981.

Dew, Edward. *Politics in the Altiplano: The Dynamics of Change in Rural Peru.*

Austin and London: University of Texas Press, 1969.

Direcciones Universitarias de Investigaciones y de Proyección Social. "Seminario: Enfoques para el estudio de la situación de la mujer campesina." Cuzco, July 1980.

Figueroa, Blanca, and Jeanine Anerson. "Women in Peru." *Change*. International Reports: Women and Society. London, September 1981.

Girón, Cristina. "Participación social y política de la mujer rural en un contexto de reforma agraria." Xerographed, Cuzco, 1981.

Instituto de Estudios Andinos. "Mi esposo es como gallo." Serie do la Mujer, Proyecto Salud Comunitaria, Huancayo, 1981.

Mujer Andina 1, nos. 2 and 3. Huaraz, June 1982.

Nuñez del Prado, Oscar. *Kuyo Chico*. Chicago: University of Chicago Press, 1973.

Roeder Romero, Marcia; María Alicia Gamarra Mejía; et al. "Seminario sobre la situación de la mujer campesina de la microregión de Andahuaylas." April 1980.

Salas, María Angélica. "Problemas de la alfabetización." *Churmichasun* 3, Huancayo, August 1976.

Saravia, Pilar. Notes. Xerographed, Instituto de Estudios Andinos. Huancayo, 1981.

Villalobos, Gabriela. "La mujer campesina: Su aporte a la economia familiar y su participación social." Paper presented at the First Mexican and Central American Research Conference on Women, November 1977.

Webb, Caballero, Figueroa, and Iguiniz. *Distribución del ingreso en el Perú*. Lima: Proyección Social Pontificia Universidad Católica del Perú, 1981.

Chapter 4: Organizing in the Shantytowns

1. *Presencia de la mujer en las barriadas,* 2nd ed., pp. 53–54.
2. Sistema Nacional de Apoyo a la Movilización Social.
3. *Mujeres del Cuzco: Trabajo y vida cotidiana,* p. 28.
4. *Presencia de la mujer,* p. 49.
5. José Carrizo, *New York Times,* August 24, 1979, p. A25.
6. Sindicato Unico de Trabajadores en la Educación Peruana.
7. *Presencia de la mujer,* p. 52.
8. A film about El Planeta, directed by Maria Barea, features the women's organization that grew out of this struggle and its founder, Rosa Dueñas, who became a leader in the Confederación General de Pobladores del Perú, a national federation of barriada organizations. The women's organization is called Comité de Damas Aurora Vivar (Aurora Vivar was a factory worker and union organizer who died during a strike), and the title of the film is *Las mujeres del Planeta* (The women of El Planeta).
9. The electoral front Unidad Nacional de la Izquierda Revolucionaria (UNIR) came out strongest among the groupings of the Left which ran candidates for parliament. The largest organization in UNIR was the Communist Party of Peru—Red Nation (Patria Roja), which had it strongest base among the

schoolteachers of SUTEP. Women within SUTEP who challenged male leadership were, however, generally not members of Patria Roja; among parties of the Left it had the weakest record in combatting male chauvinism.

10. Belaúnde's attacks on the government were impressive at the time, since he had spent the years of military rule in voluntary exile, and his party had even refused to participate in the Constituent Assembly that was to prepare the way for elections. After his election as president, Left parties renewed their efforts to unify. The Izquierda Unida (United Left), formed at that time, won decisive victories in the municipal elections that followed the presidential election.

11. Federación Departamental de Pueblos Jóvenes y Urbanizaciones Populares.

12. *¿Por Qué No la Mujer?* 2, no. 5 (May 1981).

13. *Movimiento de Pobladores y Centralización*, p. 132.

14. Ibid., p. 133.

15. The Movimiento Manuela Ramos was instrumental in linking political parties and feminist organizations. It is a feminist organization that was initially formed by members of Vanguardia Revolucionaria, the largest grouping within the UDP. Manuela Ramos is the name of "anywoman" and not that of a specific figure in history. Other Left electoral groupings, such as the UNIR (considered "pro-Peking"), the Trotskyists, the Communists (CCP-Unidad, considered "pro-Moscow"), and ex-Velasco supporters of the PSR (Partido Socialista Revolucionaria) all had Women's Commissions by 1984. The latter also had their own federation of pobladores. However, the Women's Commission of the UDP was formed in direct response to the barriada movement in Lima, where UDP member organizations have had large bases. In 1984, a majority of the UDP membership formed a political party, Partido Unificado Mariateguista (PUM), named after the founder of the Peruvian Left, José Carlos Mariátegui. At this time, members of Movimiento Manuela Ramos declared their independence from political parties, while adhering to the Left Unity electoral coalition.

16. Rosa Alarco had been director of the San Marcos University choir and an ardent promoter of popular culture. She was founder of Peru's Human Rights Committee in 1968 and cultural secretary of the UDP from its establishment in 1978. She died in January 1980.

17. Some women pointed to international data showing that social security would probably do more to free women from the compulsion to bear large numbers of children than any other change in public policy.

18. In 1982, about one fourth of United States food relief was channeled through OFASA, one half through CARITAS (Catholic Relief Services), and the rest through such organizations as the Equipo para el Desarrollo Humano, which was at first linked with the American Institute for Free Labor Development and later worked in coordination with the Narcotic Division of the Policia de Investigaciones del Perú (PIP), both of which are reputedly connected with the United States Central Intelligence Agency. World Church Services and the Servicio Evangélico Peruano de Acción Social at one time served as channels for U.S. food relief, but discontinued doing so. In 1983, the Ministry of Health established a program for maternal and child protection (Programa de Atención Maternal-Infantil—PAMI), which also distributed food surpluses from the United States.

19. Interview with Rosa Dueñas.

20. *Presencia de la mujer,* p. 64.
21. *Vecino,* May 15, 1982, p. 6.
22. Interview with Rosa Dueñas.
23. A theatre production of *Domitilia de Chungara* opened in downtown Lima in July 1982.
24. Maruja Barrig, *La pareja en la pobreza,* p. 223.
25. *Vecino,* June–July, 1982, p. 7.

REFERENCES TO CHAPTER 4

Acción. Lima: Acción para la Liberacion de la Mujer Peruana, 1979–1981.
Ayllon Viana, Rosario. "Organización de una guardería infantil con la población femenina del Pueblo Joven Huascar." Paper presented at the Research Conference on Women in the Andean Region, Lima, June 1982.
Barrig, Maruja. *La pareja en la pobreza.* Lima: Mosca Azul Editores, 1982.
Centro de la Mujer Arequipeña. *Boletín.* Arequipa, March 1982.
Centrol do Organización para la Mujer. "Justina, mujer del pueblo." Huancayo, 1981.
Centro de Promoción de la Mujer "Micaela Bastidas." *Boletín.* Trujillo, March 1981.
Chueca, Marcela, and Vilma Vargas de Balmaceda. "Estrategias de sobrevivencia de la mujer en la actual crisis de la economía peruana." Paper presented at the Research Conference on Women in the Andean Region, Lima, June 1982.
Club de Madres Santa Clara. *Boletín Informativo.* Huancayo, 1981.
Comité de Damas del Pueblo Joven San Antonio. *Mujeres en acción.* Lima, 1981.
"Decreto ley 22611 de pueblos jovenes: Alternativa del pueblo." *Amauta.* Lima: Comité de Coordinación y Lucha Barrial de Caraballyo, October 1979.
"Dirigencia femenina y organizacín gremial." Seminario Taller no. 3. Lima: Perú-Mujer, March 1981.
Domitilia de Chungara. *La mujer y la organizacíon.* Cuzco: Centro las Casas, October 1982.
De niña a mujer: Dos historias. Lima: Flora Tristan Centro de la Mujer Peruana, 1982.
"Informe preliminar sobre el problema de la mujer en el distrito de Comas." Lima: Asociación de Promoción y Desarrollo Social, October 1982.
Lema, Linda. "Una tarea pendiente: Organización de la mujer." *Alternative,* March 1982.
Movimiento Manuela Ramos.*Boletín.* Huancayo, 1981.
⸻. *Trabajando con mujeres.* Lima, April 1982.
*Movimiento de Pobladores y Centralización.*Cuadernos CIDAP, no. 3. Lima: Centro de Investigación, Documentación y Asesoria Poblacional, April 1981.
Mujer, Promoción Cultural, Creatividad y Cambio. [A series of more than forty pamphlets published over a decade, primarily for use in barriadas.] Lima, n.d.
Mujer Levantate, 1, no. 1 and 2. Lima: Frente Socialista de Mujeres, February and June 1981.
"Mujer salvadoreña." *Busquemos La Verdad,* 1, no. 4 (March 1981). Villa El Salvador (Lima), March 1981.
Mujeres del Cuzco: Su participación social y poliítica. Serie: Mujer, no. 2. Cuzco: Asociación Amauta, May 1982.

Mujeres del Cuzco: Trabajo y vida cotidiana. Serie: Mujer, no. 2. Cuzco: Asociación Amauta, February 1982.

Partido Revolucionario de Trabajadores. Women's Commission. "Para la organización autónoma de las mujeres." Lima, March 1981.

Pezo, Cesar; Eduardo Ballon; and Luis Peirano. *El magisterio y sus luchas: 1885–1978.* Lima: Centro de Estudios y Promoción del Desarrollo, 1981.

¿Por Qué No la Mujer?, l and 2, 1980, 1981.

Presencia de la mujer en las barriadas, 2nd ed. Lima: Centro de Información, Estudios y Documentacion, 1981.

"Primer encuentro: La mujer y la organizacíon." Huancayo: Centro de Investigación Campesina y Educación Popular, International Women's Day, March 1981.

Riofrío, Gustavo, and Alfredo Rodríguez. *De invasores a invadidos: Diez años de autodesarrollo en una barriada.* Lima: Centro de Estudios y la Promoción del Desarrollo, 1980.

La situación de la mujer en America Latina. Lima: Comissión Evangélica Latinoamericana de Educación Cristiana, March 1981.

"The Teacher's Strike Ends." *The People React—The Government Represses,* pp. 15–21. New York: Peru Solidarity, 1979.

Unidad Democrático Popular. Comisión Femenina. Primer Encuentro Metropolitano de Mujeres UDpistas "Rosa Alarco." Summary statement. Lima, 1981.

Vecino: El periódico de los barrios nos. 7, 8, 9. Lima: Asociación Civil-YUNTA, 1982.

In addition to the above, information was obtained from the following Peruvian publications: *El Proletario, Marka, El Diario Marka, El Observador, La República, Debate,* and *Testimonio.*

Chapter 5: Working Women and "Development"

1. Legislation enacted during the Velasco period to promote the development of national industries probably affected women more than did programs established specifically for women. However, agencies having the express purpose of promoting women's entry into the paid work force were set up. These included COTREM (Comité Técnica de Revaloración de la Mujer), CONAMUP (Consejo Nacional de la Mujer Peruana), ACOMUP, a commission of the Ministry of Agriculture, and INAPROMEF, a presidential commission.

2. "The Teachers' Strike Ends," *The People React—The Government Represses* (New York: Peru Solidarity, 1979), p. 9.

3. Ibid., p. 10.

4. Esther Andradi and Ana María Portugal, *Ser mujer en el Peru* (Lima: Ediciones Mujer y Autonomía, 1978), p. 109.

5. Linda Lema, "Lucy: When Women Keep Struggling," *Mujer y Sociedad,* December 1980, p. 31.

6. Ann Jaffe, "Eyewitness Report: Latin America's Revolutionary Spirit," *News and Letters* (Detroit, Mich.), December 1981, p. 4.

7. Other businesses boycotted the products manufactured at CONEL after the takeover by women. The cooperative has since had to obtain grants from European foundations to begin a new business in a different location.

8. Linda Lema, *op. cit.*, p. 32.

9. Ibid.

10. "Women Manage Production," *Peru Update* (Peru Solidarity, New York), December 1981–January 1982, p. 6.

11. *El Diario Marka, a* International Women's Day Supplement, p. 7.

12. The wide range in the numbers cited in different publications indicates the difficulty in obtaining accurate statistical information. The figures may also result from the rapid increase in the numbers of registered prostitutes in Peru, even during the past few years. By way of comparison, it was estimated in 1982 that there were over 200,000 street vendors in the capital alone, at least half of them women. Vendors were said to comprise one third of the female work force. Domestic servants or household workers numbered approximately 75,000 in Lima. Factory workers comprised, according to government statistics, only eight percent of the women in the country's economically active population.

13. Adapted from a version given in a pamphlet accompanying the recorded collection *Mountain Music of Peru* by John Cohen (New York: Ethnic Folkways Library, 1966).

14. An unsuccessful campaign by the government in Huaraz to bring produce directly "from the field to the pot" caused one marketer to comment that the people affected by the project are the "little people," while the really powerful people who control manufacturing and big business would not be the target of any such program because "they are the ones who run the country." See Florence Babb, "Economic Crisis and the Assault on Marketers in Peru," p. 8.

15. "La situación de la mujer en la región de Cuzco, 1980: Justificación, diagnóstico, plataforma de lucha," Asociación Amauta, December 1981, p. 7.

16. By "orthodox leftists" I mean those who would emphasize as a basis for socialist revolution changes in the relations of production over changes in relations of reproduction, thereby failing to take into account how closely the two are related. Such a perspective would also view indigenous communities only as remnants of backwardness in society, failing to recognize the revolutionary potential of those who have resisted alienation by remaining on the periphery of industrial development. At this writing, household workers in Peru who considered themselves part of native movements were affiliated with CISA (Consejo Indio de Sudamerica). CISA's headquarters was in Lima, and it sent delegations to United Nations organizations in Geneva.

17. These quotations are from Adela Principe Diego, "Testimonio," and *idem.*, "El amor y el matrimonio."

18. *Llallisunchis*, no. 4 (June 1977).

19. *Fotonovelas* are like "comic books" *(historietas)*, except that photographs are used instead of line drawings or cartoons. The original *fotonovelas*, printed by the millions in Mexico, are "cheap romance" stories aimed especially at young women. The use of *fotonovelas* in the "popular press" is very recent, and began in the household workers' movement.

20. Women and Development is a field of study or school of thought that has emerged through the integration of women's studies and U.S. government programs in "developing countries."

REFERENCES TO CHAPTER 5

Babb, Florence. "Women in the Service Sector: Petty Commerce in Peru." Paper presented at the annual meeting of the American Anthropological Association, Washington, D.C., December 1980.

————. "Economic Crisis and the Assault on Marketers in Peru." Women in Development Working Papers, Michigan State University, May 1982.

————. "Conceptualizing Market Women in the Economy and Society: Production and Reproduction in Huaraz, Peru." Mimeographed, June 1982.

Bollinger, William. "Peru Today: The Roots of Labor Militancy." *NACLA Report on the Americas,* 14, no. 6 (November–December 1980).

Bravo, Aurora. "Testimonio de tres mujeres." *El Diario Marka* (Lima), May 9, 1982.

Chaney, Elsa, and Marianne Schmink. "Women and Modernization: Access to Tools." In *Sex and Class in Latin America,* edited by June Nash and Helen Safa, pp. 160–82. New York: Praeger, 1976.

Creatividad y Cambio. A series of pamphlets published in Lima, n.d.: "La situación de la mujer en el trabajo"; "Subordinación de la mujer: Relaciones de producción"; Susana Vidales Tamayo, "Las causas de la prostitución en una sociedad declases"; José María Salcedo, "La prostitución: Ese turbio espejo de la realidad"; "Mujeres contra la pornografía"; "La prostitución: Mujeres sin derechos"; "La prostitución: Simbolo de la condición femenina"; "La prostitución: Juicio a la reglamentación."

El Diario Marka, a International Women's Day Supplement, March 8, 1983.

Figueora, Blanca. "La trabajadroa doméstica en el Perú." Lima: Instituto Nacional de Investigación y Desarrollo de la Educación, 1974.

Llallisunchis no 4, 5, 6, 7, 8. [Publication of the union of household workers, Cuzco, 1977–1971.]

Maravi de Zuniga, Layli; Carmen Fernandez de Aguirre; Carmen de la Cruz Ormano; and Gustavo Reyna A. "Situación económica social de las trabajadoras del hogar en Huancayo." Cuadernos Sociales. Huancayo: Centro de Estudios e Investigaciones Sociales, June 1980.

Mendiburu Mondocilla, Armando. "Las lavanderas de Huaraz." Xerographed, Huaraz, 1982.

Moser, Caroline, and Kate Young. "Women of the Working Poor." *IDS Bulletin* (Sussex, England) 12, no. 3 (July 1981).

Mujer Andina 2, no. 3. Huaraz, 1983.

Mujer y Sociedad 1, nos. 1–3. Lima, 1980–1981.

Perú-Mujer. A series of talks on women in Peru, March–June 1981: Rosa Flores Medina, "Caracteristicas de la mano de obra femenina en Lima metropolitana: Analisis de las diferencias salariales"; Jeanine Anderson, "La mujer en la vida cotidiana del Perú"; Elena Espinoza Chavarry, "La mujer peruana en reclusión."

Principe Diego, Adela. "Testimonio: Las trabajadoras del hogar," *Pueblo Indio* 1, no. 1 (September–October 1981).

————. "El amor y el matrimonio: Conflictivas diferencias." *Pueblo Indio* 2, no. 2 (March–April 1982).

Sara-Lafosse, Violeta. "El trabajo a domicilio." Research Conference on Women in the Andean Region, Lima, June 1982.

Simplemente explotados: El mundo de las empleadas domésticas en Lima. Lima: Centro de Estudios y Promoción del Desarrollo, 1976.

Valcarcel Arce, Jenny. "The Broken Wing: Teaching Literacy to Rural Peruvian Women in the City." In *Latin American Women: The Meek Speak Out,* edited by June Turner. Silver Spring, Md.: International Education Development, 1980.

Villanueva, Victor. "Peru Cops Assault Factory." *The Guardian* (New York), March 7, 1979.

Chapter 6: Native Revival and Revolution

1. The puna should not be confused with the Department of Puno and its capital of the same name, which are located in the altiplano, or high plains, near Bolivia and Lake Titicaca.

2. For discussions of the male bias in anthropology, see especially Rayna R. Reiter, ed., *Toward an Anthropology of Women* (New York: Monthly Review Press, 1975), and Elizabeth Fisher, *Woman's Creation: Sexual Evolution and the Shaping of Society* (New York: McGraw-Hill, 1979).

3. See Stefano Varese, *The Forest Indians in the Present Political Situation in Peru,* International Work Group for Indigenous Affairs Document, no. 8 (Copenhagen, August 1972).

4. Richard Chase Smith, *The Amuesha People of Central Peru,* p. 15.

5. To summarize several observations made earlier in this book: Male violence toward women seems to develop where population changes and increasing separation of the work responsibilities of men and women have occurred. Both of these have apparently been accompanied by conquest of territory and a division between manual work and administrative control. Religious and political hierarchies are established to maintain control or to regulate the behavior of both women and men.

6. See G. Reginald Enock, *The Andes and the Amazon* (New York: Scribners, 1907), p. 30.

7. Quoted in Abby Wettan Kleinbaum, *The War Against the Amazons* (New York: McGraw-Hill, 1983), p. 113.

8. Smith, *Amuesha People,* p. 8.

9. See Ernesto Jiménez, "En selva central de Oxapampa nativos se organizan para defender sus tierras," p. 13.

10. The young *cornesha,* or religious leader of the Yanesha, has readopted native ways after having served in the Peruvian army for one year. Only a handful of those who are members of the federation have completed high school; none have gone beyond high school. All the members of the federation's *directiva* have made a deliberate decision to learn from their elders the things they had lost through missionary and other outside influences.

11. In regions where *ayni* continues to be recognized as defining relations between women and men, reciprocal relations of special friendship also exist among comuneros. Co-parent relations, called *awra* in Quechua, are different from godparent relations, which are used as a means of increasing social status or gaining power, a custom that is more typically European or mestizo.

12. In a ludicrous display of machismo, fifty businessmen and members of the Guardia Civil (police) in Huancavelica formed an organization of Varones Oprimidos (oppressed males), complaining of "bossy wives." See *Ojo*, September 8, 1982, p. 6. Elsewhere, Andean women have organized to defend themselves physically against the machismo of *cholos* (young men from the country who are trying to learn mestizo ways). During a visit to Huancayo in 1981, I learned that *cholas* were teaching each other karate and had organized forty female soccer teams so that they could avoid being raped or otherwise dominated by boy friends, fathers, and other men. These women were called *machonas* ("butches," or women who want to be men) by townspeople, but many have since formed homes with men. Lesbianism is laughed at or resented by men in the Andes, but is also to a certain extent admired. Near Huaraz, I learned of a woman who was president of her community and had led campesinos in successful battles against landowners. She had a reputation for "acting just like a man." After the death of her husband, she established a home with a woman friend, and continued to lead the community until her death a few years ago.

13. Virgilio Roel, *Los sabios y grandiosos fundamentos de la indianidad*, Cuadernos Indios, no. 2 (Lima, 1980), p. 3.

14. Quoted in *Voz Campesina*, publication of the Confederación Campesina del Perú.

15. Kollontai's essay was a product of the Russian working-class movement at the turn of the century.

16. See José Carlos Mariátegui, *Temas de educación*, pp. 123–33.

17. The Sendero Luminoso organization actively supported the "Gang of Four" who were imprisoned by those who came to power in China after Mao's death.

18. Jonathan Cavanagh, *Wall Street Journal*, January 4, 1983, p. 33.

19. This poem appeared in *Diario la Republica*, a Lima daily newspaper, September 11, 1982. It translates roughly as follows:

"Wild flower, fragrant and pure, accompany me in my journeys.
You are my comfort and my tragedy, you will be my own fragrance and my glory.
You will be my friend when you grow over my grave.
There, may the mountain give me warmth,
may the sky be my reflection,
and may everything be remembered, engraved in the rocks."

20. The military commander implicated in the events leading up to the death of the journalists was also relieved of his command and subsequently given a post in the Peruvian embassy in the United States.

REFERENCES TO CHAPTER 6

Amazonia Indígena: Boletín de Analisis COPAL, 1, no. 1 (July 1980), and 2, no. 4 (January 1982).

Bodley, John W. *Tribal Survival in the Amazon: The Campa Case*. International Work Group for Indigenous Affairs, document no. 5. Copenhagen, 1972.

Chauca Loaiza de Checco, Lina Edith. *Educación Popular en Apurimac*. Abancay, Apurimac, 1984.

Eacobar, Gabriel M., with Richard P. Schaedel and Oscar Nuñez del Prado.

Organización social y cultural del sur del Perú. Mexico: Inter-American Indian Institute, 1967.

Escobar, Gloria, and Gabriel Escobar. *Huaynos del Cuzco.* Cuzco, 1981.

Federación de Comunidades Nativas Yanesha, Valles Oxapampa-Palcazú-Pichis-Chanchamayo, Department of Pasco. Comunicado, no. 1. July 1982.

Fuenzalida V., Fernando; Fernando; Enrique Mayer; Gabriel Escobar; Francois Bourricaud; and José Matos Mar. *El indio y el poder en el Perú.* Lima: Instituto de Estudios Peruanos, Moncloa-Campdonico Editores Asociados, 1970.

García, J.; J. Barletti; F. Juwau; P. Süess; J. Regan; L. Roman; and F. Ballón. "La selva: Abandono y esperanza de un pueblo." *Páginas* 7, no. 44 (April 1982).

Hacia la Confederación Nacional de los Andes: Por una patria andina libre, colectivista y soberana. Comité Organizador del Primer Encuentro de los Movimientos Indios del Peru, Lima: July 1977.

Harris, Olivia. "Complementariedad y conflicto: Una visión andina del hombre y la mujer." Translated from English and distributed at the Research Conference on Women in the Andean Region, Lima, June 1980.

Jiménez, Ernesto. "En selva central de Oxapampa nativos se organizan para defender sus tierras." *El Diario Marka* (Lima), August 8, 1982.

Lavrín, Asunción, ed., *Latin American Women: Historical Perspectives.* Westport, Conn., and London: Greenwood Press, 1978.

Mariátegui, Jose Carlos. *Temas de educación.* Lima: Editora Amauta, 1973.

El marxismo Mariátegui y el movimiento femenino. Lima: Movimiento Femenino Popular, 1974, 1975.

Mayer, Enrique, and Ralph Bolton, eds. *Parentesco y matrimonio en los Andes.* Lima: Pontificia Universidad Católica del Perú, 1980.

Nash, June, and Helen Safa, eds. *Sex and Class in Latin America.* New York: Praeger, 1976.

Pescatello, Ann, ed. *Female and Male in Latin America.* Pittsburgh, Pa.: University of Pittsburgh Press, 1973.

Pueblo Indio 1, no. 1 (September–October 1981) and 2, no. 2 (March–April 1982). Lima: Consejo Indio de Sudamerica.

Reiter, Rayna R., ed. *Toward an Anthropology of Women.* New York and London: Monthly Review Press, 1975.

Sabogal, Isabel. "Algunas reflexiones sobre la posición ante la mujer en nuestro mundo." *Mujer Andina* 2, no. 3 (January 1983).

Shoemaker, Robin. *The Peasants of El Dorado: Conflict and Contradiction in a Peruvian Frontier Settlement.* Ithaca, N.Y., and London: Cornell University Press, 1981.

Smith, Richard Chase. *The Amuesha People of Central Peru: Their Struggle to Survive.* International Work Group for Indigenous Affairs, document no. 16. Copenhagen, 1974.

———. "The Summer Institute of Linguistics: Ethnocide Disguised as a Blessing." In *Is God an American?*, edited by E. Soren Hualkof and Peter Aby. International Work Group for Indigenous Affairs. Copenhagen, 1981.

———. *The Dialectics of Domination in Peru: Native Communities and the Myth of the Vast Amazonian Emptiness.* Cambridge, Mass.: Cultural Survival, Inc., 1982.

Suskind, Janet. *To Hunt in the Morning.* New York: Oxford University Press, 1973.

Information about the guerrilla movement and other recent events in Peru was obtained in part from the *Wall Street Journal, Washington Post, Philadelphia Inquirer, Chicago Tribune, New York Times, Baltimore Sun, Rocky Mountain News* (Denver), *The Guardian* (New York), *Christian Science Monitor, Fôlha de São Paulo* (Brazil), *Agencia Independiente de Prensa* (Costa Rica), *Semana* (Colombia), *Uno Más Uno* (Mexico), and the Lima newspapers *El Observador, La República, El Diario Marka,* and *Ojo.*

Chapter 7: Feminism and Popular Struggle

1. By July 1982, Peru's National Commission for the Defense of Human Rights (CONADDEH) also had a Women's Commission. It assumed active defense of women arrested under the "antiterrorist law" at a time when others were silent for fear of being implicated in the guerrilla cause. In August 1984, feminists broke through police lines in Lima during a mass demonstration called by all opposition parties in Peru, protesting the massacre of peasants in Huanta (Ayacucho). Police were surprised by the action of the women, which opened the way for thousands of other demonstrators to break through police lines and defy orders to disperse.

2. The United States government was already heavily involved in military operations in the jungle. A largely unsuccessful operation to destroy cocaine bases there resulted in the dislocation, harassment, and brutalization of natives, who also complained that the anticocaine operation, UMOPAR, was being used as a pretext to establish U.S. control of the area. Both the antinarcotic and counterinsurgency efforts in Peru gave the United States a new foothold in the military, which had been receiving equipment and advice from the Soviet Union in the defense of its borders for over a decade. The Peruvian military is reportedly close to the Argentine military, whose relations with the United States were strained as a result of conflict over the Malvina (Falkland) Islands, in which the United States sided with Britain.

3. Noteworthy among these is the Movimiento Revolucionario Tupac Amaru, which had bases in Lima and Cuzco by the end of 1984 and carried out dramatic actions demanding publication of its demands in the United States press and on Lima's Channel 2 news. The latter action resulted in revelations that this movement, too, was characterized by active female leadership and feminist political positions, but differentiated itself from the Communist Party of Peru (Sendero Luminoso) by its intention not to carry out political assassinations.

4. Marlise Simons, "Peru Toughens Tactics in Its War on Guerrillas," *New York Times,* August 18, 1984, p. 1.

5. When I asked one man if his union was likely to go on strike in solidarity with striking teachers, he answered sardonically, "At least two professors will have to die first."

6. Principal sources of aid were the government of Holland and the Red Cross of the Soviet Union. Barrantes had also gone to the United States in an

effort to solicit aid. United Nations organizations and the United States government provided aid to mayors in several provincial towns where APRA had won municipal elections. Popular support for APRA began to grow as Alan García, APRA presidential candidate, distanced himself publicly from the right wing of his own party and called for a dialogue with guerrillas. Many were fearful that a Left Unity victory would result in an ultra right-wing military coup. In April 1985 García was elected by a wide margin and assumed office in July. A run-off election between García and Barrantes, scheduled for June, was forgone by the latter. Belaúnde's party won only 6 percent of the popular vote.

7. A case in point is the city of Talara, in northern Peru, where a former Aprista mayor gained fame by establishing brothels to make the town solvent.

8. See pages 207–208 for further discussion of the new civil code.

9. Left-wing council members had resigned their positions in protest over what they declared to be fraudulent assumption of power by an Aprista mayor and other council members.

10. I am referring especially to the publication *La Tortuga* (The tortoise), which resembles the United States publication *Ms.*, and is directed at middle-class women. The more left-wing publication, *Mujer y Sociedad*, the first feminist magazine to be distributed nationally in Peru, was discontinued in 1982.

11. A report on the first meeting can be found in *ISIS-Women's International Bulletin*, no. 22 (March 1982). A report on the second can be found in *Off Our Backs* 13, no. 10 (November 1983), and in *ISIS—International Women's Journal*, no. 1 (March 1984).

12. The growth of lesbian movements in Peru and other Latin American countries during the 1980s is not explored in this book. Information can be obtained by writing to Apdo. 11789, Lima 11, Peru.

13. *Revista Mensual*, publication of the Comité de Mujeres Aymaras "8 de Marzo."

14. See *Informe Evaluación*, Primer Encuentro Departmental de Mujeres Campesinas de Puno, Equipo de Educación Popular de CIED, December 1982.

15. One student organization seeks to unite some dozen indigenous organizations based in the selva, among them Aguarauana-Huambisa, Shipiba-Conibo, Ashaninca, Yanesha, Mashiguenga, and Kichwaruna. It is their aim "to form a united front against those who would like to see *indígenas* disappear altogether" and to remain faithful to traditional models in the production of *artesania*. Apart from these efforts at organization, other native groups continue to carry on sporadic warfare against those who are invading the jungle. When some fifty Piramascos attacked jungle-based petroleum crews with poison arrows, Peruvian government officials demonstrated the arrows on television newscasts as evidence of the valor of those who are engaged in the dangerous mission of "developing" the jungle.

16. The *Comunidad* sought, by 1984, to represent all working women of the popular classes in Lima, although its base was still largely among household workers. In 1985 the organization received funding to establish a center to replace the one from which it was evicted in 1982.

17. The quotation is from "El feminismo: Cambiar la vida," *Debate*, October 1981. For two views of the development of feminist organizations in Peru, see Ana María Portugal, "Hacia una comprensión del feminismo en el Perú," Publicaciones ALIMUPER, no. 1 (Lima, April 1978); and Virginia Vargas Val-

ente, "El movimiento feminista en el Perú: Balance y perspectivas," Centro de la Mujer "Flora Tristan" (Lima, January 1982). ALIMUPER was the first women's organization in Peru to seek contact with feminists in Europe and the United States. The group organized a demonstration in Lima in 1979, in coordination with feminists outside the country, to call attention to the need for the decriminalization of abortion. ALIMUPER was officially dissolved in 1984. The Centro de la Mujer Peruana "Flora Tristan" is primarily dedicated to research and documentation. The two groups shared space for a number of years in a building also occupied by a small library, Cambio y Creatividad, located at 411 Jiron Quilca, Lima. Other resource centers, bookstores, cafés, and media centers emerged as funding became available and middle-class bases grew. Among the most visible of these is Asociación Perú-Mujer, funded by U.S. foundations and employing men as well as women on its staff. Perú-Mujer and the Catholic University in Lima jointly sponsored a Research Conference on Women in the Andean Region which I attended in June 1982.

18. Florence Babb, *Women and Men in Vicos, Peru: A Case of Unequal Development*, Michigan Occasional Paper, no. 11 (Ann Arbor, Mich., Winter 1980), p. 31. This view may be contrasted with those generally held by scholars affiliated with the Women and Development school, who see women as a "neglected" sector of an economy that requires more "international cooperation" in order to function efficiently.

19. Mario Vargas Llosa, "Inquest in the Andes," *New York Times Magazine*, July 31, 1983.

20. In later testimony before an Ayacucho court, Vargas Llosa admitted he had relied heavily on assurances by General Clemente Noel y Moral that the military was not involved in the massacre. The trial was suspended indefinitely in June 1985 when the Peruvian government accused the judge, Hermenegildo Ventura Huayha, of leaking information to the Spanish press.

21. A useful discussion of how production and reproduction are related in countries such as Peru and how these concepts are used by Marxists and by feminists can be found in a paper by Jana Everett, "The Analysis of Women's Oppression in Dependent Capitalist Countries: Strengths and Limitations of Marxist Theory," prepared for delivery at the annual meeting of the Western Political Science Association, San Diego, California, March 1982. In this paper production is identified as "the organization of activities that create articles for subsistence and/or exchange," and reproduction is identified as "the organization of activities which reproduce the labor force on both a daily and generational basis." The author says: "Even if most societies have been patriarchal, we believe it is important to think of patriarchy in historically specific terms—shaped by a particular set of interconnections among the forces of production, the relations of production and the relations of reproduction and characterized by a particular set of power relations and ideational frameworks." She says most Marxists as well as bourgeois theoreticians usually use a functionalist perspective instead of a dialectic perspective when discussing women, failing to recognize women as actors in history.

REFERENCES TO CHAPTER 7

Carroll, Elizabeth. "Mission in Chimbote." Typescript, 1984.
Causa Indígena 1, no. 2 and 3 (January–February and June 1984). Associación de Estudiantes Shipibos en Lima.

Dirigentes Femeninas de la Provincia de Santa. IIo Encuentro. *Report.* Chimbote, June 1982.

Equipo de Educación Popular de CIED. Primer Encuentro Departamental de Mujeres Campesinas de Puno. *Informe Evaluación.* December 1982.

Herencia, Cristina. "Ideologia andina en la mujer urbana de clase baja." Typescript, Lima, 1982.

Pueblo Indio, "Suplemento ideo-politico." Lima, November 1982.

Revista Mensual. Comité de Mujeres Aymarás "8 de Marzo" de la Provincia de Puno, Federación Femenina Interdistrital Base de la FDCP y CCP, Puno, 1981.

Sindicato de Trabajadores del Prostíbulo Zoila Zapata de Huarote "El Botecito," Sindicato de Marina Oviedo Rodríguez, and Trabajadores Independientes del Prostíbulo "La Salvaje." Joint press release, April 1984.

Tocón, Carmen. "La mujer en la industria conservera de Chimbote." *Informes Chimbote,* no. 9 (February 1984): 4–31.

———, Elizabeth Carroll, Marí Rodríguez, and Carmen Urbina. "La iglesia y los comedores: Un desafío." *Informes Chimbote,* no. 9 (February 1984): 32–55.

Vasquez, Cristina Ciudad. "Situación de la mujer campesina: Valle 'Lacramarca-Baja.'" Universidad Nacional de Trujillo Programa de Ciencias Sociales, March 1983.

Feature articles and news items from the following publications were also useful in preparing this chapter: *La República* (Lima), *El Observador* (Lima), *El Diario Marka* (Lima), *Obrero Revolucionario* (U.S.), *New Orleans Times-Picayne, Eco-Andes* (New York), *Agencia Latinoamericana de Información* (Montreal), *New York Times, Wall Street Journal, Rocky Mountain News* (Denver), and communications from Movimiento Indio Tupac-Amaru (Peru).